We Ain't Making Sausage Here!

We Ain't Making Sausage Here!

Marshall Cobleigh

*There are two things you don't want to see being made —
sausage and legislation.*

— German Chancellor Otto von Bismarck (1815-1898)

*To Ken Hawkins & Joyce
To my successor as Joyce VP
Marshall Cobleigh*

PETER E. RANDALL PUBLISHER
PORTSMOUTH, NEW HAMPSHIRE
2005

Published by:
Peter E. Randall Publisher LLC
Portsmouth, New Hampshire 03802
www.perpublisher.com

ISBN:1-931807-35-3

Library of Congress Control Number: 2004118308

Dedication

To my parents, "Lady and Jebb," whose guidance and love are responsible
for my values, drive, and desire for recognition, the motivation that
inspired me to serve others.

To Dick and "Sister," who were always supportive and caring.
To my daughters, Laura and Kim, and the children they have given us.
They are my greatest legacy.

My family shared in my triumphs and
helped make the heartbreaks bearable. I love them.

*Cartoon by Louise "Lee" Adams entitled, "Center Court," shows many of
Marshall's friends in what we called the "Half-Dead Club."*

Contents

Acknowledgments

To Sue Beaudoin Forcier, whose loyalty, skill, and diligence kept this book project going. To Louise "Lee" Adams, who was there in the beginning and again at the end. To Carole Milliken, who was always at my side when I needed her. To Peter and Gale Thomson, whose friendship and support are dear to my heart.
To Steve Duprey, who organized the support of my friends.

I could not have succeeded without the tangible support of:
Mike and Betsy Dingman
Mr. and Mrs. Paul M. Montrone
Ambassador Joe and Augusta Petrone
Kimon and Anne Zachos
Joe Bellavance
Forrest D. McKerley
Jim Coburn
Governor Walter Peterson
Stan Hamel
Fred Seigel
Henry M. Powers
Paul J. McGoldrick
Peter F. Wells
Jay and Sherry Lucas
Will Infantine
The NH Political Library provided in-kind support as well.

The debate quotations are based on the Senate and House *Journals*,; daily newspapers covering the events described (primarily the *Concord Monitor* and the *Manchester Union Leader*), and my memory of the events.

Introduction

Young Men Can Change the World.

My head is spinning like a tornado as I return home to Nashua, New Hampshire, from Hartford, Connecticut. Tally Klimas and I have just attended a spectacular presentation. They call it the U.S. Jaycees' Ten Outstanding Young Men's Program.

It is a dramatically staged presentation, with all the theatrical gimmicks, about the accomplishments of the ten honorees chosen each year, all of whose success has come before they reached the age of thirty-five. I thought, I'm twenty-nine and I've accomplished nothing. Look what each of these people, through will, purpose, dedication, and hard work, has accomplished in his life. I have done nothing other than running a small, halfway successful business. I need to settle down like they did, study their results, and see if it's true that young men like me can change the world. This will be the motivating force in my life.

I listed a microcosm of the honorees' achievements in my mind:

J. Howard Edmundson, governor of Oklahoma at age thirty-three; Homer Babbage, assistant commissioner of the U.S. Department of Education and president of the University of Connecticut; Congressman Robert Griffin, of Michigan, who helped write the Griffin-Landrum Labor Relations Act. Congressman Dan Innoyue, who lost an arm in World War II and then was elected to Congress; Osborn Elliot, the editor of *Newsweek*. There were a couple of others who, despite physical infirmities of great magnitude, have been successes in their fields.

It was quite an event. The centerpiece of the program is the Hands Trophy. One hand is reaching up to God; the other is reaching down to help you focus on your goal. This really made an impression. I want to serve others, I thought. If they can do it, I can too. After all, I'm only twenty-nine years old, still young enough to qualify for the limit set by the Jaycees. "Yes, Young Men Can Change the World." I'd better get moving.

CHAPTER 1

Getting Started

Icame home to Nashua all fired up to change the world, and soon an opportunity arose. My father received a letter asking him to attend an organizational meeting to set up a committee to elect Hugh Gregg as governor. Gregg had already served as governor for one term but then resigned to go off to war. Some considered the senior Gregg rather spoiled: Now he was home, he wanted a new toy.

Anyway, the war was over, Gregg was back, and he was looking to run for governor against his sworn enemy, Wesley Powell. The letter asked my father, a former ward alderman in Nashua, to attend the Gregg meeting and plan strategy. My father suggested that I go. Jebby, as we called him, had had enough of politics. He told me, "You're in the insurance business. It's a good way to meet people. Perhaps you can sell some insurance to the people you meet and finally pay us some rent."

I attended the meeting and soon was heavily involved in the campaign. I was put in charge of my ward. The Gregg people asked me to run for the legislature from my ward. They promised that I could not possibly win. When they finish counting the straight tickets in this ward, they told me, you'll be mathematically eliminated.

If you run, they said, some of your friends will vote for you, but they might cross over and vote for Hugh Gregg, too. We'd like you to run, they said. I ran, and they were right. When they finished counting the straight tickets, I had been mathematically eliminated.

Just before the election, the Gregg people, noting that in me they had a new live wire, asked me to run the parade and citywide rally the night before the election. I took on the job and was completely frustrated by the budgetary constraints that I was under. I jumped right in and organized a huge parade. It was one of the most memorable parades in Nashua's political history.

Alas, it was all in vain. Gregg lost to his old nemesis, Wesley Powell. And, of course, I had been eliminated from the legislative race when the straight tickets had been counted.

I had caught a bad case of the political bug. I was eager to go again. In fact, I was so ready that I moved to another, more friendly ward so that when I ran for the legislature two years later, I at least had a fighting chance.

There were six candidates for four seats. I waged an extremely aggressive campaign, stressing the need for new blood. I ousted an old incumbent to the legislature and led the ticket in my district.

I received eleven hundred votes, Mabel Cooper had 839, George Underhill 823, and Martha Cole won the fourth seat with 766 votes. Alderman Jim Milliken, with 698 votes, and Public Works Commissioner Howard March with 561, were defeated.

There had been several other young representatives elected for the first time that year, but the median age of the New Hampshire legislators at that time was sixty-eight. I was rewarded with a spot in the New Hampshire legislature.

Now, forty-one years later, I am convinced that my election was due not just to my aggressive age-oriented campaign. My win was primarily due to the fact that my grandfather Marshall Day Cobleigh, who had been a city assessor and a respected legislator and a model of the old-school gentleman, had the same name as mine. Although our middle names were different, the people thought that they were voting for Grandpa—even though he had passed on twenty-eight years earlier!

CHAPTER 2

1963: My First Day

On Wednesday, January 2, 1963, under sunny skies and mild temperatures, I was sworn in as a member of the New Hampshire House of Representatives. It was an extremely proud moment. I was thrilled to be in that hallowed hall, taking my place among the four hundred members.

Outgoing governor Wesley Powell swore us in, then proceeded to deliver his exaugural address. Wes lost no opportunity to tell us about the things he had done and accomplished. He lamented that he had been thwarted quite often by his in-party foes. Powell bragged that he had been helped by Democratic support.

Then came the stunner. Wes told us the state needed additional revenue. He hinted that if he ran for governor again, he would not make his same pledge against any new taxes. Powell, of course, had taken the pledge against broad-based taxes in both of his two successful elections. This was the real shocker in his thirty-five-minute farewell address. Members of the legislature sat quietly through his talk, but gave him a rousing ovation when he finished. It was an emotional moment for me.

The legislature then went through the organizational matters that were necessary to set up the House. I was thrilled to participate in the re-election of Stewart Lamprey, of Moultonborough, for his third term as Speaker. Stew immediately announced the appointment of my friend and ally Walter Peterson Jr. as the Republican majority leader. This pleased me because "Pete" was the one who got me involved in running for the state legislature. I was proud to see Pete moving up the rungs of the leadership ladder.

The incumbent veteran representatives from Ward 2 in Nashua, Mabel Thompson Cooper, George Underhill, and Martha Cole, who hated the aggressive way I campaigned and made age an issue in my race for the legislature, were barely courteous to me. They made it quite clear they were not fond of me.

Historians note that the 1963 legislature set a record on the first day even before the opening gavel because we had sixty-two women members, including three in the Senate, which was a record for any legislature in America.

Members of the press corps were quoted as saying that Wesley Powell's exaugural histrionics didn't make a lot of sense. "It sounded wonderful and almost angelic," they said, when Powell said in his speech with his typical blarney that no governor "has ever had a group of advisers more dedicated or who have been more unselfish in their service at this table as my Executive Council."

Veteran scribe Leon "Andy" Andersen wrote, "Powell has never used advice or counsel from the Executive Council as the law says he should." Andersen continued: "Aw, he didn't take advice from anyone else for that matter."

It was a historic day, one that I was pleased to take part in.

Powell and I had a decent relationship even though I had supported Gregg in my initial political effort. But when Gregg lost, I—being a good party man—went ahead and endorsed Governor Powell as the Republican nominee. Most of the rest of the Gregg people did not endorse Powell and were, in fact, angry with me for doing so.

I told them I didn't go over to Powell. I was, in fact, returning home. I was a Republican. I always supported the Republican candidates.

Later I saw Governor Powell quite frequently as he traveled around the country. At one stage, Powell had aspirations of becoming vice president of the United States. Wes was chairman of the National Governors'

Conference and thought he was a contender. I was vice president of the U.S. Jaycees at the same time. Both of us were traveling around the country speaking a lot. We met up with each other on numerous occasions, at airports and in hotel ballrooms.

On one particular occasion I saw him back in New Hampshire a couple of days after we had gotten together. I told him how enthusiastic people were about his speech. He said he had told them that he was not a candidate for vice president. I said, "Yes, they told me that, but I told them that if it was offered to you, you'd jump at it in a minute."

He got angry and screamed, "What are you doing, calling me a liar? When I say something, I mean it. I'm not a liar." He just went off his rocker because I had flattered him about the fact that he was almost a viable candidate for vice president. That was typical of Wes. He had a quick temper and a bad sense of humor.

<hr />

CHAPTER 3

Inauguration Day

The next legislative day was even more memorable because we had the inaugural speech of the first Democratic governor in forty years, John W. King. The House Visitors' Gallery was closed for the first time in memory. Only people with reserved passes (notable Democrats) could get in to hear the ascension of their Democratic solon to governor.

It was a day of joy and celebration for the Democrats, one of rabid partisanship at the statehouse. It was a colorful event, and I was honored to take part in it. Former governors were in attendance. All the Republicans sat together, except Wesley Powell, who sat on the other side of the hall with the Democrats who had supported him and whom he had helped to get John King elected.

There were prayers by the carload. Bishop Primeau offered the invocation; Bishop Hall, the Episcopal bishop, the benediction; and Rabbi Samuel Uman, of Manchester, gave the thanksgiving.

I had never been to an inauguration before. It was thrilling to see the members of the Superior and Supreme Courts in attendance, including my father's friends Eddie Lampron and Bob Griffin. The governor's five sisters were there. His mother and father sat proudly, watching their son inaugurated as governor. It must have been a wonderful moment for them.

It had been forty years since there had been a Democratic governor, the last being Fred Brown, of Somersworth. One of the five portraits on the wall behind Governor King as he gave his inaugural address was that of Franklin Pierce, the only man from New Hampshire to be elected president. Of course, Governor King pointed out to us that Pierce was a Democrat as well. King advocated the adoption of home rule for New Hampshire communities and also a consolidation of the courts as the major planks in his inaugural platform.

One of the highlights of Governor King's speech was when he said, in typical legalese, "I have not been elected to act as a trustee in bankruptcy for the state of New Hampshire." King commended outgoing governor Wes Powell, who had supported King in the election. Governor King told us that Powell had made many improvements in state institutions and that the scope and intent of his government reorganization laws were laudable.

King also appealed to us Republicans for cooperation with his Democratic administration. He said, "I call upon you and upon all of the citizens of our state to unite with me in a common effort to make this state the kind of state that all of us want it to be." He pledged to continue fiscal solvency. He said that his administration "would heed demands for increased state school aid to local communities."

He reiterated his opposition to a sales or income tax. He went on at great length telling us what he would do for education.

All in all, it was a historic two days. It got me all fired up about my legislative service and the joys to come with it. I was part of a team of young turks who had run for the New Hampshire House that year. We were all activists, eager, aggressive, and obviously vying with one another for the opportunity to be the next great young legislative leader.

I was one of the leaders of this pack, which included Bill Johnson, a Dartmouth College graduate, who was an attorney with a high IQ. Bill was obviously politically ambitious.

Another shining face among the young turks was the nephew of a former New Hampshire gubernatorial candidate, a well-known hotel operator. George Stafford was flamboyant and articulate and loved his tea. He gave a spellbinding speech that culminated with his turning around and pointing to the portrait of Daniel Webster on the wall. Stafford proclaimed that "Daniel Webster would be ashamed of what we're doing here today, so we'd best not do it."

From that day forward, the New Hampshire press dubbed him

Daniel Webster. George was smitten with the nickname. This caused him a great number of problems because he tried to live up to Daniel Webster's reputation. He became a laughingstock more than he became a replica of the famous Daniel Webster; however, they both loved their tea.

Another member was a son of a distinguished Supreme Court judge. He was also quite articulate and ambitious. He got into trouble, though, when he was down in the so-called skid-row section of the New Hampshire Highway Hotel, where Larry Pickett and Pat Angus held court. These veteran legislators were furnished samples from liquor brokers who were allegedly required to do so by the Liquor Commission.

The cagey pair used their larder to host nightly get-togethers and supplied their guests with free sauce, countless stories, and much political advice.

They accused the young freshmen of raiding their larder when they were away. This ruined his legislative effectiveness.

The longtime legislators loved to watch the young and eager legislators vie for attention. They analyzed the preening newcomers. They discussed at length each one's potential for political leadership.

There was a wizened old Yankee character in the New Hampshire legislature who was widely respected for his judgment and perspicacity. Bowdoin Plumer would look at the new members of the legislature, all aspiring to be better than the others. They all wanted to move on to greater legislative and gubernatorial accomplishments.

The other members would ask Plumer who he thought was going to succeed. Plumer always said that the key question was "Is he sound?" If a new legislator was judged to be "sound," his future was unlimited.

Members would look at these upstarts who were looking for glory. They would use and paraphrase Bowdoin Plumer's judgmental question, "Is he sound?" Sound was the great characteristic one needed to succeed in the legislature, according to this venerable patriarch.

I, although no shrinking violet, was less flamboyant than several of the other would-be upwardly mobile young turks. In fact, my chance to shine didn't come until the final days of my first session.

CHAPTER 4

Harry Makris's Funeral

The tragic death of young Harry Makris, the Democratic state chairman and a political leader of great promise, was a sad time. Makris had a heart condition and was under doctor's orders to curtail his activities substantially. He wasn't the type of man who could go at less than full tilt: He continued to help his constituents and to do the things he'd been doing all his life. He died at an early age.

His funeral was in a small, poor Greek church in the ghetto area of Nashua. The church was filled with people paying their final respects to a man who had performed a great many services to his community. All the political dignitaries, with their fancy cars, were there. Many of them had to stand at the services because they didn't get there in time to rate a seat, despite their prominence and influence.

In the Greek Orthodox Church, everything is done in threes. In fact, there are three doors at the front and back of the church for historical religious reasons. During the service, a neighborhood cat came into the crowded building and proceeded to walk down the main aisle.

The black alley cat stopped at the head of the casket and crouched, ready to jump into it.

Makris was divorced. His former wife was sitting next to the casket. She spotted the cat as it was poised to pounce. "Get that cat out of here!" she screamed.

With that, four elderly Greek patriarchs, who had been chosen as ushers, went after the cat. It ran through one of the three doors at the front of the church. The ushers, distinguished in their blue suits, continued chasing it. The cat went back in through the middle door, the four Greek pallbearers in hot pursuit.

When the cat reached the casket, it headed back for the third door, again followed by the ushers. This went on until finally the cat was chased from the church. By this time, the congregation was in hysterics at the Chaplinesque spectacle.

CHAPTER 5

Larry Pickett's Board of Education

I had read in books about Washington that famed House Speaker Sam Rayburn had what he termed his board of education. He invited sympathetic lawmakers into his office at the end of the day for drinks and discussion. Much of the business of Congress took place during those meetings.

I was susceptible, therefore, when I was invited to attend meetings before and after the legislative sessions, first at Angelo's Restaurant in Concord and later at the Elks Club. Holding forth were the legendary House minority leader Larry Pickett; the crusty Republican Pat Angus, Ways and Means chairman; and north country leader Malcolm Stevenson. They usually had lobbyists around, such as Joe Moriarty of the AFL-CIO, who would buy the drinks. The men would talk about the day's legislative business and wow us wide-eyed freshmen with stories of legislative legerdemain from years before—at the same time trying, of course, to persuade us to support their causes on a day-to-day basis in the legislature. These sessions, during which the booze flowed freely, were a lot of fun. Along with several of the other young turks who had been invited, I came to look forward to these "meetings."

Pat Angus, Malcolm Stevenson, and Larry Pickett, veteran legislators all, were skilled at questioning us to find out our goals and aspirations, what kind of legislation we were trying to get passed. They would, if they didn't care about what we were doing, leap in to assist us. They would show us what great friends they were by helping us get our goals accomplished and our bills passed out of a committee. This gave us almost instantaneous success with some of our pet legislation.

They also constantly tried to suck us into supporting their legislation. They encouraged us to take up causes we wouldn't get caught dead supporting. They knew that if they could get us publicity, we would do their dirty work for them. They were master manipulators.

This was before one man, one vote. In those days, the smallest of towns in New Hampshire had a representative only two years out of ten; a small town had a representative four years out of ten; large towns were represented six years or eight years out of ten; and if your town's population was more than eight hundred, then you got a legislator every two years.

There was an attractive woman legislator from Hebron who wanted a bridge fixed in her community. Her sad tale was that Hebron was so small it had a representative only two years out of every ten. Thus, if she didn't get it accomplished while she was here this year, it would be a decade before the topic would even come up again.

Pickett, Angus, and Stevenson jumped on this and got us young turks involved, including Zandy Taft, who was the chairman of the Public Works Committee. They obtained the bridge for the woman from Hebron. This is an example of how they ingratiated themselves with new members. They would return later, of course, to collect their payback, demanding we support the things they wanted that were against our basic principles. They would help us and then try to get us to help them.

One of the most colorful episodes in my first session of the legislature was when Representative Peter Charland, a seventy-five-year-old Franklin Democrat and a grandfather, put in legislation to outlaw female hemlines that were more than an inch above the knee—this included shorts! Charland was old enough to know better, said one pundit. Charland said he filed the measure in dead earnest. He was prepared to ward off the big bats wielded by angry women. The bill caused all kinds of comments in the media, such as that portly Peter was no prize sight himself when it came to viewing his shape from any angle.

Others said the Speaker should have sent the bill to the Judiciary Committee for burial arrangements, or he could have turned it over to the Public Improvements Committee for airing. When they finally had the public hearing on Charland's legislation, it was hilarious. He was the only witness to speak in favor of his bill. Charland told the committee that some people said he didn't need to look at women if he didn't like it, but he said he thought his bill would be a good measure to get passed in New Hampshire.

The hearing came to a climax when a crusty old lobbyist named Barry T. Mines, the executive vice president of the Taxpayers Association, a well-known statehouse curmudgeon, got up and recited the following poem:

Here I am at seventy-four,
Old age knocking at my door
All my passions spent going over the hill
And along comes Charland with his goll-darned bill.
HR82 will take away one of the few pleasures I have today.
What's wrong with looking, it does no harm.
And a well-turned leg has a certain charm.
Let us remember that the older we get,
We may slow down, but we don't forget.
So fellas, take action, before it's too late.
Make this bill inexpedient to legislate.

Another highlight of each legislative season was the Order of Women Legislators (OWLS) meeting. When a woman got up once to announce an OWLS meeting, all the men started hooting, *hoot, hoot, hoot.*

I attended these meetings because I was supposed to try to get to know all the legislators.

In those days, most of the legislators stayed over in the Highway Hotel, although the ones from the north country, who couldn't afford the Highway Hotel, stayed at the Endicott. It was basically a north country legislators' hangout. Many of them were active in the 76 Club and attended the OWLS meetings as well. The Berlin delegation used to get one or two rooms on the third floor of the Highway Hotel. They slept four to a bed, which amazed the rest of us. It was a case of trying to live like the big boys while economizing at the same time.

The 76 Club meetings were often a laugh. Mabel Richardson, of Randolph, was a chairman of the 76 Club. After she had served several terms, she was told she couldn't continue these consecutive terms. To get around this rule, she schemed to get her husband, Herb Randolph, who was the doorkeeper, not a member of the legislature, elected president of the 76 Club. Herb would get up there at the front of the hall; Mabel would be in the back. He would be presiding but she was running the meeting, saying, Herbert, tell them this, Herbert, tell them that—it was a funny scene to watch.

CHAPTER 6

Jilted

When I got out of the Navy, I decided I was in love with one of the women I left behind. She was a co-captain of the Waves basketball team that I had coached to national prominence. I drove all the way back to Patuxent River, Maryland, to visit this lady and tell her of my affection.

I was a very nervous, uptight young man in those days. When I called her to ask her out for lunch, the first thing I said was "Where are you?"

Despite the fact that I had called her at her office, I asked, "Where are you?"—not an auspicious way to start a conversation. We had lunch together. She told me I was a wonderful guy. She liked me very much as a friend, but she had no interest in a relationship with me.

I was devastated. After I took her back to work, I took myself to the Spinning Wheel Bar to drown my sorrows. In the middle of the afternoon, a woman with a low-cut dress and a wound above her left breast came in. We spent the next couple of hours drinking steadily. It was obvious that we were enamored with each other. When she went to the ladies room, the bartender, who was a friend of mine, said, "Marshall, leave her alone. She's Phil Gray's girlfriend." Phil Gray was the head of the Mafia who ran the slot machines in St. Mary's County, Maryland.

The bartender told me that the wound over her breast was from a bullet; Phil had shot her when he caught her with another man. "You'd better steer clear of her," the bartender said.

I was broken-hearted. I didn't give a damn about anything. I ended up with the woman. She took me to her apartment. We were in bed when the phone rang. She picked it up and whispered to me, "Don't say anything, it's him." Of course, Phil Gray heard her whisper to me and said, "Who's there with you? Who is it? Put him on the phone."

The woman handed me the phone. A man with a southern accent said, "Who is this? What are you doing there? What are you doing in my girlfriend's house? Who are you?" My quick mind still functioning, I said to the southern voice of Phil Gray, "This is Boston Blackie, and who the hell are you?"

I hung up the phone. I wasn't drunk enough not to realize that I'd better get the hell out of there. I got up, dressed, and drove back to New Hampshire from southern Maryland nonstop, except for gas.

CHAPTER 7

A Tale of Two Bills

Passing legislation can be a quick process or a long one, as we learned during the 1963 session. Toward the end, the governor and his attorney general told us about problems that were going to occur at the motorcycle races in Loudon that weekend. These motorcycle races were the predecessors of motorcycle weekend in Laconia and the NASCAR races of today.

The attorney general had heard through police sources that the Hell's Angels and other motorcycle groups would be coming to Loudon. The opportunity for mischief was tremendous. The state police told Governor King that under the current laws, they couldn't regulate the bikers adequately. The governor told us we needed to change the law right away (this was on a Thursday).

The leadership were briefed on the problem, and they in turn briefed the appropriate committees. Legislation was drawn up. We had a joint public hearing of the House and Senate in the morning, both bodies approved the bill in the afternoon. The state police drove the bill up to the Balsams Hotel, where the governor was giving a speech—the governor signed it into law that same night.

The police now had the tools to deal with the bikers when they arrived the next day. So here we have an example of legislation conceived, written, reviewed in a public hearing, drawn up, drafted, amended, and enacted into law all in one day. Thus, when we really needed to do something, we proved that if there was a will, there was a way. Legislation on this occasion would completely go from the germination of the idea up to final passage in one day.

In contrast to that was the dominant bill of the 1963 legislative session, the sweepstakes bill, which was sponsored by the charismatic Larry Pickett. Pickett first introduced the sweepstakes plan in the 1955 legislature. That year both the House and the Senate approved it, but it was vetoed by then governor Lane Dwinell. The veto was upheld.

Pickett reintroduced the bill each year thereafter.

In 1961, the House once again approved the sweepstakes bill by an overwhelming margin, but the Senate never allowed it to come up for a vote in its chamber, as the Senate leadership was against it.

In his 1963 revival of the gambling measure, Pickett proposed to have the sweepstakes operated by the state and would limit the event to twice a year. Tickets could be sold only within the enclosure of a racetrack where parimutuel gambling was legal. In an effort to gain support for the bill and get votes from the pro-education, anti-gambling forces, Pickett earmarked the proceeds of the sweepstakes for education, which was under fire at the time for not spending enough money on the school systems. Pickett estimated that the sweeps would net the treasury four million dollars a year, which he said would pay off state bonds issued for school construction.

Pickett was a colorful character. A former mayor of Keene and a square dance caller renowned in country-western circles, he had courtly manners and a stentorian voice. He was constantly polite and well mannered to everybody. He ran a seminar early each legislative session to show new members how to speak to the legislature. Having been a vaudeville performer himself, he occasionally broke into a soft-shoe routine. Pickett would urge freshman members to look across the sea of four hundred. Find a friendly face, he'd say, and talk to that face. He knew every trick in the book. He'd been in the House twenty-two years, eleven terms. In 1963 he was fifty-eight years old, short, stout, with a protruding beer belly and the phlegmatic red face of one who enjoyed his beverages way too much.

He had no visible means of support. On occasion, he married well. Each year his friends organized a testimonial for him, at which he received a purse of money. At the testimony at the end of the 1963 session, his pals gave him a used car—his car had broken down.

Pickett also was afforded a room at the Dunfey Hotels whenever he needed one, as he had done them many political favors. Quite often he would be the Democratic nominee to run against friendly Republicans in races where there was little chance of his winning. Crafty Republicans, like U.S. Senator Styles Bridges, would surreptitiously encourage Pickett to run against them so they would not have a tough contest. Pickett would pick up campaign funding to sustain his lifestyle as he went through the motions of being part of a contested political race. He was always good for colorful speeches and press releases.

The liberal segment of the New Hampshire media was not swayed by his earmarking the sweepstakes bill for education. Among the headlines, on their anti-sweepstakes editorials, were the following: *Claremont Eagle*, "How to Tax the Poor"; *Concord Monitor*, "Laying for the Suckers"; *Milford Cabinet*, "Something for Nothing"; *Somerville Free Press*, "New Hampshire Deserves Better"; *Manchester Free Press*, "Shame of the Sweepstakes"; *Keene Sentinel*, "Needed, More Courage."

Pickett convinced a couple of Manchester Democrats, Claude Dupont and Donald Conover, to sponsor a bill calling for the tickets to the sweepstakes to be sold at state-owned liquor stores, an idea that has been revived lately by Senator Ted Gatsas.

The hall was jammed for the first legislative hearing on the sweepstakes bill on January 15. More than two hundred were in attendance. A parade of clergymen and other lay workers told the committee the sweepstakes would be an irresponsible and immoral method for the state to raise revenues. Reverend Raymond McFarland, superintendent of the Christian Civic League, said, "Just because a proposal would produce money doesn't make it right. Heaven forbid that our fair state should lead the way." My minister, Reverend Paul Walker, speaking on behalf of the New Hampshire Congregational Christian Conference, said, "Sweepstakes is an immoral way of raising revenue that would leave New Hampshire open to a process of bootlegging lottery tickets. If you gentlemen are really interested in taxing sin," he said, "I'm sure I have some interesting examples that never occurred to you. You haven't even scratched the surface yet."

Prominent Concord attorney and liberal leader Dudley Orr said, "The sweepstakes will be an unpredictable source of revenue," and he didn't think it would bring in four million dollars. He concluded by saying, "I know of no country where lottery tickets are more vigorously sold than Cuba. If you want to make New Hampshire into Cuba, then vote for the sweepstakes bill."

Reverend Charles Hall, the Episcopal bishop of New Hampshire, called the sweepstakes "a cheap expedient" and said it would "tarnish New Hampshire's historic reputation for courageous and forthright political leadership."

Pickett argued back, "There's no moral question here whatsoever. We run nine races daily at Rockingham Track. That moral issue has already been dealt with." He continued: "The state is already in the business."

An Andover representative, Martin MacDonald, rose to speak: "The churches pay no taxes and most of their ministers pay no taxes, yet they holler if the state tries to think of ways to raise revenues," he said. "Something has to be done to aid the overburdened taxpayers who are confronted with supporting schools that take from four to five times more revenues than any other town obligation." He urged the selling of the sweepstakes tickets not just at the racetrack, but also at state liquor stores throughout New Hampshire.

On a personal level, the lobbying was intense. I kept track. I got 321 calls against the sweepstakes and only one for it. I received weekly, and at times daily, visits from a neighbor, one of New Hampshire's most prominent citizens, Elliot Carter, the millionaire owner of the Nashua Corporation and a distinguished public servant. Carter was adamantly against the sweepstakes. He believed that people would gamble away their wages and end up in deep financial trouble. This would be a calamity for the community, he said.

Carter was persuasive. He would drop by the house to reiterate his opposition to the sweeps. Carter was elderly, and on one visit tripped over a bunch of empty beer cans we had in a bag waiting to be taken out to the rubbish. They rolled out across the living room floor, causing him great embarrassment, and me as well!

An interesting sidelight to the sweepstakes debate is that when it finally passed, it required a referendum in every town and every ward to see if the people were for or against it before tickets could be sold in the ward. In my ward, where I had the 321 calls against the sweepstakes bill and only one for it, the referendum on March 10, 1964, during a presidential primary election, passed by a two-to-one margin. Thirteen hundred forty-three citizens in Ward 1 voted in favor of selling sweeps tickets and 672 voted against the measure.

This showed me that the telephone calls were an indication of not what the average citizen thinks, but of what the activists in the ward think. That experience reinforced my deeply held bias against governing by polls, which I'll discuss later.

The British orator and statesman Edmund Burke said, "Your Representative owes you not his industry only, but his judgement; and he betrays, instead of serving you if he sacrifices it to your opinion."

The first vote in the House was to send the sweepstakes bill to the State Supreme Court for an advisory opinion on its legality. That was defeated by twenty-seven votes. I supported sending it to the court for the decision. So on the key vote, I voted against the sweepstakes bill, but on all the subsequent votes I supported its passage. I thought that it made sense to get an advisory opinion on its legality before we enacted it. There was a two-and-a-half-hour debate. The thirty-vote margin of victory was unexpectedly close. The key vote was to postpone it indefinitely, which means it can't come back that session and virtually kills it. I voted in support of the sweeps on that vote.

The vote to kill the sweeps was defeated 199 to 153. There were several other procedural votes, and in all of them I voted to pass the thing. On the final vote, it was 215 for the sweepstakes and 151 against. I voted for it.

Two years earlier, the bill had passed by the lopsided margin of 240 to 101, but it had died in the Senate as then governor Powell held a veto threat against the legislation. In 1963, Governor King maintained a hands-off policy on the issue. He had voted in favor of the sweepstakes when he was in the legislature, and most people thought he would sign it if the bill reached his desk.

An interesting sidelight is that when the legislature first passed parimutuel gambling (the first one in New England), Oliver Jenkins wrote in his old *Mercury Magazine:* "If the Old Man on the Mountain was to do a hula hula down Concord's main street, it would be no more startling than having Lou Smith aided by Damon Runyan sell parimutuels racing in the sturdy Granite State."

In the Senate, where the bill was expected to go down, machinations were going on. The first public indication that the bill was going to pass was when Franklin's senator, Nelson Howard, said he was going to vote for it. He had changed his mind on gambling, he said, because he claimed the bill had been amended to satisfy him. Howard was a man who could find a million reasons to accomplish what he wanted to do. His switch made it clear that the bill would probably pass thirteen to ten.

It turned out that Howard and Robert Whalen had made a strange pact, a private agreement with Senator Russell Carter, of Hooksett, that they would vote as a bloc for or against the sweepstakes. Thus, when that nefarious group went for it, that was an important key to the bill's passage.

For years there had been poker games at Russell Carter's motel. I always felt that the state was really run by the participants in those poker games. Whalen was not a regular there, but played occasionally. That group of players, many of whom were on the House Appropriations Committee or Senate Finance, were the power structure of the legislature. They often made clandestine deals while playing poker.

One personal irony is that when I got divorced, my wife went to live at Russ Carter's motel. We'll have more about that story later.

The first disclosure of the agreement among Howard, Whalen, and Carter came in the committee meeting when Carter switched and voted for the bill. The rest of us didn't know then that Howard and Whalen were going to vote the same way as Carter. Howard claimed he was won over by amendments to the bill, but that's difficult for this skeptic to believe.

The bill finally passed the Senate thirteen to ten. Then the question became, Will the governor sign it? He was getting huge amounts of mail. There was even talk that Governor King would veto the bill. Former governor Wes Powell predicted that King would veto the sweepstakes because of pressure from the Kennedy administration in Washington. King had scheduled a public session of the legislature on Tuesday to announce his decision. Powell perceptively said, "It doesn't matter that King voted for the sweepstakes when he was in the legislature; he now has the sole responsibility. There is a great difference between what a man can do on behalf of a single constituency and what he can bring himself to do on behalf of the whole state."

I found that to be true when I became a legislative leader. I also saw that premise come into play with the various governors for whom I worked.

Powell pointed out that Governor Lane Dwinell had vetoed the sweepstakes bill when it hit his desk in 1955 because of pressure from the Eisenhower administration. Powell said there definitely had been overtures to King from Washington.

Powell never had to make a decision on vetoing it because he made it clear that he would veto it if it came to him. Powell went on to say, "Sweepstakes can bring nothing but injury to the prestige of New Hampshire. It can do great harm to our people and their economy. It sets a bad example for our young people."

The poker group was coming up with statements all over the place. Senator Russell Carter reported he was given a petition with 247 signatures from the town of Pittsfield urging passage of the gambling bill. Carter said he had been informed that Pittsfield could muster up to 100,000 signatures if he wanted them. He also disclosed that members of the Pittsfield Board of Selectmen had joined the sweepstakes parade.

"Nasty" Nate Battles, another one of the poker-game gang, said that selectmen of five towns in his district urged him to vote for the sweepstakes. Battles claimed that he got fourteen letters against the bill and in each case he wrote a thank-you note and asked the anti-sweepstakes advocates what they would suggest as an alternative way to raise more cash for school aid. Battles concluded that what his informal poll showed was that sales-taxers were against the sweepstakes because they'd rather have a sales tax.

When Governor King announced that he would sign the bill, he told the legislature that he would not appoint a commission to administer the program until the legislature appropriated funds to run it. Appropriations Chairman Arnold Clement, who had voted against the sweepstakes, said he would support legislation to administer it. Governor King asked the lawmakers to give their support to the task of ensuring that the first state-operated sweepstakes in the country would be conducted honestly, efficiently, and in compliance with the laws of the U.S. government.

King, in his address to the legislature, told us, "I have signed House Bill 47, the sweepstakes measure. The decision to sign this legislation was not arrived at lightly. It was taken only after lengthy deliberations and introspection." He said that his legal counsel, Joe Millimet, had been meeting with federal officials. Millimet informed the governor that his conversations with Justice Department officials had convinced him that no violations of federal law would be involved in the sale of sweepstakes tickets to either residents of New Hampshire or nonresidents.

The governor's press people said the response was twenty to one in favor of Governor King signing the sweepstakes bill. He was criticized by Bishop John Wesley Ward, of Washington D.C., ranking bishop of the Methodist Church and a summer resident of New Hampshire. The bishop told King, "I consider April 30, 1963, black Tuesday for our nation and hang my head in shame that our beloved New Hampshire should have led the way down the road of irresponsible action. We abolished the slot machines in Maryland and legalized the sweepstakes in New Hampshire on the same day."

At one time, the Republican leadership had considered making the sweepstakes legislation a party issue. They backed off after they realized that it was too controversial. There were conflicting statements by Pickett and Bill Phinney, the lobbyist of the New Hampshire Jockey Club, about Rockingham Park's position on the bill. Pickett told the House that Rockingham had no objection to it.

When Phinney was backed into a corner, he said, "The sweepstakes business is too complex and has too many problems for Rockingham to want it. Most of Rockingham's patrons come from Massachusetts." He quoted a federal law: "There is a law against interstate trafficking in sweepstakes tickets or any similar game or enterprise." He continued, "Therefore, we have taken no formal position on the sweepstakes. Rockingham is a licensee of the state government. If the legislature should pass the sweepstakes and vote that the sweepstakes races must be run at Rockingham, such a mandate would be taken in stride. But," Phinney emphasized, "Rockingham does not favor sweepstakes. It does not want it and will not endorse it."

Andy Andersen, the liberal columnist for the *Concord Monitor*, wrote that some short-sighted intellectual friends have "insisted that Rockingham actually wants to run the sweepstakes project and is opposing it publicly only to fool the folks."

Both Senate President Phil Dunlap and House Speaker Stew Lamprey took a stand against the sweepstakes. House Republicans ran two to one against it.

At one stage, the federal government appeared to be against it. The U.S. Post Office Department ruled—and issued press releases saying—that it would be illegal to send out sweepstakes results in the mail or to publish such results in newspapers. Mike Winaroni, executive assistant to the postmaster general, said bluntly, "Sweepstakes results cannot be sent through the mail. If the newspapers publish the sweepstakes results, they cannot be accepted for mailing." He went on to say that "they can write a story about a winner, but they cannot publish the list of sweepstakes winners or operational details about a lottery."

This was used as ammunition by the anti-sweeps folks to get voters to cast their ballots against it. The sweepstakes bill passed in the House 196 to 166, meaning that a shift of sixteen votes could have killed it. Two years ago, the House passed it, 240 to 101. Democrats voted for the sweepstakes 121 to 13. Republicans voted 153 against and 75 for. The city of Concord went sixteen to one against it. Merrimack County voted twenty-seven to twelve against it.

In the days preceding King's decision, Pierre Salinger, press secretary for President John F. Kennedy, indicated that the administration was adopting a hands-off policy regarding New Hampshire sweepstakes laws. Salinger said, "I would think that would be a matter for the state of New Hampshire."

The Protestant clergy continued to discuss what they termed "the basic moral question," which, they said, "runs deeper than a question about lotteries. Lotteries are only symptoms of the disease." Said Reverend Burton Erickson of the First Congregational Church, "Ever since I came to this state, the same cry occurs in every legislative session: more sin taxes, more easy money, more painless financing, more evading the moral responsibility, more running away from the facts."

Reverend William D. Goble, pastor of Manchester First Baptist

Church, said, "Gambling encourages a bad philosophy of life. Why work when you might be able to make a killing at the track? And so the old American virtues of hard work, personal responsibilities are gradually worn away with the fever for the fast buck." Said Reverend Paul Stauffer, pastor of the Wesley Methodist Church, "Even the citizens of the Granite State cannot gamble away into prosperity, for the laws of mathematics are not capable of being repealed for their benefit."

At this same time ironically, the Senate was debating the final passage of the bill. The *Concord Monitor* ran a front-page story about a Delaware Supreme Court ruling that public whipping does not violate the cruel and inhumane punishment laws of either the state or the federal Constitution.

The rationale for final passage apparently came from Senator Laurier "Loggy" LaMontagne, who asked for a referendum in each community on the adoption and sale of sweepstakes in their community. This gave the on-the-fence members the rationale to vote in favor of the bill.

The *Concord Monitor* ran an editorial after Governor King announced he was going to sign the bill. Titled "A State Humiliated," it said that "New Hampshire may have written a new chapter in American History when King signs the sweepstakes law, but it was a clear step backwards." The *Monitor* concluded: "It is difficult for us to express our shame and humiliation as a citizen of New Hampshire without recourse to cuss words. Our disgust with the Democratic and Republican members of the legislature who voted for the sweepstakes and for the Chief Executive who signed it is complete. Our faith in a form of government which generates such irresponsible . . . [laws] . . . is even more shaken."

An interesting sidelight of the bill is that the Democratic minority leader, the highly respected George Pappagianis, who went on to become a Superior and Supreme Court judge, voted against the sweepstakes even though Governor King was for it. Normally the minority leader would be supporting legislation the governor backed.

The closing House debate of the sweepstakes bill was historic. Pickett told the committee that his sole motive in sponsoring the bill was to relieve the burden of local taxes. Pickett said he based his four-million-dollar revenue estimate on his belief that at least half the people visiting the track would purchase sweepstakes tickets.

Bill Johnson, a freshman attorney from Hanover, led the opposition and made a compelling case. He produced a telegram from a Justice

Department official saying that the government was prosecuting the sale of Irish sweepstakes tickets in Norfolk, Virginia.

It was a historic debate. After a decade of emotion, hassle, and all kinds of statements regarding its morality, the bill was signed into law by Governor King.

It took more than ten years for Larry Pickett to come up with the gimmick that enabled him to pass the legislation. Pickett's gimmick that finally got the sweepstakes law passed was to earmark the funding for education, at a time when there was a crying need for education monies. This got enough good government types and big-spending liberals to support the sweepstakes, which they would not have ordinarily done. Pickett's promise to raise four million dollars for education ended a ten-year fight to get the law enacted.

CHAPTER 8

The Antiriot Legislation

The one-day passage of antiriot legislation came about because on June 17, 1965, Governor King, who had called out the National Guard twice in ten months to deal with riots at New Hampshire resorts, convened a conference with his legal advisers and legislative leaders to discuss the possibility of authorizing the governor and Executive Council to bar a scheduled public event if there were clear signs that it could turn into a riot.

King told the assembled leaders that California sources had tipped off New Hampshire officials a week before that motorcyclists from California, known as Hell's Angels, would seek to cause trouble during the long weekend of racing at Loudon. King said he had asked the sponsors to cancel the event, but they replied that too many commitments had already been made. They couldn't do it, so King had alerted the National Guard.

This new riot-control law was sped through the legislature and signed by the governor in just one day. The bill was cosponsored by Republican Ralph Totman, of Alstead, the chairman of the House Judiciary Committee; and Representative Bill Craig, a Democrat of Manchester, the House minority leader.

The House and Senate held a joint hearing about the bill on Thursday. It passed both branches of the legislature on Thursday and the state police then hand-carried the newly enacted law to Dixville, where the governor signed it while he was attending a meeting of the New England Council.

It proved to be a wise, if somewhat speedy, decision because that weekend in Laconia a riot erupted at 10:15 P.M., started by the California Hell's Angels motorcycle group. At the start of the riot, there were eight to ten thousand bikers in attendance. In the immediate area, ninety-one people were hospitalized, at least ten of them seriously injured. More than forty arrests were made the day after the new law went into effect. The damage was estimated well into the thousands of dollars.

Some fifteen thousand bikers had come to the Laconia area for the Hundred Mile National Championship Road Races of the American Motorcycle Association. The bikers, many wearing bandannas, were otherwise dressed entirely in shiny black leather. Their hair was long, worn in a slicked-down style. Many of the bikers had chains hanging loosely around their wrists. Early in the evening, they crowded into area grocery stores buying food and stocking up on beer. The Hell's Angels started the riot by tipping over a car. They then formed a ring around the area and wouldn't allow anyone in or outside. Beer cans were omnipresent. Police and National Guardsmen moved in to stop the throwing of smoke bombs and beer cans and the ensuing fights. There had been a riot the previous year at Hampton Beach on Labor Day, and the state police and National Guard had extensive riot training as a result of that incident. They put that knowledge to good use at the Laconia motorcycle races. The legislature's quick action gave the police a tool to deal with the bikers and bring the riot under control.

When Governor King arrived on the scene, with a police escort, he said there were enough beer cans to start a dump. Concord Hospital officials said three youths had been treated for gunshot wounds and released. One man was rushed to Mary Hitchcock Hospital in Hanover with a skull fracture. He was treated and then transferred to Bridgeport General Hospital in Bridgeport, Connecticut, where surgeons specialized in that type of injury.

About forty people were jammed into the Laconia and Boscawen jails, charged with violating the state's new antirioting law. Hospital officials said that others had suffered broken bones and gunshot wounds. The legislature had acted quickly, and it was obvious that something had to be done. This action showed that the massive body, when confronted with a crisis, could speed up a usually lengthy process to protect the people of New Hampshire.

The law carried stiff penalties, including a fine of five hundred dollars or one year of imprisonment or both for engaging in mob action. There was also a one-thousand-dollar fine or one to three years' imprisonment or both for participation in mob action that caused injury to person or property. Refusal to withdraw from the riot scene when ordered to by the police called for a fine of not more than five hundred dollars or one year's imprisonment.

Contrast this again with the ten years it took Larry Pickett to amend, adjust, and recycle his bill to get it enacted into law—each time picking up a few new supporters as he tried a new technique. Both events were memorable occasions in my early legislative career.

CHAPTER 9

How Do You Handle a Democratic Governor?

It had been more than forty years since a Democrat—Fred Brown, of Somersworth—had been elected governor when New Hampshire voters chose Democrat John W. King to be our new governor with the help and support of former Republican governor Wesley Powell.

At the beginning of Governor John King's tenure, Republicans were baffled as to how to react. We started out by trying to oppose everything he was in favor of. We'd call him a big spender and talk about fiscal sanity as we tried to put a monkey wrench in everything he did.

When it turned out that the things we opposed were popular with the people, such as increased funding for education, we had to change our tactics. Now we tried to outdo him and give the people even more than he proposed. This is contrary to the Republican philosophy, but we knew we were getting clobbered by attempting to thwart King.

Speaker Stew Lamprey came forth with what he called the Republican Manifesto. He brought it before the Republican State Committee and got members to endorse it. Next Stew went to the House Republican Caucus with what he felt was a program that was better than what King was proposing.

Much of what the Republicans pledged to do Governor King claimed to be for as well. The Republicans pledged to give the University of New Hampshire a $950,000 budget increase and so did Governor King.

The Republican platform pledged a special pay adjustment for faculties at the two state teachers colleges; so did Governor King. The Republicans pledged "fair and equitable consideration of state employees"; Governor King pledged "fair treatment." The Republicans pledged to give the head-tax revenues to local communities for additional school aid; so did Governor King. The Republicans vowed neither a general sales nor an income tax; so did Governor King.

The Republicans then tried criticizing King's spending proposals. Senate President Phil Dunlap said that King's budget called for "spending money we do not have to create a planned deficit just like the President wants in the nation."

Dunlap called King's proposal for a twenty-million-dollar bond issue for schools "deficit financing that was even more serious to taxpayers than the governor's reneging on his campaign pledge to return the head tax to local communities."

The Republican leadership called for a pay-as-you-go policy on school aid. They said it would cost one dollar in interest charges for every two dollars provided in education aid under Democrat Governor King's bond issue. Walt Peterson and Stew Lamprey were both real estate agents. They knew very well the costs of financing loans for major projects.

Peterson denounced the bond issue as based on the buy-now-and-pay-later philosophy. He charged that the interest costs would run ten million dollars for the twenty-million-dollar bond issue. The Democrats pointed out that the Republicans had already endorsed ten million dollars in additional bonds for the Highway Department and five million in bonds for construction at the University of New Hampshire. We pointed out that it was one thing to bond capital spending but completely wrong to bond current operating costs. King said that bonding spending for education was a long-term investment even if it was for current expenses.

The bond issue was eventually defeated by the House 234 to 143. Lamprey, following the victory, praised his fellow Republicans for refusing to "surrender their responsibilities as legislators and hand the governor a blank check. We do not question our schools' needs," he said, "but reckless bonding as proposed by the Governor is no way to solve the problem."

Dunlap pointed out that the governor's proposal for retention of the head tax and his idea of making tax revenues available to local communities were a repudiation of his party platform and his own campaign oratory.

When Lamprey presented his Republican Manifesto to the GOP Committee, which was dominated by conservatives, Ed Edwards, of

Antrim, said the Republican State Committee ought to be asking "why we got such a hell of a licking last fall."

Edwards pointed out that what we should discuss was why two of our major nominees got a forty-one-thousand-vote shellacking at the election polls only ten weeks earlier.

The Republican leadership proposed a $30,000 "quickie study" into the tax crunch of New Hampshire. This tax study was rapidly endorsed by the party caucus.

Lamprey called his manifesto a blueprint for victory. He asked for a rebirth of New Hampshire republicanism. He sought greater cooperation at all levels of party activity and a much closer liaison between GOP legislators and the party organization.

"We must take a strong and united stand to be sure the Republican Party can and will win in '64," he said. The Lamprey program called for sustained party activity with a fully functioning headquarters, a full-time executive secretary, and a continuing fund-raising system.

In the beginning, we tried to kill Governor King with kindness. Then we tried to oppose everything he was for. When King's budget came out, Senate President Phil Dunlap called it the biggest spending program in Granite State history. Dunlap also criticized King for failing to keep a campaign pledge to give $2.8 million of head-tax revenue back to local communities to help them deal with school aid.

At the same time, Bob Monahan, who was Dunlap's floor leader, criticized the budget as vastly inadequate. Monahan, from Hanover, said it did not provide for spending for deserving new programs.

Stew Lamprey waited a day before joining the criticism. He said the King budget was "so niggardly and so lacking in spending foresight that I would sponsor a Republican budget of greater spending proportions and raise more taxes to pay for it."

The Republicans clearly were not united in their budget approaches —because they couldn't agree on how to handle Governor King.

Raimond Bowles, who headed an interim $30,000 education study commission, recommended that the state derive new income from liquor, beer, and cigarettes to be used for reorganization of our public school system on a long-range basis, and recommended other reforms as well.

It was after this report had its heyday and was getting supported editorially in the liberal papers that Larry Pickett saw the opportunity to amend his sweepstakes bill and have the proceeds go to education.

We're talking, of course, about 1963. To show how things have changed, New Hampshire collected a net profit of eight million dollars yearly for liquor and beer and $4,640,000 from tobacco along with $5,340,000 from horse racing.

Another idea the Republicans proposed was to change the primary elections for both Democrats and Republicans from September to May, so there would be more time to heal the wounds after a bitter inter-party primary election.

This was a major effort, but it didn't get anywhere. The small towns were very much against it, nor did it have the full support of the party. It was an interesting proposal because of the fractious behavior at that time between the two wings of the Republican Party. There was also a contentious fight between the governor and the legislature about whether the governor could change state employees' salaries without the legislature's approval. This was a question of the power of the two branches of government. It became quite nasty for a while.

CHAPTER 10

The Fight for Nashua Technical College

The first major policy issue that I got involved with was the siting of the new technical school. Governor Powell had talked about technical schools and promoted them. Governor King had jumped on the bandwagon.

The education bureaucracy was trying to decide where to locate New Hampshire's first technical school. The education group, of course, voted to build a school in Concord, right beyond the Highway Hotel off Route 93.

The Manchester delegation wanted it built in Manchester. The triangle formed among Manchester, Salem, and Nashua was known as the Golden Triangle. This was where the economic and technical development of New Hampshire was happening. I was pushing to locate the school in Nashua, or at least in the triangle.

I ended up supporting the more feasible Manchester (also, of course, closer to Nashua) bid. I had an opportunity to take on Franklin Hollis, one of the leading lawyers in the state, who was the head of the state school board. Hollis was in favor of the egghead solution of Concord, where there was practically no economic development. In fairness to him, however, it was closer to the center of the state.

My argument was that technical school students weren't like University of New Hampshire or Dartmouth students, most of whom lived on campus. The great majority of tech school students commuted to college. Many also worked while going to school, and often were from lower-income families. It would be best for a tech school to be near where they lived and where their jobs were. They should not have to drive up to Concord every day just to keep the education bureaucrats happy. Attorney Hollis and I participated in a major donnybrook on the floor of the House about this subject. It was my view that he was less than credible.

The education lobby had hired an architect from Durham. Irving Hersey envisioned a complex of twenty buildings, including a nuclear reactor center, that would serve some two thousand students. They were trying to build up a new university, in my opinion, rather than locating technical schools where the jobs were and where the people were.

The legislature had provided $1.65 million in 1961 for the construction of the first two buildings, a laboratory classroom and a dormitory. They gave the choice of a site to the state Board of Education, who, naturally, chose Concord.

Former Senate president Sam Green put it well when he charged that "New Hampshire is not yet ready to build a new university complex to compete with UNH." That's exactly what I felt. Green said, "In sixty-one, the legislature intended to create another technical school. It did not have to build football fields and recreational facilities. The institute should be where our technical industries are," he said, "which are located in southeastern New Hampshire. Manchester won't be in the wilderness."

Green also pointed out that the land in Concord would cost $400,000; the Manchester site would be donated to the state. The education eggheads, led by Hollis, claimed that the school was designed to prepare technical junior engineers. It would be an academic school different from vocational training, so it would be set up in five centers.

The Education Committee went along with the eggheads and recommended that it stay in Concord and not have anything to do with Nashua or Manchester. Sol Feldman, a Manchester businessman whom many perceived to be a tool of the *Manchester Union Leader,* was the sponsor of the bill to locate it in Manchester. Sol was our leading spokesman because everything he said the *Union Leader* would play up.

Feldman said there were "thirty-six technical plants in New

Hampshire and only eight of them in Concord or north of Concord. We should put the institute where it belongs, to take care of the immediate manpower needs of our industry." Mayor Mario Vagge, of Nashua, told the committee, "We need the technical institute. In twenty-five years, we may need another one in the northern part of the state. Right now the Concord location would result in great hardship due to its remoteness. Everything points to Manchester as the logical place for the institute. Concord is not located where it can help the people who need technical training now."

When the bill reached the floor of the House, I was chosen to lead the fight on behalf of the Golden Triangle. I took issue with the Board of Education's claim that the industrial trends were toward the northern part of the state. I insisted that this institute be placed where it would be more accessible to the Nashua/Manchester/Salem trio.

Shirley Clarke, the chairman of my committee, took the floor to defend the Concord site. The essence of her claim was in that in 1961 we gave the decision to the state Board of Education: They did a good job, so we should back them.

Sol Feldman got nasty, as was his wont. He denounced Franklin Hollis, chairman of the Board of Education, for alleged partisan testimony before the committee. Feldman said his only purpose for sponsoring legislation was for the benefit of the majority of the state's populace.

I found myself in a nasty exchange with Hollis, who was one of the sharpest lawyers in the state and a widely respected liberal. I enjoyed the combat, and I thought I made many telling points. When the hullaballoo was over, however, the legislature backed the education lobby and the Education Department. The site was awarded to Concord, with a promise of locations around the state down the road.

Alexander "Zandy" Taft, one of the early proponents of a broad-based tax in New Hampshire, in the legislature defended the Concord site. He said, "It would provide a good, solid base for the future of our industrial economy."

It was pointed out that the Board of Education itself split four to three on the site dispute. The Manchester interests had waged a prolonged argument that their city should host the school because it was a major center of Granite State industry. Sam Green's response was that New Hampshire was not ready for a new university to compete with the University of New Hampshire. The 1961 legislature never intended to create another university.

The depth of the animosity of the fight was illustrated by the column of Leon "Andy" Andersen in the *Concord Monitor*, where he proclaimed, "We don't expect the legislature will bow to selfish Manchester interests and shift the $1.6 million Technical Institute from Concord to that city." He urged Concord citizens to "come out and testify for the bill." Andersen wrote that "selfish Manchester groups more interested in their own immediate profits than the state's future welfare are demanding the Technical Institute benefits mostly for themselves."

He went on: "Concord citizens need to come out and testify against the proposed down-river steal." He concluded his column this way: "Life is that way. When Manchester loudmouths get going, good citizens must rise in righteous protest."

CHAPTER 11

Other Skirmishes in '63

The most emotional bill of my first legislative session had to do with where to locate a deer-hunting line. The deer line would divide the state into two parts, with separate hunting seasons. There was extreme controversy among sportsmen's groups, hunters, and the out-of-state people who came here to hunt as to where exactly the deer line should be.

I decided, because it was one of the major issues of the session, that I should get educated about it. I sought invitations to go before fish and game clubs, sportsmen's clubs, and other outfits in New Hampshire that had an interest to find out what they thought. I left these meetings utterly confused. Each individual hunter had a solution. Each club had a solution. There was no unanimity of opinion of any kind. Each was extremely vocal on saying his deer line was best. I didn't have any idea where the line should go or what we should do about it. The more clubs and sportsmen's groups I visited, the less certain I became of what the logical answer was. The dilemma was finally solved by some legislative genius who decided to eliminate the line and have the open season cover the entire state.

This was probably a good solution, but I definitely was not part of the debate. I never did understand what was happening, what was going on, or what was the best way to solve the problem.

Another highlight of the 1963 session was the appearance of Massachusetts Attorney General Edward W. Brooke. Brooke was one of the highest-ranking black officials in America. (He would later go on to a distinguished career in the U.S. Senate.)

Brooke caught my attention right away by telling a story that I thought was wild to be hearing in a legislative setting, with distinguished political officials and television watching and listening.

It was about the Boy Scout leader who was taking his troop into the woods and decided to give them a little advice concerning a possible snakebite. Brooke quoted the Scout leader: If you are bitten in the left arm by a snake, you should immediately take out your jackknife, make an incision over the bite, and suck out the poisonous blood.

There was an inquisitive young Scout in the back of the group. "Mr. Scout Leader, suppose the bite is in the back, on your hind end." There was a long and ominous silence. The Scout leader said, "That's when you find out who your real friends are."

Brooke then talked about May Day and the Communists and also about Law Day. This was why he was in New Hampshire. He went on at great length to duck the sweepstakes debate, which was still pending in our legislature. But all his serious words about Law Day, Communism, and the sweepstakes didn't stand out in my mind as much as what he said about a snake biting you on your backside.

It was during the 1963 session that I made probably the dumbest political financial decision, of a personal nature, of my career. Fellow freshman Steve Wheeler, of Exeter, and I came up with the idea of sponsoring legislation to name British war leader and historian Winston Churchill an honorary citizen of New Hampshire. Congress was considering similar legislation. We wanted to beat Congress to the punch.

Unfortunately, the Rules Committee, led by Speaker Stewart Lamprey, told us it was an excellent idea but would set a dangerous precedent. The committee refused to approve our proposal, which meant no debate and no vote by the House.

We were upset. We happened to talk to Governor King at a dinner. He thought it was a great idea. The governor said, "Come in and we'll work something out." King issued a proclamation naming Sir Winston Churchill an honorary citizen of New Hampshire.

The proclamation went on to say that Churchill was "one of the true giants of the Twentieth Century." It noted that Winston Churchill was the son of a British father and an American mother. It was full of famous Churchill quotations like, "I have nothing to offer but blood, toil, tears, and sweat," which he proclaimed during the darkest days of World War II.

Winston Churchill was renowned not only as a world leader but also as an author, legislative soldier, and artist, the proclamation continued. It went on to say, "Whereas the people of New Hampshire do not only hold Winston Churchill in the highest esteem, as one of the true giants of their lifetime, but they do reserve a warm spot in their hearts for this remarkable man of the Twentieth Century."

It concluded, "Now, therefore, I, John W. King, Governor of New Hampshire, do hereby bestow Honorary Citizenship upon that distinguished British subject, Winston Churchill." Thus was our goal accomplished by the Democratic chief executive.

Now, it happens that Governor King had been trying to get Churchill's signature for more than ten years because he was an autograph collector. Lo and behold, both King and I received letters from Churchill thanking us for the honor we had bestowed. It was a handsome note sent from the Hotel de Paris at Monte Carlo. In the famous signature, Churchill runs the s onto the end of Winston.

The governor decided, in his finest judicial temperament, that the letter didn't really belong to him and instead should be a part of the state archives. I followed Governor King's good judgment and gave my letter to the state archives as well. That letter would be worth a fortune today if I had kept it.

Sadly, my heirs will not benefit financially from the fact that I had a direct hand in making Winston Churchill, whom I believe to have been the greatest man in my lifetime, an honorary citizen of New Hampshire.

An ironic sidelight to the story is that when we were discussing the Feldman bill (see chapter 26), a public hearing was held and I was presiding. Sherman Adams was coming out of exile after his transgressions in the so-called Goldfine matter, in which Adams allegedly accepted a vicuna coat from the New Hampshire industrialist Bernard Goldfine.

Adams had been forced to resign as President Eisenhower's chief of staff, and had not made a public appearance of any kind since his public humiliation. The first time Adams decided to go public was to testify against the so-called Feldman bill to ban Communists from speaking at the University of New Hampshire. When it came my turn to introduce Sherman Adams, I said from the podium, "In my lifetime I believe that the greatest man whom history has known in the world has been Winston Churchill. As you folks know, I was instrumental in helping to make Winston Churchill an honorary New Hampshire citizen. I also believe strongly that the greatest man in the history of New Hampshire during my lifetime has been Sherman Adams, whom I first met as a little boy in my father's office. It gives me great pleasure not only to make Winston Churchill an honorary citizen of New Hampshire, but to have the personal pleasure to introduce Sherman Adams, the greatest political leader in the history of New Hampshire, in my opinion."

Adams was quite pleased with my generous introduction. At a cocktail party after the hearing, in his typical brusque manner he said to me, "Cobleigh, you're an articulate and verbose young man, and when you're articulate and verbose about Adams, Adams likes it. Thank you."

CHAPTER 12

Telling the Future

Leon Andersen wrote about *Nashua Telegraph* Managing Editor Fred Dobens: "We hope the legislature doesn't eradicate Fred Dobens of the *Telegraph* off his fancy seat on the Advisory Commission on Resources and Economic Development (DRED). One upstanding lawmaker recently picked the *Telegraph* as his paper of choice, to be paid for by the legislature. Each member can get one free paper. The efficient Forrest Bucklin, the House Custodian of the Mail, dispatched the order for the paper to Nashua. Bucklin got the surprise of his quiet-mannered existence when back came a curt note from the *Telegraph* which says if you want the *Telegraph*, pay in advance or else. Andy says we're not sure the state government pays for anything before delivery. Maybe we should try an Attorney General's ruling before somebody gets the notion that Editor Fred Dobbins doesn't trust the New Hampshire Legislature."

Some developments arose in 1963 whose significance I didn't understand at the time but in which I became strongly involved down the road. Governor King asked federal officials if the old post office building behind the statehouse could be given to the state. He went to Bernie Boutin, a friend who was the administrator of the Federal General Services Administration.

King expected to get favorable action. He said he would ask the legislature to provide the funds for renovating and turning it into another annex. Later on, when the state did obtain the post office, there was a lot of facetious debate between Lamprey and me.

Lamprey wanted to tear down the building and construct a major edifice in its place. I wanted to leave it right where it was for its historical significance. A pundit said the reason I wanted it left as was because it was a short and squat building and a statue of me would fit better in front of a short and squat building. Lamprey was tall and lanky and his statue would fit better in front of a fourteen-story structure. The pundit went on to declare that the short and squat Cobleigh prevailed and we kept the old building.

We did do a major renovation, however, and it's been a big addition to the statehouse complex. I'm proud to have had a hand in it even though there's no short and squat statue in front of it.

The House passed legislation setting up a constitutional convention for the next year. A commission was established to study the Constitution and recommend changes to it.

I didn't understand the significance of it at the time, but the Con-Cons were to play a major part in my life, as we'll soon see.

The New Hampshire Con-Con, which was to convene in April 1964, would have to examine its method of apportioning representatives in light of the decision handed down by the U.S. Supreme Court on one man, one vote. New Hampshire's Constitution called for the twenty-four Senate seats to be apportioned according to wealth, not population, which appeared to be in violation of the Supreme Court's decision.

The New Hampshire House of Representatives was apportioned in our state Constitution to weigh it in favor of rural voters. One town or ward having 822 residents is entitled to one full-time representative. A town or ward must have 1,644 residents to qualify for a second representative, and so on up the scale. The towns that don't have a population of at least 822 get a representative two years, four years, six years, eight years, in the relationship its population bears to 822. A town with fewer than 200 would get a representative once every ten years; a town with more than 400 would get a representative twice every ten years; a town with 600 gets a representative three times; and a town with a population of 800 and above, the full five times each legislative year. This then would be a topic for the Con-Con, as well as a subject in which I was to become deeply immersed.

Also in 1963, Andy Andersen wrote a column about ex-governor Lane Dwinell. In it he talked about two men riding home from a speech one night and Dwinell was reminiscing. Dwinell commented that after two years in office as governor, he found it was a very lonely and unfriendly job. When asked what he meant, Dwinell replied that the only people who visited him or paid any attention to him were those seeking favors or trying to promote something.

Dwinell said he missed friends who were simply friends and not looking for something. He lamented that his real friends felt he was so busy they didn't want to bother him by intruding upon his time. That left the governor with only the friendship of those trying to use him, which is not the kind of friendship that has lasting value. Andy went on to say that it just goes to prove that being governor is not all peaches and cream.

I was involved in one battle in 1963 along with my youthful sidekicks Steve Wheeler, of Exeter, and George Stafford, of Laconia. We were sucked in by Emile Soucy, a curmudgeon who was actually a liquor lobbyist who served in the legislature at the same time. (Many folks wore both lobbyist and legislator hats at the same time in those days.)

Soucy's proposal was basically that if a citizen won a Supreme Court challenge of an action by a public official, the person making the appeal would be reimbursed in full. We didn't get it enacted into law, but to this day I believe it makes sense. I have always favored and supported the loser-pays concept in lawsuits. The trial lawyers fight it fiercely, but it would substantially cut insurance costs.

One of the most interesting days in the 1963 legislative session came when Malcolm "Mac" Stevenson put a motion on the floor and then withdrew it, yet it was voted to victory. It astounded longtime legislative observers.

Stevenson was a north country representative for the small town of Bethlehem. He was a leader in the fight against the Education Department and a champion of small towns. (He eventually ran against me for Speaker.)

The Education Committee had filed a recommendation to kill one of Stevenson's bills. Current law basically said that a pupil had to go to outside special education facilities if the parents were not satisfied with whatever schooling the town might provide for him.

The Stevenson bill would have kept the issue within the local school district, and with local school boards having final judgment. Stevenson had waged a one-man fight against the increasing state government controls of the local school affairs. He appealed to home-rule sentiment and anti–state control resentment. He called the state Education Department "a growing monster which is eating away at home rule and the right of people to handle their own affairs." After he gave a long, venomous speech outlining his convictions, he took the House by surprise by telling members he was withdrawing his motion to upset the Education Committee and pass his bill.

There was much protest from members who had agreed with Stevenson. They were astounded that he was withdrawing his motion. Stevenson himself appeared mildly shocked. He went back to his seat, shaking his head. His pals, two veteran lawmakers, jumped into the breach.

According to columnist Leon Andersen: Larry Pickett, the Keene Democratic warhorse, got the microphone and resurrected Stevenson's fight. A minute later, Pat Angus, another veteran parliamentarian, capped the moment. He put up the motion to pass the bill again. The deluge came forth. Jim O'Neil, chairman of the Education Committee, fought vainly to kill the bill again. On a standing vote, Stevenson won 186 to 150. Another Education Committee stalwart, Betty Green, tried to send the bill back to committee for revision. That was also voted down with gusto.

Andersen explained that "Stevenson didn't think he had a chance to pass the bill. He didn't want to waste everybody's time in a losing cause. It added another demonstration that our elephantine House has the sturdy independence of a pachyderm displaying sound judgment more often than not and even in a refreshing, surprising manner when it fits the occasion."

He pointed out that it was the second time the Education Committee had been beaten that year. He asked, "Can it be that soaring school costs which are being piled upon homes and farms in forms of spiraling property taxes are finally becoming so irritating that citizens are hitting out against them? Maybe its time has come when our professional educators should take stock and stop and look and listen for a change."

Andy continued: "Nothing built or operated from the top down is democratic. To the contrary, it stifles and sullies the personal freedoms upon which our United States was founded and dedicated to preserve." This was a very strange position from the liberal *Concord Monitor*, but it reflected the tenor of the moment, and many of us felt it.

More than one cynic, including yours truly, believed that the Stevenson withdrawal, coupled with the dramatic rescue effort of Pickett and Angus, was a well-rehearsed plot to upset the applecart.

Another sign that the legislature was coming out of the Dark Ages was in the bill-drafting process. For many years a woman in the attorney general's office, Miss Marion Alexander, had drafted all of the legislation.

Lamprey, in his wisdom, decided that we needed to modify the structure and set up a department rather than depend on one fragile elderly woman. He sponsored controversial legislation to create a legislative services department. This bill came before the Committee on Executive Departments and Administration, which I was serving on. It was a modernization that was sorely needed.

We were currently hiring—for a song—another attorney, Warren Waters, to draft legislative bills to help Marion Alexander. The Senate had attorney Arthur Marx, of Alstead, on salary for one thousand dollars per month to do drafting also. Ironically, Marx's wife, Eleanor, was a member of our Education Departments and Administration Committee. She had what you could consider a blatant conflict of interest, but everybody loved Eleanor and wanted to do something to get her husband the job in the new legislative services department.

The status-quo apostles were all against this improvement in the situation; the leadership, however, was for it. After a major battle, we set up the Department of Legislative Services. In doing so, we established a permanent structure for the legislature to take care of its own drafting problems and to have a bill-drafting department staffed with attorneys. This would have happened years before except for the expertise of the legendary Miss Marion Alexander.

Another change in this direction for which Lamprey led the way was prohibiting the putting of legislation into the budget bills. One of my early lessons was that when the budget came out, you didn't look at the numbers. The first thing you did was turn to the back of the budget and look at the footnotes to see what had been snuck into it. Some of it was very good; some of it was very mischievous. Most people didn't read the footnotes, because in their minds it was gobbledygook.

Lamprey had inserted in the 1963 budget bill a provision that members of the legislature could be reimbursed for their expenses for official duty when the legislature was not in session. At that time, there was no committee mileage and there was no reimbursement of any type for the legislators once the session was formally adjourned. Attorney General Gardner Turner pointed out that the legislature had to vote such spending, or the vote from the authority at least, to make it legal. They, basically, put in the budget bill that the Senate president and chairman of the Senate Finance Committee would be given authority over such interim spending on the Senate.

In the House, the Speaker and chairman of the House Appropriations Committee would have similar authority for their side of the legislative fence. This important change allowed for committees to meet in the off-session, and brought us, finally, into the modern era.

CHAPTER 13
How Do You Stand on Whiskey?

I often used in speeches an old bit (author unknown) entitled *How Do You Stand on Whiskey?*

"If, when you say whiskey, you mean the devil's brew, the poison scourge, the bloody monster that defiles innocence, dethrones reason, destroys the home, creates misery and poverty — yes, literally takes the bread from the mouths of little children; if you mean the drink that topples the Christian man and woman from the pinnacle of righteous, gracious living into the bottomless pit of degradation, despair, shame, and helplessness, then certainly I am against it with all my power.

"But if, when you say whiskey, you mean the oil of conversation, the philosophic wine, the ale that is consumed when good fellows get together, that puts a song in their hearts and laughter on their lips and the warm glow of contentment in their eyes; if you mean Christmas cheer; if you mean the stimulating drink that puts the spring in an old gentleman's step on a frosty morning; if you mean that drink, the sale of which pours into our treasury untold millions of dollars that are used to provide tender care for our crippled children, our blind, our deaf, our dumb, pitiful, aged, and infirm, to build highways, hospitals, and schools, then certainly I am in favor of it. This is my stand, and I will not compromise."

I also like and used this poem by Marvin Ruth:

> **Swinger?**
> *He's a born politician,*
> *flexible and hyper.*
> *He changes sides more often*
> *than a windshield wiper!*

My old friend California House Speaker Jesse Unruh was famous for saying: "Money is the mother's milk of politics." When I embarked on my legislative career, I soon found out that liquor was the mother's milk of New Hampshire politics. Liquor affected funding in a million ways, as I continued to learn all during my political life.

One of the first pieces of legislation I sponsored as a freshman young turk was to allow patrons of bars and restaurants that sold liquor to be served standing up. The Liquor Commission had for years had a regulation that you had to be seated to be served a drink. If you were at the bar, you couldn't carry your drink over to a table. This was done, in theory, to keep the prohibitionists happy and to prevent men from hitting on women who were seated at tables.

It caused a lot of consternation in the barrooms that I frequented. My bill was to repeal this regulation. I expected a major battle, because it was a major change in the way liquor laws were administered in the state.

We had a liquor inspector in Nashua who wouldn't let men wear hats—even baseball caps—in barrooms. He had his own set of rules along with the official regulations of the Liquor Commission. He was a dictator in the sense that if he reported a bar, a club, or a liquor vending establishment for a violation of the law, it could lose its liquor license or have it suspended or be fined. He became an absolute tyrant, and his one-man rule made him widely disliked.

When my bill had its hearing, and was reported favorable out of the committee, I expected (and the whole press corps expected) a major battle on the floor of the House because here we were liberalizing New Hampshire's archaic blue law, letting people actually stand up when they drank and letting them move from the bar to a table to join a friend or to meet a lady.

The bill came up. I spoke on behalf of it and, lo and behold, nobody opposed it. The Speaker was perplexed. He kept asking for somebody else to speak but nobody did. We couldn't figure out why the moral-majority types, the drys, and the other anti-liquor folks just sat on their hands. Apparently they were not organized for the fight, and my bill passed the House.

A few days later, two pieces of liberalizing liquor laws passed the House, again without any real opposition. The *Concord Monitor*'s pundit, Andy Andersen, reported it this way: "Never before this week have we ever seen lawmakers pass two bills on the same day to liberalize our state liquor control system. They did it on Tuesday much to the surprise of more than a few folks—wets and drys alike. The House voted to let hotel cocktail lounges sell booze on Sundays and Election Days and they sent a bill to the Senate. At the same time, the Senate passed a bill to let restaurants sell booze in dry towns and shipped that to the House for further study."

Andy continued: "The amazing thing about this House bill was that it passed without a murmur of dissent. Observers and even Speaker Stewart Lamprey had naturally expected a hot floor fight, for a strong segment of the legislature in both branches traditionally is chary about opening the doors to booze more than is absolute necessary.

"It was so surprising, in fact, that the following day one of the religious leaders of the House, Representative Paul B. Maxham of Concord, tried to resurrect the issue and let the House reconsider and have another crack at the liquor measure. But it was too little, too late and he got snowed under a voice vote."

The Senate bill concerned a dry town, Newington, which had one of the state's best restaurants, Flagstones. The bill would allow the sale of liquor in the restaurant but at no place else in town. There hadn't been a referendum in Newington on the subject.

When the Senate passed the law to allow Flagstone's a liquor license, it specifically prohibited the town of Hampton, which includes, of course, Hampton Beach, from benefiting from this law. Lots of parents liked to send their kids to the beach, where it was dry. They didn't want to have any booze in Hampton, including in the Dunfey family's restaurants and hotel. The Dunfeys were major Democratic political players in the King administration.

Liquor laws were gradually being liberalized. The liquor inspector in Nashua continued to enforce his arbitrary rules in my home community. The Berkshire Motel and Cocktail Lounge, which I frequented, had undergone a major expansion after the change was made to allow people to stand up at the bar. To get the local liquor inspector, Emile Bozek by name, to allow it to expand the function room in which it served booze, the restaurant agreed that it wouldn't let people stand at the bar because Bozek didn't like the idea.

I came in one night and was told I could not stand at the bar and have a drink.

Having just passed a law in Concord saying that patrons could stand at the bar, I protested, but I was refused a drink because they were afraid of Mr. Bozek.

I complained to Liquor Commissioner Chick Tentas, and he brought in his enforcement chief, Bill Tassie, who was Bozek's boss. They said I was right. Bartenders could serve me and all others while we were standing. What Bozek had done in Nashua was illegal. They ordered Bozek to stop doing it. This turned out to be a disaster for me. I won the battle but lost the war.

One night, when Bozek was making his rounds in the Berkshire, he observed me standing in the bar. He also noticed that I was on my way to drinking too much.

Bozek called a friend in the Nashua Police Department and had him wait outside the bar until I left. When I started to drive home in a light snowstorm, I was pulled over and charged with drunken driving.

With family friend and noted criminal lawyer Dick Leonard to defend me, I was acquitted on several grounds. The police had entrapped me, there were major discrepancies in the police report, and they lied about tests they performed.

Dick asked the cop where he was parked when I came out of the bar. The policeman replied, "We were at the gas station across the street to get coffee." Leonard badgered the cop to the point where he admitted he'd been there three hours. Leonard then established that the garage had not been open for those three hours. The cop obviously wasn't getting coffee: He was waiting for me because he was tipped off by Bozek.

The police have a test they call the coin test, whereby they drop coins on the ground and you're supposed to pick them up in order of their value—in other words, penny, nickel, dime, quarter. A lot of drunks get fooled by picking up the dime before the nickel because it's smaller. Thus, they've proved they don't know the value of the various coins; ergo, they must be drunk.

There was a small trace of snow on the ground that night, which Leonard established when the officer said he followed my tire tracks in the snow because I was swerving. Leonard asked, "How could you tell?" The officer said, "I could tell because his snow tracks were swerving around the road."

When the officer said that I failed the coin test, Leonard asked him, "If there was snow on the ground, how could he have any chance of picking up the coins?"

The officer had clearly dropped keys, not coins. Even though they call it the coin test, he had dropped keys. I was positive of that. When Leonard badgered the second policeman, he finally admitted that they had dropped keys, not coins.

Leonard also found out that the report charging me with arrest had different-colored ink halfway through the statement. Again, he questioned the officers until they admitted they had written some of the stuff that morning, not on the day I was arrested. For all these reasons, I was acquitted. Frankly, I was guilty as sin, and this was not a proud moment for me.

By proving that it was now legal to stand in a bar in such an unintentionally drastic manner, I paid the price with the great amount of publicity that accompanied (and still does) a public figure's arrest for drunken driving. Even though I was exonerated, people were convinced that I must have been guilty.

The jovial chairman of the House Liquor Laws Committee, Lyman "Colly" Collishaw, was a colorful character in the legislature in those days. Colly had a flushed red face and always smiled when he took the floor.

The standing committees in the House all had twenty-one members—that is, all but Colly's Liquor Laws Committee, which had forty-four. This was a profile in courage by the legislative leadership at the time. A lot of representatives wanted to serve on that committee because it took two or three junkets annually to various breweries. Occasionally members were flown by the big beer or liquor companies to breweries far outside the state for a big-time party paid for by their hosts, the liquor vendors.

Colly was a throwback to the olden days. He ran a happy ship, and the Liquor Laws Committee was the prize landing place for many legislators who didn't want to work hard and wouldn't say no to a few free drinks.

Proof of liquor law influence on the legislature was the fact that when the legislature came to Concord, the liquor commissioners would open the Concord liquor store on Wednesday afternoons. Liquor stores in those days traditionally closed on Wednesday as the half day off for employees.

The Concord store remained open on Wednesday so that legislators could buy booze for their evening libation if they couldn't get it free from Angus and Pickett down on skid row.

It was not unknown in those days for legislators to be given liquor "samples" to take back to their rooms from time to time. If a legislator had a son or daughter or another family member getting married, or if there was a major birthday bash or a wedding, it was not unusual for a liquor salesman to drop off booze at the celebration so that a legislator wouldn't have to buy his own booze for the memorable occasion.

The do-gooders, of course, howled about this procedure, but the apologists for the Liquor Commission pointed out that it was not unusual in New Hampshire business circles for a salesman to drop off free liquor to some special customers during the holidays and at other festive occasions.

A major source of evildoing in the liquor business lay in the decisions as to what products were actually sold in liquor stores. A liquor broker had to be "listed" to get his product sold in liquor stores. Each brand of booze had a specific salesman whose job it was to get listed in these New Hampshire liquor stores.

Some of the top-selling brands in other states, for one reason or another, were not listed in New Hampshire because they didn't have the right kind of sponsorship in the form of a liquor salesman. The Liquor Commission, it was believed, wielded a lot of power over who got listed to sell what products. Thus, they could build up their favorite brokers and get them a number of products listed, which increased their income as they got a percentage of every bottle of booze sold in state liquor stores.

Many of the so-called brokers were politicians, retired politicians, and friends of politicians who made their living by this kind of nefarious practice. As the legislative scribe Andy Andersen reported in February 1963: "It becomes more evident as time goes by that New Hampshire had a strong and respected state liquor system for some thirty years because of the late Senator Styles Bridges. All the huffing and hassling within the Liquor Commission began after his death nearly fifteen months ago."

Andy went on: "It now appears that strange as it may sound to many folks, Styles Bridges had more to say about Granite State liquor sales and our thirty million booze retail business than we, for one, realized. Most of the liquor we sold down through the years was through salesmen of time-proven political loyalty to Styles Bridges.

"Quietly and without any public knowledge, Styles Bridges was the man behind the scenes. He kept the Liquor Commission running smoothly and without any ill winds blowing into the public spotlight. Now that the king is gone, the wolves are snarling over the spoils. It's as simple as that. All concerned are claiming that their motives and maneuverings are pure as the driven snow."

Andy concluded with this warning: "Unless Governor King quickly gets a strong man onto the Liquor Commission within a short time, the mess may blow up in the Republican Party's face."

That was prophetic.

Wes Powell had appointed Costas "Chick" Tentas to serve as a liquor commissioner. Eventually he put Chick in charge of the whole mess. Chick was a master at making friends and wielded quite a bit of power among the liquor brokers. He did a great job of improving the merchandising of liquor. Although some of his methods and means would not win the approval of today's do-gooders or even some of the ones in his days, he effectively built the New Hampshire Liquor Commission into a modern, businesslike machine that greatly increased the take for the state of New Hampshire.

Of course, Chick took care of his political friends and enemies along the way in establishing this economic bonanza.

One of the great stories of Liquor Commission history is that we established a procedure at holiday time to increase sales. Massachusetts had a tax commissioner, Henry Long, who was upset because Massachusetts citizens flocked to New Hampshire to buy the much-lower-priced liquor here and then bring it home for the holidays in Massachusetts. Long would dispatch his Massachusetts tax collectors and have them park at the liquor stores near the border towns. They were instructed to take down the license plates of people from Massachusetts coming out of the liquor stores with booze purchased in New Hampshire. His people would then bill the offenders for the tax on a case of Seagrams Seven, which he claimed was the usual purchase by these out-of-towners.

This, of course, caused outrage in Massachusetts and had the effect of decreasing New Hampshire liquor sales. Commissioner Tentas, with the state police, devised a solution to the problem. We would have our police arrest Tax Commissioner Long's agents in our state liquor store parking lots for being vagrants with no visible means of support or they'd arrest them for loitering. Of course, we would publicize the fact that we were doing this.

The Massachusetts people would holler to high heaven that it was unfair of New Hampshire to arrest their tax agents. All this did was to publicize even more the fact that New Hampshire had lower liquor prices and that Long's tax collectors had disappeared from our stores, which brought back our sales volume.

When I was in the various governors' offices during the years, we had a set of identical press statements that we issued no matter who the governor was. Once we started the first arrest of Long's tax agents, we reissued the statements promoting the facts of New Hampshire's lowest liquor prices on the East Coast. We heralded the ending of Commissioner Long's harassment of out-of-state liquor buyers.

Back to the liquor lists . . . When Governor King came into office and discovered the details of what was going on with the liquor lists, he was flabbergasted. One of the first things King found out was that Governor Powell froze the enactment of the liquor list for ten months and then released it just before Christmas to stir up the liquor salesmen and brokers, who would be fighting for additional plums.

The fighting over which kinds of booze would be listed had on one side Chairman Flanders and on the other side two Powell appointees, Chick Tentas and Mary Walsh-Caron, a former powerful West Side Manchester state senator.

When King got in, Flanders wanted to put eight new items on the list and close it for good. But Mrs. Walsh-Caron and Tentas insisted on additions of more than one hundred items that they voted on a year earlier. To that end, they wanted their list of the products printed to build up and engender political support for adding the whole hundred items. Of course the listing of these and who their salesmen would be was a list of who's who in New Hampshire politics. This would cause a good deal of consternation, so there was a major battle that King had to deal with in getting this matter settled. It occupied a lot of time in the legislature—and in the political headlines.

One fight involved my friend and lawyer, former attorney general Bill Phinney, and Judge Shaw, a politician from Newport.

Phinney claimed he had been the lawyer for more than a year for a Boston man who sold one of the top-ranked scotch whiskys in the New England area. Phinney said his client handled this best-selling item and after trying for years to get his brand onto the New Hampshire list, he'd hired Phinney to be his attorney. All three of our liquor commissioners told Phinney at one time or another that it was an excellent product. They freely said the brand would go on the new list once it got published. Phinney claimed that he "never dreamed so much detail was involved in getting a liquor brand onto a New Hampshire listing until I tried to do an honest job of representing an honest client with an honest product."

The commissioners still weren't sure they were going to put the brand on the list—I believe it was J and B Scotch. Governor King then said it's about time that "the Liquor Commission began selling booze on the basis of merit rather than hit-or-miss personalities and who knows what else."

Governor King soon got fed up with Liquor Commission Chairman Franklin Flanders. It was a virtual certainty that he was going to replace the former Weare egg expert when his six-year term expired on July 1,

1963, which was coincidental with the end of the legislative session.

King, in his term on the House Appropriations Committee before he became governor, had fought with Flanders all through the year trying to get information about the state's thirty-million-dollar booze business, but Flanders squirmed behind legal barriers and refused to let the lawmakers know what was going on behind the Liquor Commission's self-made curbs on public information.

The Liquor Commission at that time was divided up so that members had different duties. Chick Tentas was in charge of law enforcement. Mrs. Walsh-Caron supervised the liquor stores; Chairman Flanders mostly handled the booze buying and related details, which, of course, was where the power lay. King eventually told them they had to put out their list by a given date and he wanted all the products in all the stores by that date.

Driving to work a few mornings later, King was amazed when he heard on the radio that they weren't going to be doing it by that date because it was impossible to do. They hadn't even told him they couldn't do it. They just put out a press release on the radio, which, of course, activated King's Irish temper.

King demanded Flanders's resignation: "Flanders has been guilty of an inexcusable lack of leadership," he said. Flanders rebutted by saying that since he had been commissioner, sales had gone from $22.5 million to $32 million, or an increase of 41.8 percent. There had not been a single increase in liquor prices, according to Flanders. Flanders went on to say that by the constant application of sound business procedures, we had maintained the lowest level of liquor prices in the country to benefit our New Hampshire users, attract peripheral business, and at the same time produce the highest per-capita revenue of any other state except Washington.

King demanded at a press conference to know why the governor's office had not been told that the new price list had been reopened and fifteen more items had been added. King made plain not only that he was upset by having to read in the papers what was going on in this major state agency, but also that he intended to do something drastic about it.

Robert Hart, the administrative assistant for the Liquor Commission, told King at the press conference that the department had never bothered to tell other governors what it did, so it felt no obligation to tell Governor King. King claimed that he could never get out of Flanders any kind of satisfactory explanation "of what sort of yardstick and what factors were used in putting one hundred and twelve new items on the liquor list, then adding another fifteen items later."

King said, "This was a lack of good business practices." Commissioner Tentas, playing up to King, said they wanted more conferences and Flanders said he had no comment. It was reported by Andy Andersen that Chairman Flanders and Hart told the governor that most of the new brands were not worth their salt and should be removed from the new list. Flanders pointed out that he had nothing to do with the addition of one hundred and twelve brands made ten months ago by Walsh-Caron and Tentas, both of whom were ex-governor Powell's political appointees.

King was shocked by such a stand by the chairman of a major state agency—Flanders said he left these hundred and twelve things on the list because he thought the two other commissioners would outvote him. Once the new list became public, it showed that the hundred and twenty-five items had been added to the liquor list in the package stores. Two members of the State Senate were among the thirty-five people listed by the Liquor Commission as brokers for these products. They were Republican Senator Paul Karkavelas, of Dover, and Senator Paul Provost, of Manchester, a Democrat. Each was listed with nine items.

Another big-name politician on the list was Bill Styles, of Grovetown, a former liquor commissioner, who had ten items. Styles, a Democrat, had been replaced by Governor Powell. Benjamin Mates, of Manchester, Republican state finance chairman, was listed as an agent for a Jewish wine. Other politicos were Nate "Nasty" Battles, Harold Goldberg, Charlie Hunt, and Clarence Merrill.

King claimed that he'd been told that the list of one hundred and twelve new brands had been increased to one hundred and twenty-five by the Liquor Commission on January 11. Powell then froze it on his desk for eight months and freed it just before leaving office. King disclosed that the thirteen items added to the list January 11 were sponsored by Chairman Flanders and Tentas, with Mrs. Walsh-Caron dissenting.

King said that he himself had recommended no inclusions or deletions on the proposed list, but he had asked the Department of Administration and Control to review the list with the Liquor Commission. Thus, when the list was made public, the state knew what some of the politicians knew, and the public suspected that the liquor-broker thing was a politically motivated deal full of shenanigans.

Eventually, they said senators couldn't be on the list, so Provost put in his wife's name as the broker as he and Karkavelas left the Senate. Senator Nate Battles, who was a major liquor broker, left the Senate shortly after that, but remained a powerful player until he was murdered a few years later.

Another important change made by Chick Tentas was to eliminate an old commission policy or regulation, thereby allowing women to be employed in liquor stores and as bartenders.

CHAPTER 14

Finishing the Budget

We were at loggerheads on the budget until the House fiscal experts came up with a tactic that I was seeing for the first time—a tactic that had been repeated many times. They increased revenue estimates by three million dollars. They used that newly found money to finance increased aid to education and meet other needs on several fronts.

Appropriations Committee Chairman Arnold Clement made the proposal based on facts from Remick Laighton, the legislative budget assistant. The legislators claimed that Laighton's figures were more reliable than those that had been given to the legislature by Governor King the previous month and developed by Comptroller Len Hill.

When the head-tax debate was going on, I at one time got some newspaper publicity saying we should double the head tax, but instead of calling it a ten-dollar head tax, we should call it a five-dollar head tax and a five-dollar tail tax. We would then have a head and tail tax rather than just a head tax. That would solve the state's problems.

This idea made good press but it was never seriously considered. Governor King, of course, criticized the Republicans' three-million-dollar spending proposal as "just another Republican leadership exercise in indecision. It represents a third head tax switch in three weeks. Fiscal solvency cannot be projected by juggling figures." King commented: "When you're dealing with estimates, it can be like quicksand."

The Republicans had been all over the House in dealing with Governor King's proposals. First they said they were too high. Then they said they weren't high enough. Then they increased them after criticizing him for spending too much. But in the end, the budget problem was solved—just when it looked like it couldn't be—by increasing revenue estimates.

The Democrats always claimed foul play at this because the Republicans controlled the estimating process, but the fact is that when you're estimating two and a half years in advance, the closer you get to the time you're estimating for, the greater the accuracy of what the economic situation will be. Most of the time, the legislative budget estimates have been quite good overall. They have been met on most occasions.

The governor's estimates by necessity must be made by the comptroller in the fall, before the legislative session, so they'll be ready for the gubernatorial budget hearings in November. The legislature makes its estimates in May, so there is a six-month period to get a better look at what's actually happening.

CHAPTER 15

Sneaky Petes

Late in the 1963 session, crafty Speaker Stewart Lamprey asked me to check legislation coming over from the Senate. Unbeknownst to me, the Speaker had read all the legislation himself the night before. He knew that the Senate had tacked on extraneous amendments to almost every bill.

A group of senators was trying to resurrect dead legislation that the House had killed. Their trick was to put the substance of bills previously killed by the House back onto Senate bills. They thought they could get their way by fooling the House into adopting amendments that were ostensibly innocuous.

These new Senate amendments actually contained all the pet legislation that the devious duo of Nasty Nate Battles and Nelson Howard were trying to pass for friends and lobbyists but had already been killed once by the House. Their technique was to tack on their legislation in the last days of the session. I, as requested by the Speaker, started studying these new Senate measures.

I was amazed by what I saw: pensions for favored state troopers being granted beyond what the ordinary trooper gets; roads being built to mountains to help a ski developer; and legislation that could not stand public scrutiny. I reported back to Speaker Stewart Lamprey and then said, "What should I do?"

The Speaker suggested that when he'd call up the next bill for debate, instead of asking questions on the Senate amendment, I should get up and explain to the members of the House what the amendment did and then ask them to defeat it. I did my part.

I fought every amendment and explained what the original bill did and how the members of the House were being hoodwinked by these "sneaky petes."

I urged the House to kill each amendment. I sensed that the term *sneaky petes* was striking a chord with the members. The House was soon aroused. They killed the first three or four measures loudly and, of course, wily "Daniel Webster" saw a good thing and jumped into the fray.

He started railing against the dastardly acts of the cowardly Senate in trying to foist these sneaky petes on the unsuspecting House. Between Daniel Webster and me, we managed to defeat I think eleven pieces of legislation that had been sent over from the Senate.

This set up a major confrontation with the Senate. In negotiating how to solve the problem, I was able to get my legislation enacted into law, which the devious duo had kept killing. The saga of the sneaky petes increased my stature in the House substantially. The Speaker had chosen me for this role because he knew, being a Realtor and an insurance agent himself, that the devious duo had been killing my pet anti-coercion insurance legislation at the bequest of the auto dealers' lobbyist.

CHAPTER 16

Other 1963 Session Highlights

Because the New Hampshire legislature is so large, it quite often reflects the will of the constituents, at least it did in my day.

One of the hot floor fights was about a bill to force motorists to submit to a blood test if suspected to be DWI (driving while under the influence of alcohol). The fight was on the so-called implied-consent issue, which had been repeatedly killed in past legislative sessions.

The people now trying to kill it wanted to delay the vote until the following week because fifty members of the House, including most of the Liquor Laws Committee, were in New Jersey to visit officials of that state but primarily a brewery that was sponsoring the free trip and a New York Yankees baseball game.

The vote to delay the liquor law implied-consent thing was voted down without the fifty votes of the Liquor Laws Committee. The trip was made in a plane chartered by the brewery.

Near the end of the session, we got a proposal from my friend Zandy

Taft, of Greenville, to repeal the antiquated stock and trade tax. Zandy wanted to replace it with an income tax. That never really got anywhere. We did replace it a couple of years later with the business profits tax.

We also heard a proposal from the New England governors—primarily Governor Reed, of Maine, and Phil Hoff, of Vermont—for an east–west highway from Maine to Albany. This led me to sponsor legislation a few years later to construct an east–west highway.

While we were in session in 1963, Charles Barnard, the former State Senate president, who was in prison for embezzling from a trust fund he represented as an attorney, asked for a pardon. It brought back into question some of the things you saw in the legislature when you knew that the former Senate president was currently in jail.

One headline in the papers during this period is of interest—Wednesday, May 8, 1963, front-page story of the liberal *Concord Daily Monitor:*

"Riot-Trained State Troopers Ready for New Negro March. Police finally scattered the marchers. Fire hoses were brought into play to disperse the crowd. No confirmed reports of any Negroes being injured. New arrests were mostly for hurling rocks."

It is unlikely that the *Monitor* would have a headline and story like that in today's climate, when recalling what Sheriff Bull Conners did to Dr. Martin Luther King Jr. and his Freedom Fighters.

Stewart Lamprey was always a modest man, and shy, not nearly as flamboyant as I was. He was set to have his testimonial dinner, an annual tradition for every Speaker no matter how good or bad. Stewart shared the dinner tribute with the political columnist of the *Concord Monitor.*

This was Stewart's third testimony because it was his third term as Speaker. The words of Congressman Louis Wyman speaking about Lamprey at that event are worth repeating:

"We can all take great satisfaction in the fact that we have a really knowledgeable man at the helm of the House. Lamprey is both a successful legislator and a successful businessman. There is a third quality of Stewart Lamprey that outshines both of these things. In large part it is because of this quality that successes come to Stewart, and that is his sense of integrity. He keeps his word.

"Many times Stewart depended upon his skill as a parliamentarian, but finally Stewart Lamprey depends on his word. Never have I ever found his word to be lacking, nor have I ever heard anybody say the contrary. Such a quality is vital. Stew has it in spades."

CHAPTER 17

1965: Subversives, Sweepstakes, and Salaries

My second term in the legislature was dominated by the Feldman bill, a bill seeking to ban Communist speakers from University of New Hampshire facilities.

The notorious Chicago three, Jerry Rubin, et al., were scheduled to speak at the university. This became a major donnybrook throughout the session and caused a great deal of excitement.

Another major battle was over the implementation and updating of the sweepstakes legislation, with last-ditch efforts to harass it and make it impossible to succeed. The fight between two Irishmen, Governor John King and Health and Welfare Commissioner Jim Barry, was something to behold.

The sweepstakes commission and the governor supported a bill that would expand the number of outlets where you could sell sweepstakes tickets. Originally, the tickets could be sold only at the forty-nine state-operated liquor stores and two racetracks. The new bill would allow their sale at four state parks; two county recreation areas; and hotels, motels, resort areas, and fairs that were interested in doing so.

The bill passed the House, and then in a surprise was killed by the Senate, thirteen to eight. This set into motion a monumental parliamentary struggle. The Senate vote consisted of twelve Republicans and just one Democrat. At the center of the turmoil was Republican State Chairman Bill Johnson, who had led the fight against the sweepstakes in the 1963 session.

Bill was a Hanover Republican who was widely revered by the good government types. Governor King, in a strongly worded statement, denounced those who voted to kill the bill and said they "showed contempt for the people of New Hampshire." The Senate indefinitely postponed the bill, which was supposed to mean that it was killed for the rest of the session.

Sweepstakes Director Ed Powers said the bill could have meant more than one million dollars in gross revenue for the lottery over the next two years. King said, "It could have meant hundreds of thousands of dollars in extra revenue to help finance local school budgets." He concentrated his attack on the Republican majority in the Senate and in particular Bill Johnson, the GOP state chairman. King accused them of demonstrating an utter lack of concern for our cities and towns. He said the Republicans were conscious that "a successful sweepstakes operation would reflect credit on a Democratic administration."

The Republican leadership chose to sabotage the bill in an effort at political gain. Of course, the *Concord Monitor* editorialized against expanding sweeps outlets, saying, "Anyone who wants to buy a lottery ticket has a reasonable access to them at the forty-nine liquor stores and the state's two racetracks."

The *Monitor* went on: "New Hampshire's lottery is skidding in the seven and a half months since the running of the sweepstakes race in '64. Ticket sales for the '65 lottery have amounted to only half of the number of tickets sold last year in the first month of sales. Prospects are that mid-May '65 sales will be about equal to the first two months in February."

The *Monitor* editorialized that "the novelty of the lottery was gone. It was oversold anyway, and gamblers were taking a second look. The odds were better at the racetrack. Chances could be bought more cheaply there, and one didn't have to wait even a week to know he'd lost. As in the lottery, only a fraction of those who bet will win."

The *Monitor* concluded that "the lottery had become insignificant as a solution to the state's funding problems, raising barely enough revenue to salve the state's bad conscience. Certainly it was far from enough to balance the unfavorable reputation it earned for New Hampshire in the rest of the country."

The *Monitor* editorial claimed "that residents of the State of New Hampshire had a guilt complex about the lottery. They would prefer the state didn't have a lottery. They accepted it only because they like even less to pay taxes, but their conscience still bothers them. They don't swallow the pious spoutings of the sweepstakes commission, the lottery director, or the governor. Instead they subconsciously are ashamed of it."

The fight got more interesting when Stuart Hancock, a Concord representative, teamed up with Democratic Minority Leader Bill Craig to take advantage of the resentment in the House about the Senate's actions. Johnson, the leader of the Senate fight, was also state GOP chairman.

One of the bills Johnson was sponsoring concerned political advertising. The Democrats had put forth a successful advertising book entitled "Democrat Political Yearbook." They sold ads to major corporations and all the lobbying interests. Johnson wanted to do the same thing for the Republican Party but he, being a lawyer, came across some statute that said it was illegal to solicit advertising for political yearbooks. He put in a piece of legislation to allow political yearbooks to solicit advertising.

Newspapers like the *Monitor* said this was awful because they thought all advertising ought to be in newspapers and not go to politicians. The Senate had passed the bill and the House was about to pass it when Hancock and Craig decided they would recall the political advertising bill and hold it hostage until Johnson passed the sweepstakes expansion bill.

First Hancock was going to add the sweepstakes bill onto the political advertising bill as an amendment. Hancock was a clever politico, a gut fighter, and he figured they might just kill both bills and he would lose. Thus he said instead that the sweepstakes bill would show up as an amendment on some other Senate bill in his committee: He said he wanted to keep the political advertising bill for further study.

What he clearly was trying to do was hold the political advertising bill as hostage and release it from the committee only after the Senate had approved the sweepstakes expansion amendment. This got into a floor fight in the House. Republicans who didn't like Johnson and who were more conservative than the Hanover liberal started attacking him. Bob Stratton, of Derry, the Insurance Committee chairman, charged that the Republican Party was deserting the people, and added, "I as a Republican am ashamed of what the Senate did."

Hancock told the press that he was going to keep the political advertising bill in his committee for as long as necessary for the Senate to come to its senses. The House voted 209 to 121 to chastise the Senate for killing the sweepstakes expansion.

House Speaker Walter Peterson put the prestige of his leadership on the line—and got trampled. His pleas for restraint were swept aside. Bill Craig, the Minority Leader, tried to smooth things over. He privately urged Peterson not to leave the rostrum because his well-intentioned effort would be brushed aside by an irate House, but Peterson felt duty-bound.

The prestige of Senate President Stewart Lamprey and his Republican dominance were at stake. So Peterson made his plea and went down in flames.

Craig, ever the gentleman, jumped to the floor after the bill passed and defended Speaker Peterson, his political opponent. Craig emphasized the vote was not against Peterson: It just constituted deep personal convictions by the membership of the House against the Senate's shocking vote. This byplay showed what a class guy Bill Craig was, and still is.

Peterson and Zandy Taft, his Republican floor leader, spoke against the bill and in favor of the actions of their friend Bill Johnson, but it was to no avail. The House was angry at the Senate and was going to express it.

Many of the House members were proud of their vote for the sweepstakes legislation. They believed Bill Johnson lost the fight fairly and was still using his lawyer tricks to try and gut the sweepstakes after it had been enacted into law. The House was highly incensed.

More than two thousand people from the north country in 1965 requested a piece of legislation that Loggy LaMontagne said they could really sink their teeth into.

The primary purpose of the legislation, LaMontagne explained, was to bypass dentists in obtaining full or partial dentures from a mechanical dentistry laboratory in Berlin, which made, among other things, wooden teeth, which I thought went out with George Washington.

The Berlin delegation, on the other hand, supported the provision to allow dentists to make wooden teeth. It was basically single-interest legislation to help one man, the man who made the wooden teeth.

I remember vividly sitting in the lounge of the Carpenter Hotel one day with Judge Dunfey. The judge was a very mischievous guy who liked to kid people. We came across a Berlin citizen who had false teeth, and they turned out to be wooden teeth made by the Berlin dentist.

Dunfey, with a serious face and all the respect a judge can command during the cocktail hour, suggested that the guy paint the teeth red, white, and blue, and put a star in the center of the teeth. The guy fell hook, line, and sinker for the judge's pitch. The Berlin citizen thought this was a wonderful idea. Judge Dunfey kept saying it would be nifty, it would be neat. He had the guy almost convinced to get his teeth painted in the patriotic colors.

Another big issue in the 1965 session was teachers' salaries. The state Department of Education reported that New Hampshire's teachers' salaries were the second lowest in the New England area. Salaries averaged $5,440 a year, which was up 64 percent over the $3,310 average of a decade earlier.

Massachusetts salaries were up to $6,950 and Connecticut teachers averaged $6,975. The New Hampshire Teachers Association was pestering me, Lamprey, and Peterson, whom they considered moderate liberals, that this needed to be raised to a five-thousand-dollar minimum, with a cap of $8,800.

Eventually, both the Democratic and the Republican legislative leaders expressed opposition to the bill. We came down on the side of home rule. The Teachers Association didn't like that deal. They said that there was nothing wrong with the legislature telling communities what the minimum was.

We were mindful of the fact that the teachers' pay increases would have to be paid by the local property tax. Property taxes were already soaring in New Hampshire, and that had an impact on the decision.

Another big battle that year was whether or not to give a tax break to the new out-of-state owners of the Joy Manufacturing Company, in Claremont. Claremont was a poor area. It was represented by Pat Angus, who was fighting mightily to get a tax increase and tax break for the new company. The matter ended up in the courts, which gave Joy some small relief.

We were all aware that Joy Manufacturing operated in a number of other states. It was playing one state against another. There was not a great deal of sympathy on our behalf for the company, even though there would be a severe economic impact in the Claremont area if it failed.

Governor King was proposing to balance the budget by increasing both the beer and the tobacco tax. The beer lobbyists were fighting it fiercely. This caused me a great deal of consternation, as I spent a lot of time in barrooms. I had many friends who drank beer and thus would have to pay the tax.

Governor King was quite annoyed at the beer barons and the grocers. King figured that if he was going to have a major battle, he might as well double the tax and get more money to balance the budget, because these people were giving us a really hard time as it was.

King wanted to recommend that his original levy go up from 9.5 cents to 12 cents a gallon on beer to help support education, mental health services, and care for the elderly. He pointed out that the Vermont tax had long been 25 cents and Maine's was 20 cents per gallon, so New Hampshire would still be below the neighboring states.

King figured he might as well go for more money because the beer barons couldn't get any angrier. Their propaganda couldn't become any worse. They claimed the tax hike would drive business away from the corner stores and drive grocers toward bankruptcy. But the supporters of the measure asked, Where do they think they're going to go? Vermont or Maine? The tax is higher there. Or will they turn to milk or ginger ale?

Since when, we argued, would a tax of a penny a six-pack or even two cents a six-pack hurt the beer business? We also reminded the beer barons that it was only two years ago that the legislature legalized Sunday beer sales. This boosted their business by 10 percent and their profits by 10 percent. Why didn't they use their new profits to finance the beer tax increase instead of passing it on to the customers, we asked? We ended up passing a beer tax increase of 1¹/₄ cents per six-pack.

The vote was to kill the beer tax; only seventy-two members voted to do away with it. Three hundred and four members voted to support the beer tax even though it wouldn't be popular with their constituents.

Lamprey reminded citizens that if the legislature was going to spend money for such projects as a $9.4 million state employees pay raise, it was essential to raise the money to pay for them. He said that the store owners could actually benefit from the measure. They'd have to increase the price of beer by two cents per six-pack; they would get three quarters of a cent themselves.

We had already that session passed increases in taxes on tobacco, utilities, and inheritance, and they were all signed into law.

The education lobbyists decided to put in a soft-drink tax too, to get more money for education, but that didn't fly. Zandy Taft, who at the time was also pushing an income tax based on 3 percent of a person's federal income tax (which he claimed would raise twenty-four million dollars), said he would abolish the stock and trade tax and the interest and dividend tax, the head tax, and the property tax on farm, livestock, and poultry. The education people and the liberals loved this, but it had no real chance of passage in the House or the Senate.

The overall needs for funds, however, led us to believe we should go for the room and meals tax. If it wasn't going to get a fair shot in the '65 session, we knew that it would have to be taken up later, probably in the special session or the '67 session.

We also had the annual fight on capital punishment. The motion to indefinitely postpone the bill, which was successful and killed the legislation, was made by Democratic Representative Armand Capistran, of Manchester, who later became a notoriously heavy-handed Manchester judge.

Liberal Democrat Harry "Midnight" Spanos said that the present system was just a lazy answer to a social and economic problem. Spanos said that if the state wanted to retain the death penalty, it might as well go all the way back to the Dark Ages and hang people from the statehouse steps for everyone to see.

It was pointed out that the last execution in New Hampshire was in 1939, and it was by hanging. Two Rhode Island men, Russell Nelson and

Frederick Martineau, were currently under sentences of death in the 1959 slaying of Maurice Gagnon in a Nashua parking lot. They'd appealed their case to the U.S. Circuit Court in Boston. The Martineau/Nelson case had a personal connection to me.

Maurice Gagnon was going to be a witness against Nelson and Martineau in their trial for robbing his trailer. They all came from Rhode Island.

Nelson and Martineau then kidnapped Gagnon. They rode up to New Hampshire in his car and then shot him, thinking the state was populated by a bunch of hicks and they could get away with it.

After the murder, Martineau and Nelson couldn't drive the bloodstained car back to Rhode Island. They left it, with the body in it, in Nashua, my town at the time. They called their Mafia friends in Rhode Island to come up and pick them up. They were hanging around the back alleys of the main street of Nashua waiting for their ride when the Nashua police found them.

They couldn't explain what they were doing. Police records showed they had histories of criminal activities. The Nashua police took them to the police station. The next morning, somebody found the body. The hick Nashua cops discovered that they already had the murderers in custody, although at the time of the arrest they didn't know a murder had been committed.

I went over to the courthouse that morning to see the arraignment. I was sitting next to an elderly couple waiting for the trial to start. The fancy Mob lawyer Leo McGovern came in. The people sitting next to me got up and said, "Leo, Leo, come here."

McGovern came over and the couple asked him how Nelson was. McGovern said he had seen him and that he was all right. He would be coming into the courtroom shortly and they could see for themselves.

Then the man, who it turned out was a retired cop, asked what Nelson was being charged with. McGovern said first-degree murder. What's the maximum you can get? asked the man. The slick lawyer said, Well, in New Hampshire, the sentence for first-degree murder is death. The cop said how? McGovern answered, By hanging. The woman sitting next to me almost fainted in my lap. That's when I realized I was sitting next to the murderer's mother and father.

After Nelson and Martineau finally went to trial and the jury came back, the foreman of the jury gave the verdict to the clerk of court, Bolic DeGasis. Bolic was a friend of my family and his brother was my uncle's partner in the insurance agency that I later worked for.

DeGasis read the verdict: guilty of murder. The jury recommended that Nelson and Martineau be hanged. DeGasis then dropped dead of a heart attack. That was a dramatic ending to one of New Hampshire's most notorious murder trials. It was the prelude to an extensive court fight over the death penalty.

During the '65 session, Senate President Stewart Lamprey was hospitalized at the Mary Hitchcock Clinic, in Dartmouth, because of a blood vessel spasm. He remained at Mary Hitchcock for a couple of days. He was released and told to reduce his workload. It was the first of a series of health problems for Stew Lamprey that he has suffered from that day until now. Lamprey is now, thirty-nine years later, a vigorous old man.

CHAPTER 18

King Versus Barry

When Governor King gave his second inaugural address, it was roundly praised by both Republican and Democratic leaders. House Speaker Walter Peterson did criticize it by saying he hoped the governor would promise action to improve the state's special education program and to step up the tax on water pollution. Action on both of these items would be needed this year, Peterson said.

Peterson and his floor leader, Zandy Taft, indicated that the governor's plans for major changes in the organization of two large government departments could run into GOP opposition. Taft said he wanted to know if King's proposal to break up the Health and Welfare Department was another move in what he termed "the one-man feud between King and Health and Welfare Commissioner James J. Barry."

King and Barry clashed repeatedly over how to run the state's health and welfare programs. The unified Health and Welfare Department and the Department of Resources and Economic Development were established in 1961 reorganizations of the state government under Governor Powell. Taft said the legislature was going to have to take a good hard look at this one. Peterson said he thought Governor Powell's reorganization plans had not been given enough of a chance to work.

Governor King had proposed to create a separate department of mental health, leaving intact the Office of Health and Welfare Commissioner Jim Barry. The bill was in the ED&A Committee, and

Stuart Hancock, a rebel but a brilliant leader of the committee, was voting with the Democrats on the measure.

Speaker Peterson said the Republican leadership was firmly opposed to demands by the various professional groups, including the New Hampshire Medical Society, for a separate department of mental health. He said the GOP bill he was going to propose would feature refinement and clarification of lines of authority within the framework of the present four-year-old Department of Health and Welfare, lines of authority created by former governor Wesley Powell in 1961.

At one stage there was so much friction between Chairman Hancock and Peterson that Hancock announced he had withdrawn the health and welfare bill into his Committee on Executive Departments and Administration and then taken a leave of absence so the bill would be delayed until the following week. Peterson said that Hancock had no right to impose a delay.

Peterson quoted the attorney general's office that Peterson did not have to bow to the Hancock action. The Republican compromise plan would give division officials clarified authority to get out from under the domination of Commissioner Barry.

At a press conference, Peterson repeatedly declined to say flat out that his bill would clip Barry's control over everything, including the pantry sink, in each division. But he gave that impression without going into personalities, according to media reports. Peterson did say the bill was designed to "indicate the responsibility of the directors in initiating policy and supervising the operation of their respective divisions."

Barry claimed that the present law put squarely on his shoulders all the responsibility down to licking postage stamps in every division. That, he said, was the reason for his delving day and night into Divisional Operations. When the press asked Peterson if Barry endorsed Peterson's bill, he said he didn't know, although it included some suggestions for improvement from Barry.

Peterson's bill said the authority would include the power to establish departmental and divisional policy as well as to control the actual operations of the department and all new divisions therein. Peterson said his bill was designed to give the division chief responsibility and authority for day-to-day operations.

Peterson claimed that his bill was not an indictment of present H&W operations; rather, it was designed to improve services of the department.

The Republican leadership had killed King's bill but in doing so promised to set up a substitute bill that would limit Barry's operations.

Another iron was thrown into the fire when Attorney John R. McLean Jr., of Manchester, denounced former governor Powell at a legislative hearing. McLean had been, for more than ten years, chairman of the powerful Board of Trustees of the New Hampshire Hospital before Powell put it into the present Department of Health and Welfare. McLean's prepared statement labeled Powell "a hermaphrodite governor: one-third Republican, one-third Independent, and one-third Democrat."

McLean claimed that the Republican Party in both 1955 and 1958 mental health studies had recommended a separate department of mental health. He attacked Lamprey and Peterson in his statement: "Now we come to 1965 where we find a Republican-controlled legislature and a Democratic governor. The Republicans desire to forge a new image of the party. Individuals within the party are ambitiously seeking the nomination for governor and everybody is out for himself. A most shameful kindergarten performance.

"Nobody seems to care about the poor mentally ill 2,500 patients at our state hospital, plus many who are non-hospitalized."

McLean went on to say that the present organization was the idea of Governor Powell, who was motivated, perhaps, by the hope of securing control of a large segment of the state employees. McLean said as far as he knew, the power of the organization was never any part of the Republican platform, nor was it recommended by any official of the party.

"Thus, today," McLean went on, "the Republican Party has no more obligation to support the existing merger than Governor Powell had to support the Republican candidate for governor in 1963, namely John Pillsbury. You recall that Governor Powell, defeated at the polls in the Republican primary, deserted the Republicans and swung his weight to and endorsed Governor King. So I say to you Republicans, since this never was Republican legislation, you are free to vote to untangle the present mess."

The Republicans went on to defeat both bills sponsored by Governor King. They proposed instead a bill that would clarify the powers and duties of the Health and Welfare Advisory Commission, add two more psychiatrists to the commission, and establish a special committee within the Advisory Commission to handle the troubled Mental Health Division.

The GOP bill would redefine the duties of the superintendent of New Hampshire Hospital, require that he be a board-certified psychiatrist, and give him full charge of the medical and psychiatric operations of the hospital. Hospital finances would be handled by a qualified business administrator. The directors of both the Mental Health Division and Welfare would be given full authority to establish policy for their divisions. This indicates that some power would be taken away from Health and Welfare Commissioner Jim Barry.

But Taft went on to say that Barry would retain general supervisional authority over all divisions. He also said the power of the Advisory Commission to determine policy would be strengthened. Typically, former governor Wes Powell jumped into the fray, saying that the legislature recognized the necessity of his 1961 reorganization when they rejected Governor King's proposals. At the same time, Powell called on King and Health and Welfare Commissioner Barry to forget their differences and concentrate on a constructive approach to the future.

Powell said, "The 1961 reorganization was absolutely necessary to bring our state government and its programs up-to-date. The legislature recognizes again yesterday in the overwhelming vote of both Republicans and Democrats to kill the effort to throw the '61 accomplishments out."

Powell went on: "There is much that can be accomplished by this vital department through cooperative effort. No good purposes can be served by further public differences between Governor King and Commissioner Barry."

Powell, who at one time was Barry's lawyer, said: "I know Commissioner Barry is willing to meet with the governor to establish a constructive approach to the future. I hope the governor may be willing to meet with him. There is no reason why this attempt at harmonious operations should affect either the investigation or the court proceedings now in the process. I think that a meeting between the governor and the commissioner and a happy approach to the future would be highly approved by the people of New Hampshire.

"Were I governor now," Powell said, "I would constantly seek internal improvements in all departments including these two, while recognizing," he said, "that constant improvement is essential and that neither organization nor the human beings who run them are perfect in every respect. However, there's a difference between wrecking something and simply perfecting it."

There were similar nasty fights about the DRED breakup, but they didn't have the personal animosity and bitterness of the feuding two Irishmen—Governor King and Jim Barry.

The situation got so bad between the two that the governor and council threatened to suspend Health and Welfare Commissioner Jim Barry. He took the matter to the New Hampshire State Supreme Court. Barry had demanded that the Executive Council give him a written statement of purpose and submit questions in writing in conjunction with an investigation ordered by the governor. Barry claimed this was unwarranted.

The court ruled that the governor and council had the authority to require a department head to respond orally if need be to questions on how he ran official business. If he refused to comply, he faced the possibility of executive sanction, including suspension.

Governor King said he was very pleased by the decision. It represented a landmark in the furtherance of good government. The Supreme Court did not order the governor and council to suspend Barry, but did rule clearly that they had the authority to do so. The court said that the panoply of powers granted to the governor and council by the Constitution and statutes of this state is extensive. The full exercise of these broad powers demands an increase in investigations conducted by the governor and council into the activities of state departments and officials, to be carried out with practical efficiency.

If the inquiry in the investigation of the activities of state officials were to be conducted only after questions were reduced to writing, and the purpose of the inquiry was stated in writing in advance, information about the conduct of the affairs of the state would be incomplete and unsatisfactory.

For all practical purposes, the court went on, executive supervision and control would be relegated to a futile exercise in recording a written cross-examination. This is not the increased economy and efficiency in the conduct and affairs of the state that the statutes contemplate. We conclude that the governor and council had authority to obtain the information that was sought by them.

Ironically, Governor Powell represented Barry in this request before the court.

CHAPTER 19

The Hancocks

During the '65 session, while I was on the Appropriations Committee, by chance I had responsibility for the budgets of the entire Hancock family. The Hancocks, including Stuart, who was causing the Peterson leadership so much trouble, were a number of siblings. One brother, Parker Hancock, was warden of the state prison. Another brother was head of the Division of Safety Services, Boat Safety Division. Mary Louise Hancock was head of the state planning operation.

I had the approval of all three of their budgets. The Hancock family put on a full-court press to lobby me for the needs for all the funding they were requesting in their various budgets.

I remember Parker Hancock taking me to the state prison for a fancy dinner and telling me that's what they served the inmates. I watched an intramural basketball game there. As a basketball referee and coach myself, it was very interesting. The one rule of prison basketball is never take the ball out of bounds, because if you pass it to somebody on the court, you'll never get it back. The prisoners would put their heads down and bull through the whole opposition until someone took a shot. If it went in, he was filled with elation. If it missed, he was filled with despair.

The Hancocks were pressing me hard for favorable treatment on their budgets. The night the budget was printed, Peterson and I had gone to a high school basketball tournament at the University of New Hampshire. We had a driver with us and we consumed a number of beverages on the way back. When we returned to the Highway Hotel, everyone was saying to me, "Mary Louise Hancock wants to see you," "Stuart Hancock wants to see you," "Parker Hancock wants to see you." I received messages every place I went that night, all saying that the Hancocks were looking for me. I figured I might as well face the criticism I knew I was in for. U.S. Secretary of the Interior Stewart L. Udall had come to New Hampshire for the first Earth Day celebration. He gave a speech to six hundred people at the Governors Conference on Outdoor Recreation. I knew the Hancocks had attended Secretary Udall's speech, and there had been a hospitality room in the Highway Hotel before the function.

When I went by that room, it appeared to be quiet. I went outside the building to look in the window to see if anybody was there. The lights were on, so I went back in and knocked on the door.

When the door opened, there stood the U.S. Secretary of the Interior, Stewart Udall, in his underwear. All I could stammer out was, "Is Mary Louise Hancock in there?" He glowered at me and saw me looking at his underpants. He said, "No, she's not!" and slammed the door in my face for suggesting that he was entertaining Mary Louise Hancock, in his motel room, in his underpants.

Another turmoil in the '65 session came when the Republican legislative leadership ordered sets of state and American flags for their offices—the same as those Governor King had in his office—and it cost them $114 per set. Senate President Lamprey and House Speaker Peterson installed fiberglass drapes with valances of blue and gold, the state colors, featuring the state seal in screened silk, for their statehouse offices as well. They also installed for each office wall-to-wall carpeting, as the governor had in his suite. They considered themselves an equal branch of the government and felt they deserved these accoutrements.

On Wednesday, June 23, 1965, Edward H. Coolidge Jr. began serving a life sentence for the murder of fourteen-year-old babysitter Pamela G. Mason. My uncle Bill Esson had been one of the cops who had arrested Coolidge. The medical examiner said Pamela had been beaten, raped, stabbed four times, and shot twice in the head.

This case would have personal ramifications. I later found out from state police friends that the man who ran off with my wife had been a suspect in the case. The police had almost brought him back from Baltimore, where he was attending a convention, to question him.

They decided they didn't want to alert him. They would wait until he came back voluntarily and then question him. He was later exonerated. Another irony of the case is that it was almost thrown out on appeal because the police work, headed up by my uncle, had violated some of Coolidge's rights, which the court was in those days just beginning to establish.

Also during this session, I had some success in getting passed a couple of pieces of the insurance legislation that my association wanted. One was to ban the sale of insurance by credit cards. Several oil companies were threatening to sell insurance through their credit cards. This bothered insurance agents—for example, Creely Buchanan, who was the head of the Senate Insurance Committee and, like me, employed in the insurance industry.

Buchanan said, "Insurance is unlike most other commodities. It's a quasi-public utility but it is a highly competitive business." He allowed that credit cards were good, but, he said, "I like credit cards but I'm opposed to selling insurance in this fashion. It is not in the best interests of the people to put the insurance business on a do-it-yourself basis."

Ironically, that bill was tacked on to another bill of mine, House Bill 602. The bill originally would have outlawed coercion in the insurance business. It would have, in simple words, barred auto dealers from forcing a trusting car buyer to tie the required insurance policy purchase into the installment payment plan for the car. It would allow the car buyer to get the insurance from anyone he chose, rather than just from the auto dealer. Both of these bills were important to my association. I made certain not to speak on them, but I did tell a lot of friends to make sure they were aware of the merits of the bill.

In the *Concord Monitor* Leon Andersen's entire column was devoted to how the bills passed. Andy wrote: "Legislative monkey shines are in order at the Statehouse." He went on to say that the House Insurance Committee came up with a beaut this week. He talked about how Chairman Bob Stratton dished up a sudden gush of double talk and got the House to pass a bill that was not what it was supposed to be. Andy wrote that he thought most legislators had no idea what it is all about or what they approved.

I'm sure Andy's column came about from the lobbyists and lawyers who were against the bill, those representing the car dealers and gas dealers. They were trying to kill the bills with bad publicity.

Conflict-of-interest rules were lax in those days. As long as you didn't talk on the bill when it came on the floor, you could work behind the scenes to get your legislation passed. This I did.

CHAPTER 20

The Liquor Wars Continue

Remember the riot-prevention legislation? In it was a provision that delegated liquor law enforcement to the enforcement personnel of the state Liquor Commission. The commission had learned of the possibility of trouble during the motorcycle races.

Liquor Commissioner Costas S. "Chick" Tentas told the state news service both beer sales in stores and on-premises sales of alcoholic beverages in restaurants, clubs, hotels, and cafés were stopped in Laconia, Belmont, and the Weirs shortly after 9:30 P.M. Police said the riot began at 10:15 P.M. Tentas said similar authority had been voted to his staff prior to the Hampton Beach Labor Day riots and rumored disorders at the Plaistow/Kingston area and the North Conway area, but had never been used.

At the Weirs, however, the mounting indications of impending trouble prompted the move to close down all liquor sales. Tentas said the action was part of the standard operating procedure agreed upon by the Liquor Commission the year before. Ironically, Tentas ended up his public statement by saying he wished to emphasize that the riot was not caused by drunkenness.

Governor King took action to get control of the liquor agency. He asked the legislature to downgrade the three-member Liquor Commission and put the state Liquor Department under the supervision of just one strong man. The legislature intended to give the job to Ralph Brickett, who was state business supervisor from the Department of Administration. He was on loan to the Liquor Commission for six months. They proposed to name Brickett director of liquor operations with a salary in the $15,000-$16,500 range if the reorganization legislation was approved.

The salary for liquor commissioners, at that time, was $10,000-$12,000 for the chairman and $9,000-$10,500 for the associate commissioners. King did throw the commissioners a sop by leaving them in charge of store listings, which had been very controversial. The director would have authority to issue licenses and to suspend or revoke them, but they would be subject to review or possible change by the commission.

The legislative leaders were upset to know that when they appropriated money in the capital budget two years ago for liquor warehouses in

Concord and Salem, the Liquor Commission had decided to put stores in the warehouses and make them into combined stores/warehouses, of which the legislature was not aware.

Actually, it was a warehouse in Concord and two new stores in Nashua and Salem. One of the goals was to increase the sales of the sweepstakes tickets as well as liquor, but the bureaucracy was dragging its feet. The stores were not being built as fast as Governor King wanted and not to the specifications that Senate President Lamprey had understood. This caused another battle royal.

Lamprey planned to quiz the state Liquor Commission about the stores in Salem and Nashua, and put in legislation to do just that. Governor King told Lamprey that he would veto the bills if they came to him. King would not hold up the construction of the new stores and the resulting sales just for legislative scrutiny.

Lamprey wanted to know whether or not the state should be in the business of building its own stores. If the state was going to do it in Salem and Nashua, why not in other places as well?

Lamprey, too, claimed that when they put the warehouse in the capital budget, he did not know that it was going to include funding for two liquor stores in Nashua and Salem. Lamprey said that the $150,000 in the budget for stores was supposed to be for renovations, not for new construction.

Marshall greets Nancy Reagan before a Congressional drug hearing. Congressman Bill Zeliff is in the background.

New Legislators from Hillsborough County meet with Speaker Cobleigh. Seated: Catherine G. Lamy, Speaker Cobleigh, and Frances Abbott. Standing: Bob Monier, Dennis J. Murphy, Chris Spirou, Howard Humphrey, Sr., John Harvell and Emile Boisvert.

House Minority Leader Bob Raiche, Marcel Vachon, Costas "Chick" Tentas, Speaker Cobleigh, and Lyman Collishaw discuss a proclamation on New Hampshire liquor laws.

Governor Walter Peterson signs legislation creating turnpike liquor stores sponsored by Speaker Cobleigh as liquor commissioners Jim Nadeau, "Chick" Tentas, and John Ratoff look on.

John Muir, Governor Walter Peterson, Speaker Cobleigh, and Governor's Councilors Lyle Hersom and John Walsh visit New Hampshire National Guard troops at Camp Drum.

Marshall proudly pins his daughter Laura with her nursing degree pin from Health Careers Technical College, which he sponsored legislation to create.

Governor Mel Thomson enjoys Marshall's humor.

White House — View from the East Garden

Christmas Greetings from
the President and Mrs. Truman, 1952

Christmas card greeting that Marshall received from President and Mrs. Harry Truman while serving on the president's yacht, the U.S.S. Williamsburg.

Marshall, Governor Mel Thomson, and Peter Thomson enjoy Mel's closing days as governor. Thomson wrote "To Marshall Cobleigh—an outstanding aide who contributed greatly to our success and whose friendship I value."

Governor Walter Peterson delivers his inaugural address as his friends and allies Senate President Stewart Lamprey and House Speaker Marshall Cobleigh listen.

To Speaker Marshall Cobleigh —

Governor Walter Peterson presents Speaker Cobleigh with the pen that has just signed HB1, which created the Governor's Task Force. Looking on are other key supporters of that legislation, including Senator Bill Gove, Jim O'Neil, Rob Trowbridge, Sam Reddy, John Goff, Harlan Logan, and Jack Bradshaw. Seated is Senate President Arthur Tufts. Peterson's inscription says "To Speaker Marshall Cobleigh—Peerless Leader and warm friend—on the occasion of a most significant event."

Senate President Stewart Lamprey, Governor Walter Peterson, and Speaker Cohleigh discuss the day's legislation

To Marshall,
Thanks for your help.
John H Sununu

White House Chief of Staff and former governor John H. Sununu greets Marshall in his White House office with the words "Thanks for your help."

President George H. W. Bush and Barbara Bush.

Marshall and President Ronald Reagan at the Wayfarer.

President Richard Nixon inscribes his picture with the words "To Marshall Cobleigh with appreciation for his dedication to the Republican Party."

Bob Dole and Marshall.

Senator Ted Kennedy greets Marshall with the kidding remarks, "To Marshall—glad you could join us."

Best wishes

Marshall as vice president of the U.S. Jaycees presents the Teenage Safe Driving Road-e-o winners to President Lyndon Johnson.

CHAPTER 21

The Concord Liquor Warehouse

This is Chick Tentas's statement of how the liquor store warehouse situation came about:

"In 1963, I suggested to the commission that with new items being added to the list and if sales were to grow with self-service stores, we should look into the possibility of a new warehouse.

"I contacted a friend in Boston who set me up with a meeting with Mr. Buck Dumaine of B&M Railroad.

"I asked him if he would be willing to sell the state of New Hampshire some land at the Capital Center, which he owned—for the purpose of building a new liquor warehouse.

"He said he would be willing to sell the land to the state, if the state of New Hampshire and the Liquor Commission would also consider putting a liquor store on the property. I told him I would meet with my fellow commissioners and state officials.

"The commission decided any plans for the new warehouse should include a liquor store and the Liquor Commission offices. I met with Mr. Dumaine again and laid out our proposal, which he agreed to. Dumaine ended up selling the state 155,000 square feet for one dollar per square foot—that's how much he wanted a liquor store to generate traffic for his center.

"I tried to get Peterson to name the new facility warehouse store and offices for Robert Hart. This never did come about. I then proposed it to Governor Thomson. I told him that Bob Hart's sister, Irene, was a schoolteacher and active in the State Employees Association.

"Thomson agreed and the building was named the Robert Hart Building. At the dedication, Irene, who didn't like Thomson, came together at the dedication and she thanked Thomson and then praised him and planted a kiss of thanks on him."

Liquor Commission Chairman Arnold Clement came up with a good line in opposing the governor's plans for an appointed director to oversee the operations of the state Liquor Commission. Clement questioned the efficiency of one-man supervision. He said, "Someone apparently thinks we should have a one-member commission. Maybe we should think about reducing the size of the legislature from four hundred to one hundred." This, of course, got the legislators on his side immediately.

There was a bill to allow liquor sales in golf clubs and, lo and behold, when it got to Governor King, it included not only letting golf clubs sell liquor but also allowing liquor and beer sales on Sunday and election days. Ironically, that legislation passed the Senate on April Fool's Day.

CHAPTER 22

Annual Sessions

One piece of legislation in 1965 that had a real impact was a proposal for annual budget sessions, which I supported enthusiastically. I did not believe you could budget effectively two and a half to three years in advance. If you budgeted once a year, you'd be a lot closer to the facts than guessing what the economic conditions were going to be two or three years down the road.

The leader in the fight for annual sessions was the patrician state senator Robert "Bob" English, of Hancock, Republican. He went into the history of the thing. He told us that the legislature had not met annually for almost a hundred years because of the long-forgotten railroad scandals of 1878. Those scandals caused a switch from annual to biannual sessions.

As you will see in chapter 32, the State Supreme Court overturned our efforts to enact this reform.

CHAPTER 23

Thrown Out of the Governor's Office

The capital budget was also a significant fight. By this time I was the pet protégé of Appropriations Chairman Joe Eaton. He came to me one day on the Capital Budget Subcommittee and asked me to cut thirty-seven million dollars from the proposed spending for the University of New Hampshire. I set forth to do that, and managed to accomplish it in several hours.

The capital budget was coming up on a Friday late in the session. I went on the floor to ask for the suspension of rules to bring up the bill without the usual advance notice. The motion was shouted down. I then demanded a standing vote and my motion carried, 187 to 70.

The only member to speak on the measure was Majority Leader Zandy Taft, of Greenville, who said he opposed the allocation of funds for a new supreme court building in Concord. The money should go instead to the provision of an adolescence wing at the New Hampshire Hospital, he claimed. Of course, we knew that Governor King was the one who was pushing for the new supreme court building. This became a fight toward the end of the session as well.

Another battle that went on during this session was when I was chairman of the subcommittee on executive branch funding. I set up an appointment with Governor King to talk about his requests for the Executive Department and the governor's staff. It was the first time I'd ever been in the governor's office. King made a big deal about having me there and how he had first come into the governor's office when he sat in the same chair as I did as a member of the Committee on the Executive Branch Budget.

King told me I should carry out the traditions of the House and flattered the living daylights out of me. Everything was going very nicely until I said, Let's look at the specific items in the budget, Governor. In the Executive Branch Budget, of course, the first item is the salary of the governor. The governor, at the time, got a salary of $16,667 and King was proposing to raise that to $30,000.

I asked him innocently, "Governor, as an attorney, would you speak to the concept of law that salary raises for elected officials should take effect for the next elected official and not the incumbent in any case?" King became irate and his Irish temper exploded. "If that's the way you want to be, you son of a bitch, you can get out of here right now," and he tried to kick me out of his office.

Fortunately, his administrative assistant, Tom Powers, was in on the conference. Powers calmed King down. We eventually agreed to discuss the thing further. It was ironic that the very first time I ever was brought into the governor's office, I was almost thrown out bodily by the governor.

The House did eventually set the governor's salary at $30,000. It made sense to me. Later, the Senate tried to cut it back to $20,000 for bargaining purposes. The House was trying to get money to establish the Legislative Services Division. Lamprey wanted to use the salary cut as a bargaining chip with the governor.

CHAPTER 24

Pete and Stew

Andy Andersen said the following about Walter Peterson: "Peterson is a respected legislative leader. He's fair and moderate and he goes out of his way not to hurt anyone's feelings. He's ever courteous and he's such a kindly person, it's almost a handicap in the oft times rough and tumble game of politics.

"Speaker Peterson is such a quiet-spoken man that this mannerism at times fools folks into thinking he's an easy mark. But he has purpose and rigid standards of conduct, which stand out sturdily when they break through the inherent kindliness of his personality. Peterson is a realtor. He was in business with his dad and brother. He's a native of Nashua . . . and becomes 44 this session ('65). He's a Dartmouth man, a Navy veteran and a former President of the New Hampshire Realtors Association besides being an Episcopalian. Most of all, though, Peterson has long been a behind-the-scenes counsel and key cog in the political life of Norris Cotton. It has been in this role that Peterson has acquired political savvy and has earned the respect and confidence of Republicans in general. Peterson is serving his third legislative term. He was Majority Leader two years before."

This information was printed by Andy on the night of the Speaker's testimonial, May 26, 1965.

Andy also spoke in glowing terms about the Senate president Stewart Lamprey on Wednesday, June 9, at the time of the annual testimonial for the Senate president. Andy said: "This youthful realtor has wrung up a historical legislative record. We expect it will stand for many years to come. President Lamprey served three terms as Speaker of the House, an accomplishment without precedent in modern New Hampshire annals.

"Then he set another mark, becoming Senate President in such an outstanding manner that he won his high post without opposition. Lamprey served five terms in the House before going to the Senate. Where he moves from there, politically, remains unknown. When this legislative session opened, President Lamprey loomed as the front-running GOP gubernatorial candidate for 1966. He then appeared a top choice to carry the Republican banner in a rejuvenated party effort to recapture the statehouse from Democrat John King.

"In the past five months, two developments have clouded Lamprey's potential gubernatorial future. First off, Lamprey ran into editorial censure and general public criticism for an all-out effort to discredit the King Administration in the Republican cause. Observers agreed Lamprey had the right idea, but he overdid it.

"More important though, Lamprey ran into another hospitalization siege with a chronic nerve condition. So for the past month, President Lamprey has been under wraps. He's been quietly, but rigidly, protecting his health, presumably under firm doctors' orders to avoid another breakdown. Because of health reasons, it now appears, Lamprey must forgo a possible run for the governorship next year. President Lamprey has long been one of my favorite lawmakers. We have said so more than once over the fourteen years since he first became a legislator in 1951 at the age of 30.

"We've been critical of Lamprey's wield, especially in this session as he sought to use his position as the top elected Republican in state government to pull the Republican Party image out of the shambles of the last election. We, like most of the New Hampshire press, did not pan Lamprey for his aim so much as for the manner in which he tried to achieve the objective.

"The commendable Lamprey characteristic is his innate modesty and lack of egotism. He stems from humble origin in the best American tradition. Lamprey went into the real estate and insurance business in 1942 after graduating from Concord Business College. Then he went to war for three years. Lamprey has an excellent business centered around Lake Winnipesaukee with his brother, Robert, four years his senior. They have ten employees. President and Mrs. Lamprey have two children, Diane, who is headed for Western Michigan State College to become a psychologist, and George, 14, is facing high school. We expect that with the grace of God, Lamprey has not come to the end of his political career."

CHAPTER 25

The Power of Prayer and Other Gospel Messages

Legislative prayers have been a subject from time to time and Episcopal chaplain Peter Floyd, whom I got elected when I was Speaker, once prayed on the morning of a data-processing-bill debate saying, "Do not fold, mutilate, or spindle your conscience as you consider this legislation."

Another guest clergyman, Reverend Jack Clark, a Protestant chaplain at the Laconia State School, said, "Forgive our immature, irresponsible, and unprogressive legislature for passing a sweepstakes lottery to support the education of our children. Give our government the vision and courage to bring out the best in the people of New Hampshire," he prayed over the errant flock. The *Concord Monitor* put Reverend Clark's prayer on the front page and then on June 3 editorialized about it in a piece entitled "Wanted by the General Court: A Conscience." The *Monitor* said that Chaplain Jack Clark dared to speak out with this specific application of his interpretation of the meaning of Christian morality in the presence of those whom he was indicting.

He was concerned, no doubt, as to how his religious principles applied to the most notorious piece of legislation enacted in the state in many years. The *Monitor* went on to say that they've listened to and read many other prayers made to the legislature, but they often dealt with current events or matters currently under consideration by the legislature.

The *Monitor* claimed, "None ever made specific reference to a particular bill and none ever appears to have created a sensation provoked by Clark's invocation or to exert a visible influence on the course of legislation." The *Monitor* said, "Chaplain Clark deserves a medal he won't be getting from the governor or the General Court for his fearlessness and the thanks of the people of New Hampshire for so accurately describing the chief executive and the legislature as a whole. He obviously was interested in public service or he wouldn't be chaplain of the Laconia School. We suggested a possibility of running for election into the House of Representatives. The legislature needs more members like Chaplain Clark."

During 1965, we had a fight about elevators, which was really about whether or not there would be elevator attendants. Most of us felt that we could push a button. We didn't need any help. However, when elderly Hilda

Brungot, of Berlin, got stuck in the elevator door, it gave Peterson an opportunity to put a couple of friends on the payroll as elevator attendants.

Elderly lawmakers became upset as they had to hurry to the back of the elevator before they got caught in the automatic doors. Pete eventually pulled off the elevator operators because he thought they could not be justified economically, but Superintendent Arthur Petell, of the statehouse grounds crew, took the blame.

Eventually, a compromise was hammered out: There would be an attendant on the elevator with the snappiest doors. You had to push your own button if you took the elevator on the House side.

There was a fight on legislation to bar ticket agencies from handling sweepstakes tickets for nonresidents for a service fee. George E. Stafford and I opposed it, and Stafford claimed it was a shame to clip the service to tourists on vacations.

I pointed out that the bill's penalty called for a maximum fine of five hundred dollars and a year's jail time. This was a much stiffer penalty than a first offense for drunken driving. Why should the sale of sweepstakes tickets warrant a higher penalty than drunken driving? I asked.

Governor King, to his credit, started a student internship program. There was publicity for one of his interns who was later elected to the House. Dennis Murphy, of Pittsfield, worked as an intern in the Department of Purchase and Property and came up with an idea that would save considerable money: Why not let University of New Hampshire officials use the state purchasing powers to make economies in purchasing?

He pointed out that the state paid $6.59 for toilet paper and the university paid $8.85. The state bought tires for $9.87; the university paid $16.14. For one gallon of paint the state paid $2.25; the university paid $3.82. Murphy's bill would compel the university system to use the state's purchasing office to get bargains on procurement. The savings would be earmarked for other educational purposes.

Ironically, Murphy, when he was an intern, used to babysit for my wife and me when our children were young. Years later he was a legislator and still bragged about the fact that he babysat my children. He recently retired from serving as a lobbyist for the National Education Association (the teachers).

One of the pieces of legislation in which the Pickett/Angus gang involved us was to reduce small interest loan rates in New Hampshire. A couple of legislators who were lobbyists also had put in bills to raise the interest rates.

We got them very angry by taking on the finance companies and going for the lower rates.

One of the significant factors in the 1965 session was that because it followed the Goldwater disaster for president, there were more Democrats elected in New Hampshire than ever before.

Because we have the first presidential primary and because we lost a congressional seat and the governorship, Republican national figures were coming into New Hampshire to get us back on the right path. We had both Republican Chairman Rogers Morton and later Republican Chairman Ray Bliss speaking to us.

Bliss told us: "We've got to stop blaming ourselves. We must be concerned with the people and prove it. We must appeal to a broad spectrum of citizens across the United States. Mud slinging and negative thinking will win neither supporters nor elections. We must become a constructive force in the eyes of the average American. We must transmit a sense of sound responsibility to all our citizens—young and old, rich and poor, black and white, employer and employee, city-goer and farmer. We must become a party of awareness and concern and hope for the men and women of America.

"To do this we must first determine and then act upon pertinent issues, issues that are of deepest concern to most people, issues around which our fellow citizens organize a political response."

It was a great speech by Chairman Bliss, even though he was not a colorful speaker. It's as true today as it was when he gave it in 1965.

Here are Andy's words of wisdom about Larry Pickett: "Pickett is a twelve-term legislative war horse who fathered the New Hampshire Sweepstakes into being as his claim to Granite State fame. He sponsored a lottery for five consistent sessions to the House of Representatives and hit the gong in 1963 when it landed on the desk of Governor King and became the nation's first legal lottery in the Twentieth Century.

"Even more significant has been his quiet, but ever warm friendship to the novice legislators. No stranger to the giant house, Pickett has had his ups and downs like most of us but he never complains nor does he hold anger or indulge in any regrets. Instead he offers a helping hand for the new lawmakers when they become tangled in a parliamentary tape. And his booming note of levity often is welcomed oil on troubled waters in the heat of partisan debate."

In 1965, the John Birch Society went public and my old friend Mel Thomson was one of its guiding lights in his formative days in New

Hampshire. He later served on its national board of directors.

An interesting battle was fought when Bill Johnson, one of the rising stars, passed a compulsory jury bill for women. When the bill hit the House of Representatives, George Stafford got up to fight it fiercely. The League of Women Voters was solidly behind the bill. Stafford argued that most women do not want to bother with jury duty. Being forced to perform such service would mess up family life in situations where only one auto was owned and the man of the house needed it to drive to work.

Representative Greta Ainley lit into Stafford. Furious, she argued that women should not be limited to the kitchen for the convenience of males, because they now had deep freezers. Stafford stuck to his stand and shrugged aside Mrs. Ainley's assault. The House then killed the jury bill by a rousing 214 to 82 standing vote.

I talked my way into a problem at the New Hampshire Municipal Association's meeting, where they had a panel discussion on the state's tax needs featuring Professor Kenneth Howard, of the University of New Hampshire. Howard was a loud and clear advocate for a broad-based tax to help curb soaring property taxes on homes and farms.

Joe Eaton challenged Howard, saying that slashing government costs was better than raising taxes. I then got up and asked Howard "if efficiency was not a better alternative than more taxes." Howard then landed on me like a ton of tar. But I got a good deal of press coverage for my fighting the taxes. That was fine with me.

When my first daughter, Laura Lee, was born, on April 24, 1965, I sent out a birth announcement informing everyone of a brand-new Republican on the Granite State scene. I pointed out that she hit the scene on April 24 at 3:21 P.M., bouncing in at 6 pounds 11 1/2 ounces. Andy Andersen couldn't let the card go by without comment. "God knows our grand ole party needs new life, new blood and fresh ideas," he wrote. "It'll need plenty of Laura Lees in the years to come. Meanwhile, the enthusiasm of Rep. and Mrs. Cobleigh perhaps is a bit overboard. They said in their elephantine announcement that Laura Lee joined the GOP at birth. We imagine that once Laura gets swinging, she may say otherwise. She may want to shop around and not swallow old-fashioned ideas just because her folks are that way."

Andy proved to be right and my daughter, who is now a nurse and runs the Neo-Natal Intensive Care Unit at Children's Hospital in Boston, now is on the liberal side of many issues. Economically, however, she's very sound and a good business manager.

My other child, Kimberly Ann, also has her early press clippings. Jim Morse, in his Boston Hub-Bub column, wrote that "in an effort to wind up the NH legislative affairs by July 1, Speaker Cobleigh remained in Concord for a week. Consequently his family didn't see him during that period. Imagine, if you will, one Kimberly Ann Cobleigh—age 16 months—in the House Gallery at the end of that week hearing her dad's voice come through the speakers in the ceiling.

"With screams of ecstatic joy, 'Daddy, Daddy,' this entrancing little doll brought the 400 wheels of the legislature to a grinding halt. Daddy was forced to wave from the podium, bringing more loving squeals of delight from the balcony. Mrs. Cobleigh finally had to remove Kimberly from the rafters, but not before the precisely built argument on the floor had been dashed to bits. She is now regarded as Speaker Cobleigh's secret weapon."

Kim, now a certified public accountant, is chief financial officer of Predix Pharmaceuticals.

Legislative pay was once more an issue as the House voted to increase substantially the mileage for legislators. The *Monitor*, in an editorial, suggested that they had taken it to court twice before and might very well do so again.

Also in the '65 session, Governor King signed into law legislation that gave the Senate president authority to set pay scales for Senate help subject only to the approval of the Senate Finance Committee. The Speaker would have authority to set pay levels subject to the approval of the House Appropriations Committee.

The governor went along with this—which governors in the past likely would not have because of the equality of branches—but King said when he did sign it that if the time came when we couldn't trust our legislative leadership, then we would have to face up to doing something about it. King said he signed the bill with the assurance that there would always be full disclosure at all times on legislative pay scales and legislative personnel roles. This was a significant step in starting to upgrade the caliber of the legislature.

I always remember Governor Lane Dwinell, who couldn't believe that I had the number of employees I had when I was Speaker. He had one employee during his tenure as Speaker.

Bob Preston, of Hampton, was appointed supervisor of Commercial Development for the state department of DRED. He worked for the seacoast regional plan at an annual salary of $7,500. Preston was one of those elected to the Senate in 1964, but he was ousted on a party-line vote when the Republican majority questioned his qualifications, saying he did not meet the Constitutional requirement of having inhabited Hampton for seven years. N. Doug Hunter was seated in his place.

We passed four tax hikes in 1965. The beer tax eventually settled on 1 1/3 cents a six-pack, which was expected to produce $620,000. A hike in the tobacco tax from 3 1/2 to 4 1/2 cents on each package of cigarettes was expected to produce five million dollars. An increase in the utilities tax, from eight percent to nine percent, was expected to produce $220,000. A hike in the inheritance tax, from eight and a half to ten percent, was expected to produce $700,000.

There were a number of budget-cutting tricks that we used over and over. The state police were asking for twenty-two new state troopers and the Finance Committee whizzes, in their wisdom, suggested that they take seven troopers who were then on communications duty out on the highways and replace them with lower-paid workers. We used this device many times to cut requests for their budget.

We told the state Liquor Commission to keep the forty-nine state liquor stores open six days a week and on shopping nights. This was expected to raise another $400,000.

In 1965, I saw my first broad-based tax bill debated in the House. Laconia businessman and liberal politician Larry Guild had sponsored an income tax bill. It was obvious that the question was ahead of its time by the number of speakers against it. An interesting note was that Alexander "Zandy" Taft, the House majority leader, who had been advocating and talking about running for governor based on the fact that there should be a state income tax and replacing the stock and trade tax, did not speak in favor of it. A roll call was started in Hillsborough County and the vote stood at ten to one when Taft's name was called. He voted to keep the bill alive and for the income tax. Bill Craig immediately called off the roll call once they had Taft on record as being for an income tax, because they figured he was running for governor.

It was Minority Leader Bill Craig who withdrew his request for the roll call as soon as the name of Zandy Taft had passed and voted and Taft had gone on record for the income tax. This irritated Representative Ellerton H. (Bill) Edwards, the only other member to have voted for the income tax. He took the microphone and turned to Democrat leader Craig and said, "I think we just witnessed a pretty stinking little trick."

Speaker Peterson warned him to avoid personal references and a crisis was averted, but the Democrats had succeeded in getting Zandy Taft on record for the income tax in this, the first broad-based-tax debate I had seen in the House.

In late May, the Republican leadership wanted to spend five million dollars more than they had. They held a conference with Governor King to come up with a solution. King played politics and said, "This is a legislative problem and I would insist that GOP leaders make the decision. I am not going to be involved." He agreed to meet the following week to give them time to make up their minds as to what they want to do.

The Republicans claimed that the governor had more than five million dollars in pending spending requests. They wouldn't be able to pass his spending requests if he didn't come up for a joint tax with them. The Republicans really wanted a room and meals tax, which had been defeated earlier in the session. They wanted the governor to be in favor of it with them before they would propose it.

Lamprey proposed that it be a room and meals tax or a soft drink tax, but they needed to have agreement with the governor. To make matters worse, the usual technique of increasing revenue estimates was not available. Legislative Budget Assistant Remick Laighton had told them that he was going to have to reduce the revenue estimates by $1.4 million because revenue trends had decreased since he had set the figure in December.

One of the other big fights at the end of the session was about the Park Expansion Program (PEP). The governor had proposed a $250,000 bond issue, which generated a lot of federal funding because we were providing the matching funds. It was to improve the state parks and provide one hundred and fifty jobs each summer for unemployed men and college students, and this became a major political football.

The legislative leaders were claiming that the governor's program was five million dollars underfunded and that amount needed to be raised. They would propose to pass a commonsense budget to do it, and King, in essence, said that if you want to spend five million dollars more, you raise it. They had previously told him they would cut his spending request by that amount if he didn't join them in supporting a tax.

King brought up the issue of broad-based taxes. They cornered him, and he said that he did not believe broad-based taxes were inevitable in the near future. "That's been the cry since 1950," King said at his monthly news conference, "yet we've gotten along very well without one."

King blamed the legislature for its decision to provide additional funds for the University of New Hampshire and because they wanted to spend more on the state employees' pay raise than he proposed. King said in his press conference that the problem was to find sufficient revenue to again balance the budget. He claimed the budget he had submitted was balanced. The two items mentioned above had put it out of kilter.

King made his press statement basically a broad-based-tax issue: "There's always maneuvering for a sales or income tax, but I don't think that we need broad-based tax this session." He was convinced the Republicans in the legislature didn't want such taxes.

The frugal Appropriations chairman, Joe Eaton, got into the battle and set up an interim committee to cut spending further. I was heavily involved in helping Eaton reduce spending from existing agency players. When the Appropriations Committee budget came to the floor, it set a new record of eighty-five million dollars, which was approximately four million over Governor King's recommendation, which had been filed with the legislature back in February.

Lamprey eventually proposed a solution whereby we would okay a $1,250,000 increase for the University of New Hampshire for the next biennium. They approved a footnote to finance the extra aid out of a surplus in the second year of the biennium or by issuing a temporary loan for it. Lamprey claimed that anticipated General Fund revenue would increase over estimates sufficiently in the second year to finance the special augment for the university. But if the funding did not materialize, the state Treasury would be authorized to borrow $1,250,000 against future income to turn over to the school.

Lamprey's plan also gave a $77,000 biennial increase to hire more personnel so that all state liquor stores could be kept open six days a week and on shopping nights in communities that had them. Lamprey said this new policy was expected to increase liquor profits and help finance the University of New Hampshire's budget boost. Governor King said he would veto the state's budget for the next biennium if it reached his desk in the form approved by Lamprey and the Senate Finance Committee.

In a letter to Lamprey, Governor King said, "I have no desire to quarrel with legislative prerogatives. However, your sponsorship of a borrowing policy against the future demands that I speak out. If new revenue is needed, the legislature should have the courage to face up to that. We should not condone possible deficit state operations for a lack of courage to face up to the problem."

During the debate on the deficit financing, it wasn't said, but was widely known by both sides, that the governor's pay, which was currently $16,000, was scheduled to go up to $30,000 as voted by the House but was back down to $25,000 in the Senate version, and Lamprey was using the difference for leverage. One committee member said there was no question that the governor's salary should be on a par with justices of the courts. This was not intended as an insult to the governor; we just wanted to leave some room to bargain with.

In the end, Governor King prevailed, and the Senate was forced to back down before the budget was unanimously approved by both branches.

The final budget allowed a $4.5 million increase for the University of New Hampshire, down $500,000 from the Senate allotment. It did boost the governor's salary back to $30,000 and also restored a $1,000 cut in the salary of Comptroller Leonard Hill, who was the governor's budget expert. The final budget also cut to $750,000 the amount that would go to the University of New Hampshire if the funds were there, but it would be done subject to approval of the governor and council, not the legislature. Thus was the budget battle settled for another year.

CHAPTER 26

The Feldman Bill

The most explosive and emotional piece of legislation in my career came up in the 1965 session. Manchester Representative Saul Feldman introduced the so-called Feldman bill, most people believed at the request of the *Manchester Union Leader.*

The bill at first proposed to ban subversives, and later all Communists, from using state facilities to advocate their position. The legislation was controversial. It was heavily support by the *Manchester Union Leader* and its puppets and widely opposed by liberal politicians of all stripes.

Many of us felt that its author, Saul Feldman, was coached by the *Union Leader*. His floor speeches were allegedly written by *Union Leader* editorial columnist Jim Finnegan. That was never proved, but one of the amusing aspects of the discussion was that Feldman, who had bad eyesight, would be up there reading a speech with a magnifying glass to aid his vision. He would mispronounce many of the words contained in his own speech. This indicated to a lot of enemies of the bill that Feldman didn't write his own speech.

During the research for this book, I was told that the actual author of the bill and of Feldman's speeches was the late congressman Louis Wyman. I asked my friend Jim Finnegan who was right. "Were you the author or was it Louis?" I asked. Finnegan, in his enigmatic manner, replied: "Why don't you simply say that the Feldman bill and concept had several authors."

The controversy began when a Communist was invited by students to speak at the University of New Hampshire. At the time, Governor King objected strongly to providing a tax-supported platform for a subversive paladin. King rekindled the controversy when he said he would propose legislation to turn his objection into law.

Representative Saul Feldman, of Manchester, attempted to submit a broad, antisubversive bill to the House but was discouraged from doing so by the House Republican leadership. Feldman was trying to do this after the deadline had expired for new legislation to be filed, and he had to get the permission of the House Rules Committee to do so.

His efforts to accomplish this were widely publicized in the *Union Leader*. The Republican leadership decided that they would throw the issue back into Governor King's lap. They said the House Rules Committee would consider Feldman's bill if the governor would state in clear terms that the legislation was needed. King's support of the bill seemed to have waned some; he outlined at a press conference that he would sign the legislation but not introduce it.

Speaker Peterson said he would support a move to allow formal introduction of the proposal if the governor said it was needed. Otherwise, Peterson indicated, he would use his vote and influence on the House Rules Committee to prevent the bill from being introduced.

Feldman's bill provided that no tax-supported agency would be able to make available its facilities for use by any official representative or member of a subversive organization. Any agency head who willfully violated the ban could be removed from office by the governor and Executive Council.

When King appeared to be ducking the issue, Peterson sent him a letter: "In view of your position as Chief Executive of the state of New Hampshire, the Committee on Rules would value your opinion as to the advisability of this motion. I believe it is essential that we have a clear expression of your position relative to this important legislation at this time."

Peterson sent similar letters to the presidents of the University of New Hampshire, Keene State, and Plymouth State, and to the trustees of the university system. In the letter to the education leaders, Peterson said if the governor stated in clear terms in answer to his letter that the following bill was needed, then he would vote to allow the bill to be introduced into the House. "I will so vote," he wrote, "because I believe that the governor is entitled to have any bill considered by the House which he believes to be necessary for the sound operation of the university."

King then said he would endorse the Feldman proposal, but suggested it be amended to specify representatives of the Communist Party and the American Nazi Party. Speaker Peterson, after getting Governor King to endorse the legislation with an amendment, indicated that he and his supporters would vote to allow the introduction of the Feldman bill, but this would not prevent Peterson's opposing the bill once it had been introduced.

The *Concord Monitor*, on March 1, ran an editorial entitled "What Loeb Hath Wrought." The *Monitor*'s position: "The more one studies the Feldman Bill, the more ridiculous it becomes as a badly-drawn piece of legislation. Quite aside from the issue of freedom of expression, which it raises, it has been pointed out that the bill would punish public officials or employees who permit the use of public facilities or premises by agents of subversive organizations, but would not punish such agents."

The *Monitor* claimed that hundreds of public officials and employees would have to, in order to avoid dismissal from their public jobs, "enforce the Feldman edict on private facilities and premises, or they would be trespassers. For this a governor loses his head, a legislature is disrupted, citizen is set against citizen, and a sovereign state is cast into turmoil."

This led to a series of letters exchanged between the leading players. John W. McConnell, president of the University of New Hampshire, sent a letter to all the members of the legislature. It said, in part: "Historically and currently the record shows consistently that the most effective means of defeating objectionable and dangerous ideas and their advocates is to permit free expression subject to critical questioning of a man's analysis. This is what the University does and will continue to do through the exercise of trustee and faculty discretion. Prohibition of certain types of speakers and certain ideas places a false and attractive lure before the young minds that are probably anxious to explore the world of ideas. It presents an exaggerated challenge to these young minds, which the authors of the prohibiting legislation almost certainly do not intend."

Governor King then sent a letter to Speaker Peterson: "Inherent in the right to academic freedom is the corresponding duty of academic responsibility. The notion that if a student is to learn about Communism, he must entertain a Communist on the campus is silly.

"The world has all sorts of evils about which we can learn without entertaining them. We don't need to be bitten by a rattlesnake in order to understand the power of his venom. We do not have to taste arsenic to know it is poison."

Peterson replied that he supported the bill in the Rules Committee to clear for introduction without a public hearing a controversial bill to bar representatives of subversive organizations from speaking on state property. Peterson said he was still strongly opposed to the measure. "My vote in favor of allowing this measure to be presented to the House should in no way be taken as an endorsement of this bill," he wrote. "I shall so vote because I feel the bill is strongly endorsed by the Administration and should not be blocked on procedural grounds."

He went on: "I am strongly opposed to this measure as an affront to the University trustees and faculty in a serious threat to the freedom of a great educational institution. If the membership of the Rules Committee votes to allow the bill in, I shall assign the bill to the Education Committee for hearing, at which time the University officials and other interested parties will have ample opportunity to fully discuss the merits of the legislation."

The *Monitor*, in another editorial, this one headlined "How Silly Can They Get?" points out that "to be forbidden the use of public facilities, one first has to be proved an agent of an organization. Next, the organization of which he is the agent has to be proved to advocate the overthrow of Constitutional Government in the nation or state, or in any of the political subdivisions. This all shakes down to guilt by association."

The editorial continued: "Who is to list what are, by definition, subversive organizations? Why should any subversive not a member or agent of listed subversive organizations be privileged if other alleged subversives are not? Here again, the folly of the Feldman bill is revealed," according to the *Monitor*. "The governor would have to have been party to a willful violation to be guilty. Suppose he was. He would be punished but not the subversive intruder.

"How silly can the witch hunters get? Lee Harvey Oswald could have spoken at the University of New Hampshire with impunity, even if the Feldman Bill had been law," the *Monitor* concluded.

The hearing on the Feldman bill was set by the Education Committee for Wednesday, February 24. The university immediately sent out a letter saying that it was anxious to present its position on the bill. The letter said, "The threat which is presented to a free university in this legislation demands complete exposure. The principles of trustee and faculty direction of a free university and that of a full academic freedom are so basic and so much a part of our national education heritage, that we welcome any opportunity to defend them against anyone who would demean them or inhibit their exercise."

The presidents of St. Anselm College and Keene State College also voiced opposition to the proposal. The ban was triggered by an appearance at the University of New Hampshire in 1964 by James Jackson, editor of the *Daily Worker,* a Communist newspaper published in New York City.

The newspapers on both sides of the issue were full of expressions of sentiment supporting their respective positions. The University of New Hampshire Alumni Association ordered its chapter president, Doris Desautel, to draft a letter to President McConnell and the trustees backing their stand against the bill. Dick Blaylock, a trustee of the university and publisher of the *Portsmouth Herald*, told the *Monitor* he was violently opposed to the Feldman bill. There was no need for it, he said.

Another university trustee, Dean Williamson, wrote to Peterson: "[E]nactment of this proposed legislation would be a great misfortune for the University of New Hampshire. Any university exists only as a place of learning and learning can be achieved only by opportunity gaining knowledge of understanding by study and instruction or investigation. The proposed legislation would restrain this opportunity."

Andy Andersen wrote, "The down-river publisher is once again baiting the University of New Hampshire. He's done it for years, claiming to be more of a patriot and loves our country more than UNH officials or most of the rest of us. Loeb is having a field day because now he's got another governor to tool along with him on this pet subject. Governor King, to the amazement of many of his supporters, insists Loeb is right in wanting to curb freedom of inquiry at our respected Durham education center."

He continued: "Governor King and Loeb say Communist speakers are dignified when allowed to display their un-American nonsense before UNH students. This is foolish. The more we Americans know about Communism, the more we see it in action, the less regard we have for it."

The *Monitor* ran an editorial entitled "Feldman Spells McCarthy." It said: "[I]f the governor permitted a subversive to enter the Statehouse and come to his office for any purpose at all, the governor, under the provisions of the Feldman bill, would be required to remove himself from office. Nothing happens to the subversive under the law. The Feldman bill does not prohibit subversives from using state property or premises. It only prohibits state officials and employees from letting them do so.

"A known subversive could cross the state highway in the presence of a state policeman. The law gives the policeman no authority to prevent such use of state financed property or to arrest the subversive. Yet the law would penalize the policeman by taking his job away from him if he did not somehow prevent the crossing."

The *Monitor* concluded: "What a lark Messrs. Loeb and Finnegan are going to have if the Feldman bill becomes law. They will have a license to go witch hunting to their snooper hearts' content. Their victims won't be Communists either, but public offices and employees, the state's universities and colleges and the reputation of New Hampshire itself."

The liberal clergy, of course, jumped into the legislative fray as well. The Right Reverend Charles Francis Hall, the Episcopal bishop of New Hampshire, said, "A proposal to bar certain speakers from state property today is legislative mischief. This is not an anti-Communist bill, it's an anti-education bill."

John Sloane Dickey, the president of Dartmouth, said he would testify in opposition to the bill.

Feldman did have some support, of course, besides the *Union Leader*. His proposal drew endorsements from the New Hampshire Conservative Union, the New Hampshire Department of Disabled American Veterans, and House Minority Leader Bill Craig, of Manchester.

Bishop Hall, in a letter to the committee, said he was going to be out of state on the date of the hearing and could not testify. "But as a concerned citizen of New Hampshire," he wrote, "I cannot see such dangerous legislation as the Feldman bill come before our legislature and remain silent."

The bill, Bishop Hall charged, "is not only a serious attack on free inquiry, but is an affront to the trustees, the president, and the faculty of the University of New Hampshire. If this legislative mischief becomes law, not one subversive person would be injured, but our state University will become a smaller place."

University students were organized and gathered through Manchester's Ward 1—to ring doorbells over the weekend explaining to householders their opposition to the bill. Among the houses they called on was Feldman's. Feldman's wife answered the door and was given a courteous explanation of the students' position and handed a copy of the campus newspaper, Feldman said.

The Intellectual Freedom Committee of the New Hampshire Library Association issued a statement opposing the bill, saying, "It was well-intentioned, but faulty in reasoning. We view with alarm any state action which would encourage misguided groups of individuals to continue their attacks on the free flow of information."

Sherman Adams told the hearing that the Feldman bill would open the floor to possible further attacks on the powers of the trustees of the state university system. Adams said, "If you were a trustee of the university, you would be most reluctant to allow a person pledged to work for the overthrow of the United States government to speak there. If you were a member of the legislature and were concerned about the trustees' policy, I would recommend an administrative approach. I would consider legislation as a solution with insurmountable reluctance."

Adams went on to say, "The heart of any institution such as the university is to provide the best education within the capabilities of the trustees, administration, and faculty. There is not one of us who wants a New Hampshire student to have an education opportunity that is anything but the best. Such a proposition now confronts this committee, lays bare the whole corporate body of which the trustees are the principal members to legislative censure and to compromise of their powers."

Governor King released the text of the letter to President John McConnell, of the University of New Hampshire, where he had protested proposed visits by American Nazi George Lincoln Rockwell and Communist Party leader Gus Hall. Neither ended up speaking at the university.

Soon afterward, King spoke to students at the university and said, "I strongly resent your using my tax dollars to provide the forum for these vermin. The issue is simple. It offers choice between what we call academic freedom and common sense and I choose to take the road of common sense. I bitterly oppose providing a public-supported platform for an enemy agent who would destroy everything that is near and dear to every person in this room tonight."

One hundred students came to Concord to demonstrate on the issue. They met with the governor, who reiterated his feelings. King told the students he was concerned with extremists, and not people like Norman Thomas, a Socialist leader, and Robert Welch, the head of the John Birch Society. King called Thomas a good American and Welch "confused, a bit of a crackpot, but not extreme."

The rug was pulled out from under King by President McConnell, who said to his students and faculty: "I will uphold the University's policy guaranteeing the right to invite outside speakers to the campus." He said that "ill-motivated or political criticism would destroy the university. As I understand it, even speakers as objectionable and insubstantial as Jackson may come to the campus if properly invited.

"I believe, I voted for, have authorized the Dean of Students to approve with no strings attached the request of the Socratic Society to invite Mr. Jackson."

Testifying for the Feldman bill, King's top aide, Tom Power, repeated the governor's endorsement of such legislation as the Feldman bill and the governor's suggestion that it be narrowed to apply only to members of the Communist Party and the American Nazi Party.

Power quoted from King's letter to Peterson, saying that "the notion that if a student is to learn about Communism, he must entertain a Communist on campus is silly. The world has all sorts of evils about which we can learn without entertaining them." Power also disputed the argument of the bill's opponents that it encroached on the right of free speech and assembly. "If a group of citizens want to invite a Communist to speak, they should have to hire a hall," Power told the committee. Governor King believed that should a group of students of the university want to hear a Communist, they should have to hire a hall.

Feldman's bill, Powers said, "in no way denies students the right to hear a Communist or the right of a Communist to speak to a group of students. All it does is deny the Communist a state-supported platform to air his views."

In addition to Adams, noted figures speaking against the Feldman bill included Manchester attorney Maurice Devine; Keene attorney George Hanna; and Mrs. Mildred McAfee Horton, of Randolph, former president of Wellesley College and the head of the Waves in World War II.

John Sloane Dickey, president of Dartmouth, also spoke. He said, "Any attempt to restrict open discussion at a University is a distorting and distracting influence on the educational climate at the institution. Undoubtedly a few speakers come to or are brought to our campuses primarily as a form of defiance or to raise trouble rather than enlightenment," Dickey said. "But whether this be annoying or just amusing immaturity, it is still infinitely better than to permit these felons on the campus to poison the climate for everyone by giving them a freedom of speech grievance. In the business of higher education," Dickey said, "freedom of speech is not a nice luxury. It is, in fact, the profit principle of the enterprise."

Reverend Placidus Riley, president of St. Anselm's, released the text of a letter in which he labeled "any legislative version elitist, futile, and wrong-headed." Father Riley said that he's "opposed to any legislation which would limit the freedom of a guest lecturer to discuss what he considers important or the freedom of students to hear and debate controversial or unpopular views."

One of my favorite professors, Bob Dishman, said that "backers of the Feldman bill were showing a lack of faith not only in the trustees, faculty and administration of the university, but in their own sons and daughters who are or may be students. Students today cannot easily be won over to any doctrine. The surest way to arouse the curiosity of our young people about a baseless ideology like Communism or Fascism is to forbid their hearing about it firsthand from an active believer."

Dishman pointed out that if the Soviet ambassador should someday come visit Concord, Governor King might be hard put to find a place to receive him without violating the proposed Feldman legislation.

Feldman himself was the lead-off speaker at the hearing. He charged that a Peking-oriented Communist, Levy Love, attempted to organize a group at the university without interference from the school's administration.

Feldman said, "A number of secret meetings were held on the campus at Durham attended not only by students but also by members of the university faculty." Reading what many in the audience felt was a Finnegan-written diatribe, he said, "What we are concerned with here is the law of the land. Communists may hold contrary opinions but I am confident this body will not cringe before charges of Nazism or instituting a McCarthy-type witch hunt."

Feldman went on: "These were Communist charges." He said his bill, out of necessity, had to be approached from a nonpartisan basis. Feldman added that the very definition of Communist-activity organizations mentioned in his bill would exempt diplomatic representatives, for example, of Communist nations from traveling to and from New Hampshire on official business. This was a rebuttal of the *Concord Monitor* editorial that suggested the governor couldn't see the ambassador.

Feldman testified that "the Communist Party [is] not a legitimate political party, but a conspiracy to overthrow the U.S. government." He compared himself and his bill to the U.S. Supreme Court and its 1954 decision on the Communist Control Act. He insisted that the outcry, which would accompany the passage of his bill, would be similar to that which greeted the Supreme Court's decision on Communists.

Feldman said in making his decision whether to file the legislation, he was reminded of Hitler, of Yalta, of the chicken plucker in Cuba, of Vietnam, and of Winston Churchill. He decided that his bill must be filed despite the pressure and threats directed at him. He saw himself as a reasonable man who had listened to views not his own. He also said that "academic freedom must not be academic license."

Another former governor jumped into the fray on the Feldman bill. Governor Robert O. Blood, in a letter to Education Committee Chairman Jim O'Neil, wrote that "there has been no indication in testimony given before your committee that New Hampshire either on public or on private platforms is being overrun by Communists or subversive persons. If such people are a menace to the safety and well-being of the country, surely Congress would recognize the fact and enact necessary legislation."

Blood said, "I am opposed to any legislation that would take from these eminent people the responsibility of education policy which has worked for one hundred years in New Hampshire."

A noted conservative spokesman, Dr. Thomas Ritzman, of Hopkinton, said, "Free speech is one of the great inherent rights in our system of government, but for every right there is a responsibility. Sooner or later everyone must exercise the responsibility that goes with each right."

Ritzman charged the trustees of the university with not exercising their responsibilities. "We have become so obsessed with the right of free speech that we've reached the point of now abusing it," Dr. Ritzman said. "The trustees acted irresponsibly by permitting an agent of an enemy country to use a tax-supported platform."

All in all, the hearing on the Feldman bill lasted more than nine hours. Among those who testified against it was the rabbi of the temple attended by Saul Feldman. During the two-day hearing, seventeen supporters spoke in favor of the bill and thirty-six opponents were heard.

Governor King's legal adviser, Joe Millimet, testified against the bill, saying that he was "for the governor, against the bill, but believed the governor had been mousetrapped on the issue."

Judge Bernie Sneirson, of Laconia, had a good line when he said, "[T]he proponents of the Feldman bill are the finest press agents the Communists could ever have."

There was some talk among legislative pundits that if the bill passed the House, it still could be killed in the Senate if Governor Powell came out against it. Others thought that because Powell was so close to the *Manchester Union Leader,* he would not do this.

Senate President Stewart Lamprey and Senate Majority Leader Bill Johnson said they could not discuss the bill because it was before the House and thus ducked taking a stand. The liberals felt this was because Lamprey's conservative ties to the *Union Leader* and Johnson's liberal-moderate views interfered with his duty to the Republican Party as state chairman.

Andy Andersen took Lamprey to task for avoiding the issue: "President Lamprey is talking through his hat. He says the Feldman bill is before the House and he doesn't want to appear to be interfering in House prerogatives. That's for the birds," he wrote. "Governor King's budget bills are in the House Appropriations Committee and will not actually hit the Senate for months, but that hasn't stopped Lamprey from barking like blue blazes against them. As for the Feldman bill, it is officially before the Senate Education as well as the House Education Committee. So Lamprey and

Johnson should cut the mustard and pass up the custard."

Andy concluded: "Lamprey and Johnson should speak out the sooner the better, on this Feldman foolishness. They are against it. They are working against it as they should, so why are they being coy? They are not fooling anybody except possibly themselves."

The House finally took up the measure on Thursday, March 11. More than forty speakers were listed to air their views, most of them opposed to the measure.

Zandy Taft, the GOP majority leader, one of the first speakers against the bill, testified that it would not be a practical one. He said, "The bill cannot be enforced. It places an enormous legal liability on any state official who attempts to determine and announce publicly who is and who is not a subversive because it is libelous to call a person a Communist. It must be proven."

Bill Craig, Governor King's Democratic minority leader, explained that the governor favored its passage, but it was not a party-line issue. Craig told the House that "the governor had informed the Democratic legislators that they were free to vote as their conscience dictated."

There was a packed gallery for the debate. National television crews set up their equipment before nine o'clock in the morning and tied it into the regular House microphone system. It was the second time in history that giant TV cameras were set up in the gallery. (Two years earlier they invaded Representatives Hall for Governor King's dramatic announcement that he had signed the disputed sweepstakes bill.)

Feldman announced that he had a clarifying amendment designed to win votes and he would change the bill covering subversives to apply only to Communists. The Feldman amendment would also restrict the Communist ban in relation to the University of New Hampshire and affiliated colleges rather than all state property, as he had originally proposed.

Debate lasted five and a half hours, during which forty-two people spoke. These two facts are believed to have set records. The House voted 205 to 176 to kill the Feldman bill. The vote was on Jim O'Neil, chairman of the committee's motion, to indefinitely postpone the bill, which killed it for the rest of the session of the legislature.

Feldman appealed, unsuccessfully, for the House to vote on a substitute version he was ready to offer. Strongest support for the bill came from the Manchester area, which is the base of *Union Leader* circulation, and some parts of the north country. The opposition came from Rockingham and Strafford Counties and the areas around Durham, where the university is located.

Feldman tried to be a good guy and move that the vote be made unanimous, but his supporters screamed No! No! The vote to kill the bill comprised 159 Republicans and 46 Democrats. Voting to keep it alive on the floor so it could be amended were 122 Democrats and 54 Republicans.

Significant is the fact that the debate was televised by UNH-TV, which was the first time an entire debate had been broadcast. This may very well have inspired such a great number of people to speak on the legislation—and get themselves on TV.

Democratic woman voted twelve to nine for the bill and Democratic men voted 110 to 37 for it. The ladies voted 41 to 21 to kill the bill and the male legislators voted 164 to 156 kill it. It was an emotional and historic vote and one that I shall always remember.

I voted for academic freedom and against the Feldman bill.

CHAPTER 27

Turmoil in the New Hampshire Senate

One of the ramifications of the Republicans' nominating Barry Goldwater (whom I supported) and his getting clobbered by Lyndon Johnson in 1964 was that the New Hampshire and Senate Republican majorities were much smaller than they had been in the past.

In 1963 there were 144 Democrats in the House and 254 Republicans. When the 1965 session started, it was 176 Democrats and 222 Republicans, with one split seat.

In the state Senate there had been five Democrats and nineteen Republicans in the '63 session; now there were ten Democrats and fourteen Republicans, with three seats up for grabs because of court debates (which I'll get into in a minute). Thus, there would be no second honeymoon for Governor King and the legislature in 1965.

The Democrats were claiming that they should have some chairmanships in the House, as is the case in Vermont. The Republicans said no way: The Democrats didn't let the Republicans have chairmanships in Congress, where they have a fat majority. We had to be on our tocs because the Republicans were not as firmly entrenched in the legislature as they had been in the past. A shift of a couple of dozen House votes at any given time could upset everything. Thus, the mood was different.

I felt firsthand this new mood when the battle began over which senators were going to be duly qualified as elected. This was power politics at its best—or worst, depending on your perspective.

First off, in the House, Peterson was not elected by acclamation as he had been two and a half years earlier. He defeated Bill Craig on a straight party-line vote after an hour of debate. They had a fight about whether to have the election by secret ballot, which had been the former House custom. They had a roll call on whether or not to have a roll call. One Republican, Jack Manchester, of Hanover, sided with the Democrats in favor of the secret ballot. He told newsmen his purpose was to avoid an open political showdown on the first day of the legislature. But on the final roll call, Manchester voted for Peterson.

Andy Andersen, in a column, said the official returns disclosed that the Democrats could have taken over the legislature if they had put up candidates for every seat. The Democrats in New Hampshire not only won the governorship for an unprecedented second term, but they also got a congressional seat and captured the Executive Council for only the second time in the twentieth century.

There were a couple of stories circulating about people who ran because they'd been promised they could not win. Because they were Democrats, however, they did win. They didn't really want to serve. On opening day of the legislature, the issue was not yet resolved in the Senate. There were three seats in question.

Paul Provost, a Manchester Democrat, had resigned from the '63 Senate when the state Liquor Commission set rules that legislators could not also serve as liquor salesmen. Provost had been a liquor salesman. He decided to resign as liquor salesman and give the job to his wife. He then wanted to take his seat in the Senate.

Another senator-elect, Paul Karkavelas, submitted his resignation as a liquor salesman. The Democrats, through their National Committeeman Jay Wilcox Brown, of Dunbarton, a former Merrimack County Democratic chairman, asked the state Supreme Court to order a special election in the Eighth Senate District. They also asked the court to review whether the candidates elected in the Fifth and Twenty-third Districts had met the Constitutional requirement of having been inhabitants of the state for seven years prior to their election.

The Republicans called on former House speaker Dick Upton, a noted Constitutional expert, to represent them before the state Supreme

Court. Upton, quoting the state Constitution, said that "jurisdiction of the Senate in determining election results and the qualifications of members is final, exclusive, and not subject to judicial review."

Several Democratic attorneys, led by noted criminal lawyer Fred Catalfo, of Dover, who was their gun, argued on Brown's behalf. Opening day, Governor King gave his inaugural address in a joint session of the House and Senate. That session lasted eleven hours and eighteen minutes. It was the most partisan scene I had ever witnessed.

The Republicans prevailed by a series of twelve to ten party votes. The GOP seated a contested Republican Senator, Bill Johnson, and unseated two contested Democratic senators, James Lewis and Bob Preston. (Lewis was from Newport and Preston was from Hampton.) This was a series of real power plays. The seating of Lewis and Preston had formerly been challenged by the Republicans under statutes covering residency.

To be elected a state senator, you must be an inhabitant of New Hampshire for at least seven years before your election. Members listened to Governor King's address. The dispute over the seating of members was put off until the afternoon. Senate Clerk Ben Greer called the meeting to order at 10:07 A.M. It recessed until 12:30. Fourteen members mustered for the first call. The Senate went back into session in the afternoon. At 1:40, Governor King, backed by his lame-duck council, swore into office the twenty-three senators, including the contested ones. The only one not sworn in was Paul Karkavelas, who had resigned after the dispute with the state Liquor Commission. A temporary Republican chairman, Bill Gove, was elected. Then for the next thirty minutes, the entire body erupted into parliamentary confusion.

They tried to elect a permanent Senate president. The Republicans nominated Stew Lamprey and the Democrats nominated Louis Martel. Lamprey won thirteen to ten and Martel moved to make the election unanimous.

The Senate then tried to pass a bunch of necessary opening-day resolutions to get their house in order: little things like adoption of rules, rule changes, election of the clerk and other Senate aides. Meeting times were set, and the hiring of stenographers and even the providing of newspaper subscriptions to the members were taken care of.

The first item of action was a petition from Jim Saggiotes, of Newport, asking that he be seated because of a violation of residency requirements by Senator Lewis. The petition was referred to a select committee of senators named by Lamprey to examine the returns in the Senate elections, which is the normal procedure. A recess was then called to allow the Select Committee to do its work. The report came back. It contained what was expected. All senators were found duly elected except two. The committee said there were questions on the legality of seating Lewis and Preston because there were petitions filed against them. The committee reported that the pair should not be seated until the questions were answered.

Then Senator Martel brought in his challenge of Senator Johnson. The Senate transformed itself into a committee of the whole to discuss the merits of the Johnson, Lewis, and Preston cases. Martel claimed that Johnson was ineligible because he did not become a New Hampshire resident until late 1958. When he applied for the Bar Association in 1958, he listed his residence as Arlington, Massachusetts. There's no record of Johnson voting in Hanover prior to 1958. By signing his bar application listing himself a resident of Massachusetts, Johnson, by his own admission, was not a New Hampshire resident.

Johnson, then, conducting his own defense, made a highly emotional and lengthy rebuttal of Martel's charges. He gave a legal talk about whether a man could have many residences but only one domicile, a domicile being a residence with the intent of the man to remain there. Since 1952, Johnson maintained that his domicile was in Hanover, where he had gone to Dartmouth, left personal property, had a continuing bank account, tried to register to vote, tried to register his car, where he had sent his only application for employment, and where he and his wife had made their home since Johnson graduated from law school. For ten years, he'd been physically present in the state. Hanover did deny him the right to register because he was a student.

Johnson pointed out that the law allows a man to leave the state for military service. Johnson was in the Army for two years. Johnson attended Harvard Law School without being required to give up his residency. He had continually stored property in Hanover since 1952.

He said, "The essence of my case is I came here in 1949, I wanted to make it my home. I did come back. I won my seat with an awful lot of hard work. I'm convinced I'm qualified," he finished.

Senate Democrats were too. Senator Martel's motion to have Johnson unseated was defeated in a straight party-line vote, thirteen to nine. Switching his allegiance, however, was Senator Preston, of Hampton, who only a few hours later would be tossed out of the Senate. Preston voted with the Republicans.

After the Johnson vote, the Senate tackled the question of Senator

Lewis. The case against Lewis was read to the Senate by Attorney Dick Upton. Upton represented Lewis's opponent, Jim Saggiotes. Lewis, in his deposition, admitted he had not moved to New Hampshire until August 1959, two years shy of the residency requirement. Upton said that Lewis "only made an inadvertent mistake," and that "he'd run in good faith." But, he said, "the Constitution was the Constitution. It was clear he had not lived in the district the required seven years." Lewis admitted he was ineligible, "but if you remove me, you disenfranchise the voters of Sullivan County unless you hold a special election," he said.

When it came to Bob Preston, of Hampton, the case against him was made by Attorney Bill Phinney. Phinney said that Preston did not move his family to or take up formal residence in Hampton until August 1964. Prior to that, according to Lawrence, Massachusetts, city directories and tax returns, he'd lived at two addresses in Lawrence, Phinney said. What he gave as his Hampton address prior to 1964 was in fact the home of his mother-in-law. Although he owned a restaurant in Hampton, his major businesses were a restaurant and a funeral home in Massachusetts. His federal income tax, his automobile registration, his driver's permit were all from Massachusetts until recently, Phinney said during a lengthy statement.

Preston's lawyer, Wilfred "Jack" Sanders, claimed the senator was interested in living in New Hampshire, not the Bay State. Preston said he had been on the Hampton checklist since 1952 and a member of the Hampton Chamber of Commerce since 1954, and had attended both St. Anselm's College and the state university. He had family ties in Manchester and returned to Massachusetts only after the death of his wife's father to help in his wife's family's business.

When Sanders concluded, Preston made an impassioned plea on his own behalf and asked "not to be denied my right to serve." He voted for Bill Johnson, he said, "because I could not abide by party politics. I love politics. I wish they were outside this room today." He then restated what his lawyer, Sanders, had told the Senate.

When the arguments were over, the committee as a whole dissolved and became the Senate again. The Senate showed the power of the GOP majority. The Senate voted twelve to ten to strip Lewis of his powers and install Jim Saggiotes as senator. Preston made another plea. Arguments on his behalf were made by Senators Martel, Eileen Foley, and Clesson "Junie" Blaisdell. The Senate voted twelve to nine that Preston be stripped of his seat and the runner-up in the election be installed. There was a vote to reconsider. This was also defeated twelve to nine. Lamprey read a letter of resignation from Paul Karkavelas. He asked that a special election be held to name another senator in the Twenty-first District.

In the Johnson case, being a lawyer, he made a big deal of the fact that according to the statute a notice must have been given to him by December 15 if they were going to challenge his seat. The first notice he got of any person challenging his seat was a couple of days before with Martel's petition. However, Johnson claimed, "I will not hide behind a technicality."

After Martel read his petition challenging Senator Johnson, discussion ensued. Bob Preston was very bitter about his removal. Just after his ouster, he issued a blast at the Senate. He called his unseating "a personal affront to the intelligence of the New Hampshire voters, particularly those who issued a mandate for me to serve in this term in the Senate." He charged that the Senate in handling the seating disputes had not only a problem of ethics and law but also one of straight party voting. "It was evident today," Preston said, "that party lines meant the difference in the seating of a lone Republican senator and the unseating of two Democratic senators."

Lost in all the machinations of the power play in the Senate was Governor King's inaugural speech and his swearing in. We were all sworn in as legislators without controversy.

King said he "would have to ask for increased taxes to finance his program for the next two years." He said, "The last increase in state taxes was eight years ago." In his campaign, he said there would be no new taxes. He asked us to join him in a partnership for progress, and pledged to submit a commonsense budget that would include some reorganization of two departments.

He asked for new conflict-of-interest legislation, repeal of the milk controls, retail-price-fixing powers, and new laws to crack down on traffic violators. He also came out for a pay raise for the state's five thousand classified employees. He pledged his opposition to either a sales or an income tax, saying he would rely on increases in existing taxes to fund his new spending. He proposed tax increases on tobacco, beer, utilities, and inheritances.

He advocated for two more vocational training schools, which would probably be located in Keene and Claremont. He wanted to increase sharply penalties for traffic violations, more realistic speed limits, and a compulsory blood test for drunken driving suspects. He pledged support for a twenty-six-million-dollar construction program at the University of New Hampshire. He wanted laws barring judges from political activity. He wanted new laws that would prohibit state officials, including legislators, from doing business with the state government.

The House did pass an increase from 30 to 40 percent, as the state's contribution toward projects to end water pollution. The appropriation was $387,000. Before our vote, local communities paid 40 percent, the state contributed 30 percent, and the feds paid 30 percent. Now, under the new proposal, the state would pay 40 percent, the feds would pay 30 percent, and local communities would pay 30 percent as well.

This was a significant deal because it led to the cleanup of rivers all across New Hampshire. One of my accomplishments in the House of which I am proudest was supporting this provision.

Another thing that Stew Lamprey and Peterson did was to say that when we adjourned for the session, it would be after there had been final action on any vetoes left by the governor. In the past, the legislature had adjourned and then the governor could pocket-veto legislation after we were gone. Lamprey and Peterson led the way in changing this practice.

Another thing the governor did during that term was to open the statehouse dome to the public and to have guided tours. He also called for renovating the dome's interior, as well as gilding the outside the year before. A safety wall was erected around the roof so that people could tour the dome. I had the pleasure of escorting many old friends, neighbors, and children around the newly renovated dome. Everybody loved to go up inside the dome. It was a good move that Governor King made.

CHAPTER 28

A Bigger Role

Aa a result of my session-ending "sneaky pete" notoriety, I was now serving on the Appropriations Committee. I soon developed into a major player. One thing I did was my homework. I knew every bill and every appropriation. I scrutinized every account. I was ready to fight those things that I thought were wasteful government spending.

At first the chairman, Joe Eaton, had been thrilled with my efforts and research and started using me to defend our recommendations on the floor.

One day, near the end of the session, the chairman called me into his office. "Marshall," he said, "I want you to cut thirty-seven million dollars out of the University of New Hampshire's budget today because they got too big a capital budget. They're spending more than we can afford."

I looked up each and every spending item in the capital budget and put together a list of those most vulnerable to attack. I chose items that looked like they could be labeled pork-barrel spending. I then proceeded to cut the thirty-seven-million dollars out of the university's budget in the committee. The chairman was thrilled.

Of course, the University of New Hampshire went ballistic.

A major legislative development was taking place at about this time. It appeared that Stewart Lamprey was going to leave the House and run for the Senate district in his area and seek the presidency of the Senate. This was the normal course of climbing the political ladder in those days.

Walter Peterson, a basketball star and my friend, was going to seek the speakership. I immediately enlisted on Peterson's team.

As the campaign got under way, I was put in charge of recruiting people to run for the legislature from Hillsborough County, my home area. My job was to convince them to run for the legislature and commit to vote for Walter Peterson for Speaker, if they got elected.

It was in this process that Warren Rudman, who would go on to become a distinguished U.S. senator, was recruited by me for the legislature to be one of Peterson's minions. Rudman and I had been in the Boy Scouts together, in Troop 256. It was not to be, however, because Rudman then was a young lawyer. His firm decided it couldn't spare his time to be up in Concord earning a hundred dollars a year for his services. He was back at the firm earning money to pay the partners' rent.

A friendship developed among Marshall, Peterson, and Rudman, culminating in Rudman's appointment as Peterson's legal counsel. Later, when governor, Peterson appointed Rudman attorney general. This set Rudman's career on the way to the prominence he attained nationwide.

I also decided that because I had been the leader in defeating the sneaky petes in the Senate and had been a powerful player on the House Appropriations Committee, I was the logical guy to be Walter Peterson's floor leader during his second term as Speaker.

I went to Peterson and let him know I was interested in the job.

Peterson told me, "I don't think you're electable to that, Marshall. I think you're too flamboyant, you're too aggressive. I don't think that you'd be saleable in that position." He mentioned Roger Smith as a nice, quiet, well-dressed guy, a gentleman. Smith was polite and well mannered. Peterson went on to tell me that his wife thought Smith would be a "much better representative of the team as majority leader than Marshall."

I continued to seek approval of the members for the majority leader's role. I had a discussion with Henry Goode about the deal. Goode, who was close to Peterson, urged me in no uncertain terms: "You don't want to be majority leader. Why do you want to sit down on the House floor and defend porcupine bounty bills and stuff like that? If you take over the Appropriations Committee and become the chairman, you'll be the real power in the state. You can take care of your friends and you can take care of your enemies. You'll be a major player in the government of this state."

Henry Goode's argument made sense. My ego wanted to be floor leader and part of the leadership team. I did not want to be just the be-hind-the-scenes money guy. So I sought and finally was selected for the majority leader's post. This set me on my way to a leadership role with the New Hampshire legislature.

One of the most difficult things about being the Speaker of the House is that you preside. You have to give the impression of impartiality and fairness, even though you have strong feelings about the legislation. You want certain bills to pass and other bills to fail. You're not, by tradi-tion, supposed to go to the floor and fight for the passage or defeat of any measures, except on the rarest occasions when the future of the state was at stake.

In fact, Stewart Lamprey used to love to tell me that any time the Speaker went to the floor of the House, he'd already lost, because if he had the votes, he wouldn't need to go to the floor.

Invariably, the Speakers are frustrated by the way their majority leaders advocate the passage or killing of legislation. Perhaps they do it better than the Speaker. Maybe they do it more articulately, more flamboyantly. The one thing they can't do is debate exactly the same way as their boss, the Speaker, would do it.

This frustrates every Speaker who has ever presided. He wishes his majority leader would do things the way he would do them himself.

I was sharp. I was bright. I was articulate. I knew how to go for the jugular. I did it regularly and, some said, viciously. Walter Peterson, my predecessor as Speaker, had tried to persuade people to his way of thinking in the nicest, sweetest terms possible. He sought not ever to make an enemy. Peterson sought to defeat people and let them down gently. My style and Pete's were 100 percent different, and this led to constant frustration between the two of us.

Peterson, during a campaign appearance when he was running for governor, once told an audience: "I am proud to have been born in New Hampshire." Realizing that about half of the audience was from out of state and had moved to New Hampshire, he then said, "but of course we welcome you people who had the wisdom to move here rather than be born here."

This frustrated the hell out of me. I said to Peterson, "Damn it, can't you ever be proud of anything? Can't you even be proud of the fact that you were born in New Hampshire? You don't have to equivocate on everything. Stand up for what you are. Say what you are and don't be kowtowing to everybody all of the time. This is not the way to do it!"

Each of us was effective in his own way, but our styles were completely different. Walter Peterson is a mild-mannered gentleman. He goes out of his way to present a kind, sincere image to everyone he meets. Behind that image, of course, he is tough as nails. His record of accomplishments outlined in his prorogue speech will have him be recognized as one of New Hampshire's best governors. I consider him a close personal friend who provided the impetus for my career. I started in politics as a Walter Peterson disciple. I was proud to have been deeply involved in his campaigns. We went through a lot together, and remain close friends to this day.

This style conflict came to a culmination when a New Hampshire Constitutional Convention was being held. The U.S. Supreme Court had recently come down with its *Roe vs. Wade* decision. Whatever the state of New Hampshire put in its Constitution, either pro-choice or pro-life, would have no effect whatsoever on what happened in New Hampshire. The Supreme Court had ruled; its ruling took precedence over the New Hampshire State Constitution.

Nevertheless, the forces of pro-choice and pro-life were adamant that they were going to have their debate. They were geared up on both sides to fight fiercely for their cause. Peterson and I had a three-martini lunch. We discussed what a frustrating afternoon it was going to be at the Con-Con. We would have to listen to the impassioned on both sides pontificate at length about why their side was right and the other side was wrong.

All of a sudden, I got a glimmer of an idea. I said to the governor, "Look, when the first one of those wackos from the pro-life side gets up, [Peterson and I were pro-choice] and says life begins at conception, you recognize me for a question."

Peterson said, "Well, what are you going to ask?"

I told him that I was going to say: "If I follow your premise to its logical conclusion, isn't it true that any man who receives oral sex is guilty of mass genocide?"

Peterson was aghast. "You can't say that on the floor of the House!" he said, appalled.

I said, "It makes the point, Pete. I think I should!"

He said, "No, no, no. No way. I'd never recognize you."

Sure enough when we got back to the statehouse and started the session, it wasn't ten minutes before those magic words came forth from the podium from a distinguished doctor from a seacoast town: "It is scientifically established that life begins at conception."

With that, I bounced out of my majority leader's chair in the front row and brandished a question mark sign to the presiding officer, Peterson. (This is the signal that someone wants to question the speaker— that is, the person who has the floor.) Peterson kept signaling me, no, no, I can't recognize you. The members were baffled because they could look out there and see the presiding officer not recognizing his own floor leader, which is usually whom he would recognize first. They were all wondering why he wouldn't recognize his own floor leader.

After moments of frustration, I went up to the podium and said to the presiding officer, "Would you recognize me if I said 'nocturnal emission,' not, 'oral sex'?"

Peterson's gentle demeanor actually caused him a great deal of difficulty. At the end of his first term as governor, when he started seeking reelection, the polling numbers were not good. In fact, his blandness had caused the public not to have very strong opinions for or against him. Finally, his political consultant, who was one of the first ones ever hired in the state of New Hampshire, said, "You've got to start making stronger statements. You've got to start saying things that the people understand. Otherwise, you're going to get beat!"

Finally, Peterson was convinced by his kitchen cabinet that he had to let me write his press statements every day. These press releases should be put out before Peterson saw them so that he wouldn't water them down, as he had done in the past.

They set up the procedure. The first night I wrote a statement criticizing the New Hampshire Republican Congressional Delegation for their equivocation on a redistricting issue that was plaguing New Hampshire at that time, as they grappled with the results of the state census.

It was a hard-hitting statement that said the congressmen were wrong in playing politics. We should do reapportionment the New Hampshire way and do it fairly and squarely, it said. It's time for congressmen to get off their butts and do what was right for the people.

I put out the statement and then said, "I suppose we ought to call up Pete and tell him what he said in case he gets questions on it in the morning."

So we called up Peterson at the Bridges House and read the statement to him. Peterson, typically, said, "That's pretty strong, isn't it, Marshall? Don't you think we should water it down a little?"

I answered, "Pete, that's what we're not supposed to do. It's already gone out. You can't change it. I just want you to know what it says so when you get questions on it you'll say things that are consistent with the statement. But you can't water it down because it's already gone out."

Peterson said, "Well, I don't really like it. Congressman Wyman is going to be really teed off."

I said, "The hell with Congressman Wyman. We've got to get you reelected!"

And then a voice came booming over the speakerphone from the Bridges House: "Marshall! I don't like what you're saying!"

And what do you know—Congressman Wyman had been in the office just listening as I read the attack on him.

Peterson was defending the congressman partially because of the incendiary nature of the article and partially because he was sitting in front of him in the room when the article was read to him on the speakerphone.

The next day, I sought out a less controversial target and issued a statement saying Peterson demanded that the Environmental Protection Agency check out the Nashua Tannery because the odors emanating from it had been particularly obnoxious. He demanded that it be fixed immediately. We showed it to Governor Peterson and he thought it was okay. He said, "At least you're not getting somebody mad at me today."

Well, when the *Nashua Telegraph* came out that afternoon, it was a front-page story because people were upset with the odor from the tannery, including the editor of the paper, who lived reasonably near it. So now we had a front-page story on our hands. We started to get some favorable publicity for Peterson, which eventually resulted in his easy reelection.

Another vignette demonstrating the different styles of the two leaders played out when the insurance industry, which I represented, chose to honor me at a big meeting in Boston. The meeting was always attended by the governor of the Commonwealth of Massachusetts since about 1745.

When they chose to honor me, Governor Peterson came down to pay his respects. When the governor of Massachusetts, Frank Sargent, came in to read the speech in my praise that had been prepared by his staff, Sargent couldn't pronounce my last name. Sargent mispronounced it all three times that he read it.

When I received the award, I stood up and said, "Governor Sergio, or whatever the hell your name is, I want to thank you." Peterson was embarrassed by my flamboyance again.

One of the highlights of the New Hampshire political scene over the years has been the need for the Republican-nominated legislature and candidates for Congress to touch base with the people at what they call the Lincoln Day Dinners.

All of the elected Republican political leaders go off in a caravan and make speeches to the faithful about the virtues of Republicans and the great things they are doing for the state and the nation. As part of this, we usually use the same speeches every night. It gets very boring to the rest of the members of the touring band as they listen to each other give the same speech every night in a different town.

I had a great repertoire of stories, so the New Hampshire delegation decided that I should tell a different joke every night. At least they would hear something new, which I proceeded to do.

The senior U.S. senator, Styles Bridges, was not a very effective public speaker, and was usually quite brief. He had a set speech that he read without much animation. The meeting usually ended up with the junior U.S. senator, Norris Cotton, preaching about the virtues of the Republican Party and the evils of the Democratic Party and going on at great, great length.

All during this particular February Lincoln Day Dinner circuit, Senator Cotton kept saying "When we get to Dover, I've got to go first. Styles. I've got to be back in Lebanon for something at my firehouse that night, and you know how important the firehouse is to me. I'll go only five minutes, but would you please let me go first. I won't speak long, but I've got to get back to Lebanon."

Thus, Bridges agreed to let Senator Cotton go first at this particular event and, sure enough, Cotton stuck to his word and spoke for only five minutes. The trouble was that Cotton had memorized Senator Bridges's speech, and gave it verbatim.

Cotton strode out of the hall, as the moderator introduced Senator Bridges to give a speech that had already been given. Bridges, who was not very quick on his feet, was extremely upset with Senator Cotton.

I liked to tell this story at those meetings: A guy gets up at a Town Meeting and says, "Mr. Moderator, I noticed on page 34 of the Town Report that when Milly Johnson had her illegitimate child, we had to pay $212 to the local hospital." The moderator says, "That's right, sir."

The guy says, "Mr. Moderator, I also noticed on page 74 of the Town Report that we received from the State Welfare Department the sum of $500 to take care of the expenses of Milly Johnson having her illegitimate child." The Moderator says, "That's right, we did."

The guys says, "Mr. Moderator, I move we breed her again!"

CHAPTER 29

Right to Know

One of the first battles I got into as House majority leader was in support of the so-called right-to-know law. At the Judiciary Committee hearing, I told the committee that "the public has the right to know what is happening in government. The presence of outsiders at public meetings is invaluable. Government officials are more responsive to the public if they can ascertain public reaction to proposed measures in advance of any decision. The principle of open covenants openly arrived at is an old and respected one in this country, and it's worth defending."

The bill had the support of the New Hampshire media and had been before the House and Senate a number of times. This year, because of the involvement of the legislative leadership, it had a better chance.

The House Judiciary Committee gutted the essence of the bill. The House had a number of members who were selectmen, town officials of one sort or another, and some aldermen. They resented the process of right to know with the people looking over their shoulder. The House succeeded in watering down the bill substantially.

The Senate strengthened the bill again and made it worth passing. After conference, it was recommended to the full House for passage. The compromise measure would give statutory teeth to the public's right to attend all public proceedings affecting citizens of the state by any board or commission of the state, county, town, municipal, corporate, school district, or public subdivisions. The bill also made minutes of such meetings open to public inspection. The teeth was the provision that people could take alleged violations of the proposed law to the Superior Court for action. The measure further stipulated that alleged violations would be given priority on the court calendar to bring about speedy judgment.

The bill did allow executive sessions and exempted House committee records—necessary to get it passed. It was an important first step for the right to know. One proponent said that democracy is often inconvenient, but the public's right to know is basic to democracy.

CHAPTER 30

Sea of Blue

One of the most memorable fights of my career was the legislation to merge the four state-sponsored retirement systems—police, firefighters, state employees, and teachers—into one pension plan equal for all. At that time, the firemen and the police had by far better benefits, and the others kept trying to attain their level, which kept jacking up the cost of the pension plan. The issue was clear. The public, which finances the pension systems, had to be given major consideration for the first time. The merger project allowed all members of all four pension systems to remain in their present systems if they so desired. They had until May 1 to weigh and analyze the merger and decide whether or not to join the new plan.

The State Employees Association had fifty-five hundred workers. There were fourteen hundred city, town, and county workers tied into the state employees' retirement system. The plans were not fully funded then, and in fact were fourteen million dollars short. We were promising to pay that amount as a condition for granting the merger.

There's no real reason except self-interest for the state to operate four separate retirement systems, each with staff and investment policy—each exerting pressure on the legislature each biennium for more benefits.

The day the bill hit the floor of the House, the police and fire unions had told their members to assemble at the Concord Police Station. More than three hundred strong, they marched to the statehouse and started buttonholing members of the legislature to oppose the bill. Particularly for members who drank or drove too fast, it was a scary situation for local cops to watch over them and see how they voted. The police were trying to get us to vote against something that was in the public interest, but they, of course, had a vested interest. Legislators were frightened. Speakers including me repeatedly referred to the sea of blue in the gallery, as the debate went on for more than six hours. It was one of the scariest sessions in which I had ever participated.

Larry Pickett was in the pocket of the police and firemen opposing the bill. Pickett used every parliamentary maneuver available to him during the debate and parliamentary wrangle. Charges of blackmail, conflict of interest, and bulldozing were made repeatedly. The bill was supported by the teachers and state employees and opposed by the police and firefighters.

As Representative John Bednar, a town official in Hudson as well as a legislator, said, "It is thirteen hundred and forty-seven people telling us to go into debt for $18.7 million. They're attempting to blackmail us." He pointed to the gallery of nearly three hundred men in uniform. He said police and firemen made up less than 10 percent of the total enrollment of the 15,611 employees in the system. We are here to represent the interest of six hundred thousand people, he said, not thirteen hundred and forty-seven.

The police and firemen ignored parliamentary procedure. They applauded loudly and cheered every representative who opposed the bill. The sea of blue booed and hissed those who were supporting it. I pointed out during the debate that under the present system, there was a deficit of six thousand dollars for every cop and seven thousand dollars for every fireman.

I urged the House to pass the bill: "If we recommit it to committee, as Pickett is urging you to do, all we accomplish is to have to face this sea of blue another day. It means refighting on another day. This is not a partisan fight, it's a fight for responsibility for a sound retirement system and good government."

The police and firemen's supporters were saying that there should be more study on the bill if all our firemen and policemen were opposed to it. Appropriations Committee members said that if they sent the bill back to committee, they would return it to the House floor in exactly the same form. Representatives said it was clear that the intent in recommitting it to Appropriations was to keep the bill from being passed.

With his parliamentary maneuvering, Pickett demanded three roll calls. Those of us who were supporting the bill believed it was clear that the real reason they wanted the roll calls was to find out who were against them so the police and firemen could intimidate and even blackmail them.

Once roll call results were printed, police and firemen had a target of whom to put pressure on in each community. As the debate rolled on and the time got later and pressure increased, Pickett urged Peterson to put the bill over for the weekend (this was a Thursday debate) and take it up on Tuesday. He knew that once he had a roll call, the pressure would be immense over the weekend on representatives who opposed the police and firemen. I was leading the fight for the Appropriations Committee to get it passed now. Peterson was inclined to delay it. Peterson and I had a major debate up at the Speaker's platform about this.

I had a speaking engagement at Cape Cod that night for the Mutual Insurance agents, whom I worked for. I had a strong motive to agree to let the bill be laid over.

I demanded that Peterson do it that day. This is a fifteen-million-dollar deal, I said. If you let it be laid over so the cops can find out who's against them and start pressuring them, you're going to cost the state fifteen million dollars. We had to decide this tonight, I said, no matter how much Pickett stalled.

Peterson was under tremendous pressure to delay it, but my arguments finally prevailed. We pressed on so that the cops wouldn't have a chance to harass us and pressure us over the weekend.

After a two-and-a-half-hour discussion on the merits of the bill, the request for a recommit-to-committee roll call was made by Pickett, who declared, "I defy anyone at this moment to digest this bill." I told the House that recommittal would mean fighting the bill on another day. This was not a partisan battle, I said. It's a fight for a responsible, sound pension system and good government.

We defeated the motion to recommit on a close vote of 189 to 168. Pickett, the best parliamentarian in the House, then moved to send the bill to the Legislative Council for more study.

We debated this for another couple of hours and this time defeated him by a slightly larger margin, 211 to 134. It was getting later, and it was closer to the time I had to leave for my speaking engagement, but the debate went on and on and on. Pickett then moved to postpone the discussion of the bill until next Tuesday. Clearly his intention was to get those two first roll calls published so that the firefighters and police could know their enemies—and let them work on them over the weekend. Peterson was again under pressure to allow this one to pass. It had been a long legislative day. The legislators were sick of the fight and sick of the pressure.

Fortunately, a lot of the cops and firemen had begun to leave for their three-to-eleven shift, so the sea of blue (as I kept calling it in the speeches) diminished as time went on. The third roll call to postpone the bill until the following Tuesday lost, 231 to 108. This was good news because the support for delay was gradually being eroded. We got 189 votes on the first vote, 211 on the second, and 231 on the third. As our tallies increased, support to kill it decreased, of course.

We still hadn't got it passed. If we didn't get it passed before we adjourned for the day, those against it would really lobby the daylights out of those of us who were fighting for fiscal sanity. Pickett then moved to put off further discussion on the measure until Wednesday. We had previously defeated putting it off until Tuesday.

Now that was debated, and the vote this time was 234 to 90. We had gained three votes and Pickett's side had lost eighteen. People were getting tired of the dilatory tactics and were finally throwing their support to the bill. We then made a motion for final passage. This time Pickett didn't demand a roll call; he sensed he had been beaten. He knew people wanted to go home. A voice vote was held and the motion to pass carried, to my great relief. I rushed out of the hall, jumped into my car, and went tearing down Route 3 at about eighty miles an hour. I knew half the cops in the state were ready to kill me, but I felt I had to get to work to make the speech for my association.

The Senate acted quickly on the bill and passed it the following Thursday. They wanted to get away from the pressure that we had faced. They then sent it on to the governor for his signature.

They were told there was currently an $18,000 debt in the plan and that the legislature had to do something about it now. They were, of course, aware of the delaying tactics that Pickett had used to put up the six-hour fight and the parliamentary maneuvering that he admitted was to put off passage until more opposition could be mustered.

The governor signed the bill into law. Our fight for fiscal responsibility was over. It was a long, bitter, and memorable day that I shall never forget

I arrived in Hyannis in time to make my speech.

CHAPTER 31

George Wallace

It was certainly a memorable day during the '65 session when former governor George Wallace, of Alabama, decided to campaign for president in New Hampshire.

He was scheduled to address a group at Dartmouth College as well as a group of four local high schools—Concord High School and Bishop Brady as well as Penacook High and Pembroke Academy—which had invited every presidential candidate to speak at a Youth for America rally. Wallace said he would be campaigning for president on the issue of the merits of local government versus those of the federal government.

The Democrats were talking about running Tom McIntyre as a "favorite son" candidate to take away the impetus for a primary fight in New Hampshire on the Democratic side. Wallace said that while anybody had the right to run, he would campaign on the issues, not on personality.

Wallace's upcoming appearance at Dartmouth did not at first appear as controversial as was his appearance at Syracuse the week before. But three campus groups, the Dartmouth Christian Union, Students for a Democratic Society, and the Afro-American Society, threatened to stage a demonstration when some fourteen hundred people were expected to hear Wallace speak. As the time for his appearance drew near, there was more and more tension. The Upper Valley Human Rights Council called for a boycott of Wallace's address at Dartmouth. The Afro-American Society promised that members would attack Wallace on his segregationist policies.

Meanwhile, Pembroke seemed to be trying to back out of sponsoring his appearance. Their headmaster, William Marston, said that no adult group had contacted the school to make arrangements. Penacook High soon joined Pembroke Academy, saying it would not hold an assembly due to poor communication with the adult leaders.

There were also unconfirmed rumors that the American Nazi Party planned to provide a security guard for Wallace. Security in Concord was going to be provided by the city's police force and in Hanover by the local police department.

One of Wallace's theories was that he needed to get just 34 percent of the vote if the Republican and Democratic candidates split the other 66 percent equally.

No state police were requested by Concord Police Chief Walter

Carlson or the Hanover police chief. This proved to be a mistake. When Wallace showed up to give his speech at Dartmouth's Webster Hall, boos, signs, cheers, and jeers accompanied him as he walked onto the stage. He was surrounded by Alabama state troopers whom he brought with him. Shouts such as "Wallace is a racist" mingled with "Shut up, we want to hear him." After his speech was interrupted at Dartmouth, he had to wait for about five minutes before the crowd quieted down. Six or seven members of the Afro-American Society unfurled banners saying FIGHT MENTAL ILL-NESS IN ALABAMA and WALLACE, CAN YOU WALK ON WATER?

The speech was again interrupted when members of the Afro-American group, led by Colby Junior College psychologist Joseph Topping (who was white), jumped on stage screaming, "Mr. Wallace, go home!" His bodyguards removed Wallace from the stage. Television cameras were all over the place as a crowd of students started pushing and shoving Dr. Topping.

Wallace said in his speech, "The theoreticians sit in their ivory towers and tell us what to say and we're getting tired of it. Castro was called the Robin Hood of the Caribbean by the *New York Times*. Every cab driver in Alabama could look at Castro and know by instinct he was a Communist."

Wallace asked his audience to be tolerant. When they started screaming and yelling at him, he said he'd like to recommend a book called *How to Behave in a Crowd.*

When he was finally booed and hissed off the stage, Wallace ducked out a back door. A crowd of about five hundred people was waiting. They rocked his car. They pounded it with their fists, caving in the top. About two dozen Hanover campus and state police took ten minutes to move the crowd away from the vehicle.

"You have to watch these pacifists. They don't want to fight the Viet Cong, but they sure can fight police. There's a small vocal minority at Dartmouth," he said.

John Sloane Dickey, Dartmouth's president, said, "It's the old story. A few silly people got the trouble they apparently wanted. An irresponsible few demonstrated that they neither know nor care about democracy. To say that both elements do a disservice to education is simply to speak the regretfully self-evident truth."

The demonstration at Dartmouth was in contrast to the favorable receptions at Concord and Bishop Brady High Schools the day before. Dartmouth tried to put a good face on the demonstration. The *Daily*

Dartmouth editor, William S. Green, and Dartmouth Dean Thaddeus Seymour sent a message to Wallace saying they were "shocked and embarrassed by the demonstrations."

Green added that he thought the demonstrators represented only a small portion of the student body. Green invited Wallace to speak at Dartmouth after he learned the former governor was coming to address a youth rally in Concord on May 3. Green was a summer reporter at the *Concord Monitor*.

Seymour's telegram said, "I sincerely apologize that certain Dartmouth undergraduates so flagrantly abused the cardinal principal of an academic community by infringing on your rights as a guest on our campus. I speak for the overwhelming majority when I assure you that this college stands on a principle that a man's opinions, however unpopular or controversial, deserve a free and unobstructed platform."

Wallace told the press about the telegram from Seymour and said, "If pacifists fight the Communists as hard as they fight the police, we could win the Vietnam War."

The *Concord Monitor* reported a story headlined "Dartmouth Students Route Wallace": "Screaming, jeering students last night forced the former Alabama Governor George C. Wallace from the speaker's platform at Dartmouth College. Later they surrounded his car pounding it with their fists for ten minutes. The demonstration lasted for an hour and a half, breaking into violent insults when Wallace appeared at Webster Hall. A crowd of up to five hundred people closed in on his automobile as he left."

Hanover Police Chief Dennis Cooney termed the disturbance "the worst behavior I've seen in twenty-two years here."

In spite of the noise and the police chief's statements, there were no arrests and no injuries. Reporters traveling with Wallace said the demonstrations were worse than the outbreaks at Syracuse University the previous week.

Wallace was scheduled to stay in Hanover that night, but police there suggested that he leave town. He decided to drive back to Concord, to the Highway Hotel, where the legislature was ensconced for a night session.

Wallace and his entourage, clearly shaken and scared, arrived at the Highway Hotel bar just as it was closing time.

I knew a couple of his aides from the legislative leaders groups that I belonged to. I invited the Wallace group up to my room on the top floor of the hotel and gave them some drinks.

We talked for a while about the wild night they'd had at Dartmouth. They told us all the horror stories that they had gone through. They insisted on showing us their car. The antenna was gone. The roof was caved in.

"That's academic freedom. That kind of academic freedom will get you killed," said Wallace. "I'm used to it. I've been through this before. You have to watch those pacifists."

Wallace believed that those who caused the melee and refused to let his car leave the Dartmouth campus for ten minutes were the same students who jeered his Vietnam stand even as the majority cheered. "They don't represent the student body," he said. "They said they were against violence, but they seemed in an awful hurry not to be peaceful to me." He went on, "The student body as a whole was receptive. I think they were more on our side." I asked him, "Whose side?" And he said, "Our side— yours and mine."

Wallace told reporters the next day he was going back home to check on these pacifists. We discussed the matter over drinks for a while. Wallace and I agreed to have breakfast in the Highway Hotel coffee shop in the morning.

He retired to bed but members of his staff stayed around and drank with us. They were visibly shaken.

The next morning, as scheduled, Wallace and I got together for breakfast. It was interesting, to say the least. He presented his speech to me almost verbatim. It wasn't really a conversation, it was a monologue I was hearing.

Wallace tended to give the same talk every place he went. The Alabama police whisked him off the stage as fights and demonstrations broke out in the middle of his speech. He was doing it again in Concord— emphasizing rights and the importance of local government.

I didn't realize that this was his set speech until later on in the day, when he addressed the legislature. Then I realized quickly that what I was hearing in the speech to the legislators was the exact same message that I had heard at breakfast, almost word for word.

Anyway, the press somehow figured out that Wallace and I were having breakfast, and inundated us at the breakfast nook at the hotel. He handled them with aplomb. You'd never know he'd had a wild night. He told the press that he found out at Dartmouth that some of the pacifists who aren't willing to fight Communists are very willing to fight the police.

When asked about the college riots he had endured at both Dartmouth and Syracuse, he said, "Hell, we knew all this ahead of time.

There's nothing new in this to me. I'm used to these things. These are the folks who believe in free speech. They were merely exercising academic freedom, that's all. Of course, their rocking the car was academic freedom too."

It was a memorable night.

When I introduced Wallace to the legislature, the reception was a good ovation. A few Democrats did walk out, including Democratic National Committeewoman Winnifred Hartigan, a representative from Rochester and an extremely liberal partisan. She told the press, "He's nobody. He's just a governor's husband and I want to make it clear that the Republicans invited him to the legislature, not the Democrats."

I enjoyed my conversation with the feisty former boxer turned governor. Years later, when I was an aide to Governor Meldrim Thomson, we had a chance to renew our acquaintanceship at the National Governors Conference.

Thomson at the time was trying to pass some right-wing resolution through the National Governors Association. Mel decided he would lobby the moderate governors and I should go at the conservative ones to support his measure.

I went up to Governor Wallace, who, by now, was in a wheelchair as a result of an assassination attempt in Maryland. I said, "Governor, Mel Thomson asked me to ask you to support and sign on to a resolution he's going to offer this afternoon at the NGA."

Wallace looked up at me and he said, "Marshall, if Mel wants me to sign something, tell him he'd better ask me himself." So much for my in with the good governor from Alabama.

CHAPTER 32

1967: Majority Leader

The '67 session opened in a memorable fashion for me, as a day earlier, House Speaker Walter R. Peterson Jr., of Peterborough, had named me his top aide, the House majority leader.

I was replacing Alexander "Zandy" Taft, who lost out in a bid for the GOP gubernatorial nomination in 1966.

It had been a long, difficult struggle to convince Peterson that this was the thing to do, as I've outlined in other sections of this book. Pete said, in making the appointment, during a pre-session press conference in his statehouse office, "Cobleigh was chosen from a list of several excellent people. He was chosen because he is a young man of experience and ability and can be a part of a legislative team that can reach all groups."

Peterson went on: "Cobleigh would take part in efforts to build a leadership team that can establish communications with the rank-and-file members." He told the press that because I was going to be the majority leader, I would not be named to any committees outside the necessary Rules Committee.

I replied that this choice as floor leader tore me up a little because I enjoyed my duties on the Appropriations Committee and I would miss them.

Peterson had me serving as his liaison on a committee to set up rules for the new annual sessions of the legislature, along with Senator Bob English, who was the godfather of annual sessions.

One thing to worry about just prior to the opening session was that a newspaper article reported that Peterson had said in the morning that he could not reveal who his majority leader would be, but that the leading contender was third-term representative Marshall Cobleigh. That didn't do anything for my ego.

The inaugural ceremony for Governor King was steeped in tradition. With the participants dressed in formal attire, King gave his opening address. He outlined plans for the streamlining of state government and for ambitious programs in the fields of education, mental health, and economic expansion.

He surprised us by proposing that the governor's term be extended from two years to four, to give governors in the future "some relief from the nagging demands of politicking." He said this would allow a governor to devote more of his energies to his job, which had become enormously complex.

King also urged lawmakers to give the governor veto power over parts of the appropriations bills. That would save the state thousands of dollars, he claimed.

My chief rival for the majority leader's role, Roger Smith, of Concord, was named vice chairman of Appropriations, a position I could have had if I turned down the majority leader's role.

Another of the young turks, George Stafford, of Laconia, who joined the legislature at the same time as Smith and I did, was president-elect of the National Society of State Legislators, a fledgling organization, but one nevertheless with an impressive title. George succeeded in bringing its convention to New Hampshire, which was a prestigious thing for our state.

Conflict-of-interest rules, to which I was vulnerable, raised their ugly head when the Senate wanted to change one of its rules.

That rule said, "No member shall vote on any question in which he is directly interested." The Senate was proposing to change the rule to say, "A member is not required to vote on any question in which he believes he is directly interested."

The *Concord Monitor* editorialized against the proposed Senate rule: "Voting, when there is a conflict of interest, is not only condoned but encouraged by the Senate proposed rule. The Senate should do what the House does." I was a trade executive for the Mutual Insurance Agents' Association, and had to be careful of these kinds of rules. I tried very hard to make certain that I didn't ever do anything on the floor or publicly that showed any conflict of interest.

One of the duties of the House majority leader is to sponsor the bills that the Speaker doesn't want to put in his own name but which he wants to be part of the leadership package.

The first proposal of this type I was asked to sponsor, by the Education Department and public health officials, was a health careers program to be conducted on the junior college level. A state scholarship program would be established. Based on financial need, scholarships would be awarded to any New Hampshire student, including those attending private and parochial schools.

The health careers program would cost about two million dollars for the building and training. About two thirds of the money would come from the federal government if we got it passed before July 1, 1968.

We pointed out that there were now nine hundred vacancies in the positions of registered nurse, medical secretary, and dental hygienist. We proposed that the health careers program be mainly for young women, most likely in conjunction with the present state voc-tech program. I became the sponsor of this legislation.

It was ironic, to say the least, that my then one-year-old daughter, Laura Lee, some eighteen years later would graduate from the Health Careers Technical College that was built by my legislation.

The president of the college pointed out at Laura's graduation that "her father sponsored the legislation that created the college. Now he was proud of his daughter graduating from this college that had done so much to help the health careers of so many young New Hampshire women."

Laura, incidentally, went on to become the head of the Neo-Natal Intensive Care Program at Children's Hospital in Boston, where she is the top executive of that whole program.

We got into a major fight on the rules of the House as the session was starting. We had proposed a number of steps to modernize the rules. The annual-sessions question to amend the Constitution had been ratified by the public, but we were also setting up rules to call for the implementation of annual sessions.

The *Concord Monitor* brought the case to the state Supreme Court, claiming the question was misleading and the public didn't understand what it was voting on. We thought the annual sessions would be a reality. We made our rules accordingly. We had also a plan B as to how to amend the rules if and when annual sessions were tossed out by the court.

There was a group of obstructionists in the legislature who wanted to go back to the old rules, taking the power out of the rank and file and putting it into the hands of the select few. We had proposed a twenty-four-page booklet of rules to show what we were doing and why we thought they were improvements.

Don Spitzli, Bob English, and I had headed the Interim Committee, whose purpose was to set up the proposed new rules as we tried to modernize obsolete provisions. The fight against the new rules was led by Henry Newell, an architect from Concord, who was a notorious nitpicker and details guy.

There was also opposition to the rules by those who didn't want change of any kind. They were battling everything we were doing. Also opposed were those old-timers who thought we were too young and aggressive and taking away the prerogatives of the members.

We finally got our rules adopted, but Newell succeeded in requiring that there would be an amendment allowing amendments by a majority instead of a two-thirds vote for a four-day period because of the apprehension of lawmakers on two fronts.

The first was concern about what the Supreme Court would do with the *Monitor*'s annual-sessions question. The *Monitor* had claimed to the court that the question presented to the voters on the ballot was not properly worded. We sent lawyers to the state Supreme Court, including Kim Zachos, one of my key supporters in the House, who was a great lawyer and who appeared as a friend of the court for the legislative leaders.

The question as worded to the voters read, "Do you favor having the legislature meet in two annual sessions with a total limit of ninety days, but no limit on time of adjournment?" The newspaper claimed that there was no limit on the number of days—the only limit was on the mileage payments for ninety days. This was technically correct, but the effect was the same. The question was adopted by the necessary two-thirds vote, 109,847 to 53,792.

We, the leadership, wanted to keep annual sessions, but if the court decided otherwise, we wanted to be able to move ahead. We decided to adopt the rules that we had prepared for annual sessions so the Supreme Court would not think we were hedging, and thus use that as an excuse to throw out annual sessions.

The House did adopt Newell's amendment to give them four days to change the rules by majority vote instead of two thirds, once the court decision came down. This was a responsible request and it was granted. Attorney General George Pappagianis appeared before the court and testified that the voters knew what they were voting for. He said the wording of the question could have been improved, but as it appeared, it was understandable. The newspaper contended that there was a limit to mileage payments of ninety legislative days per two-year period, but this put "in no way a Constitutional limitation on the length of the Legislative sessions."

It was clear as hell that if the legislators weren't going to get paid, they weren't going to be there. The *Monitor* was correct that it didn't technically say that. Chief Justice Frank Kennison asked the *Monitor* attorneys, Did it say too little or too much? It said too much, responded Malcolm McLean, the attorney for the *Monitor*, by suggesting a limit of ninety-days on the legislature. But it could have been broad and say that the ninety days could have involved mileage compensation.

We thought it was clear, but the Supreme Court struck down the annual-sessions vote in a unanimous decision. It did decide, however, that the amendments to the Constitution to allow the House and Senate to adjourn without a time limit were validly adopted.

The court said the voters obviously intended to impose a total limit of ninety days upon two annual sessions, but the language that they ratified did not really accomplish that. The court added that the voters' guide clearly pointed out that this power could permit adjournment as needed without unnecessary expense when no work needed to be done. The effect of the court ruling was that we were back in a biennial session, and we didn't like it.

Senator Bob English, the father of the annual-sessions debate, said immediately after the decision, "I am disappointed but I can't quarrel with the court. I will, of course, consider putting through another amendment. I will get in touch with legislators and if they agree, I will go ahead with making the wording crystal clear."

Stew Lamprey, the Senate president, said, "I am disappointed, of course, because the Senate and the House had approved the amendment along with the majority of the people. I am pleased, however, the legislature can adjourn when it wants to. We got at least fifty percent of what we wanted."

This, of course, meant that we had to amend the rules we were proposing to implement annual sessions. We now needed to adopt the rule changes we had proposed. We also had to adopt the changes necessary to return to biennial sessions.

I told the House and the press that we were prepared for the possibility of losing the annual-sessions case but the rest of the revised rules would stand. This meant there still could be a floor fight on Tuesday.

The obstructionists wanted to go back to the old rules of two sessions ago. Peterson and I wanted to bring change to legislative organization and its efficiency. It took us four hours of debate to adopt the 1967 rules of procedure. We defeated an amendment 230 to 90 to return to the old 1965 rules. Don Spitzli, chairman of the Judiciary Committee, and I were the defenders of the rules. Spitzli was a good and effective ally. I told the House, "The new rules were necessary for clarity, consistency, modernization, and updating to current legislative practices."

Emile Soucy joined with Henry Newell to fight us. There were several voice votes during which we beat them back with loud NO votes. Spitzli told the House, "Many of the 1965 rules date back to 1875. It is a gross disservice to the one hundred or so members of the House to make them use rules that don't apply, in language that is not understandable. There is an opportunity to make a good change. Let's not slough it off."

The *Concord Monitor* wrote, "There was surprisingly little opposition to the adoption of the new rules and the House leaders clearly had firm control of this situation. Leaders earlier had expected bitter attacks after howls of displeasure that have echoed through the House over the last two weeks." But we prevailed, and the modernization efforts began.

The *Monitor* gloated a bit in an editorial on Monday, January 3, 1967: "At the memorial services held in the legislature for the annual session's Constitutional amendment after its sudden death following admission to the Supreme Court hospital for sick laws, Marshall Cobleigh spoke for the lawmakers."

I had pointed out that "fiscal planning is a big advantage with annual sessions. There is a danger of the law of diminished returns stepping in and we would have to wait for two and a half years to correct any mistakes."

The *Monitor* claimed that there had been special sessions, and we had corrected mistakes in the past without waiting two and a half years. Defending its opposition to the annual sessions, the *Monitor* wrote, "New Hampshire is not crippled by reason of another biennial regular session. It does not have to wait two and a half years to correct its mistakes.

"They can do it in the regular Legislative session. In fact, they are already occupied with the task of making deficiency appropriations a part of the process of using hindsight which is almost always better than foresight at biennial or annual sessions."

Bob English liked to use this example: "In the last session you remember some fifty percent of all legislation passed was during the last forty-eight hours. This suggested even now there is much we can do to smooth out our production line."

English loved to take the journal of the House (the permanent record) and open it up to the middle page, which always was in late June. The first five months were before that. The last ten days included most of the business, which he said proved the need to have annual sessions and to smooth out the workload.

The *Monitor* did admit that "our rules to modernize were working and that the 1967 session was off to a faster start than in other years. Administration bills were mostly drafted. If the legislature kept its head, it could surprise itself and adjourn maybe a month ahead of the mileage shut-off date, which caused the furious and dangerous pace set in the last forty-eight hours."

Bob English also pointed out that "most of us were aware that the . . . awkwardness of biennial sessions came from the post–Civil War scandals arising from railroad expansion."

Later in the session, annual sessions were approved by the Senate, twenty-one to one. But the obstructionists prevailed in the House. We were defeated when we tried to put the question on the ballot by the necessary two-thirds vote. We got a majority of 175 to 155, but not the necessary two thirds. Annual sessions were no longer on the ballot for the coming election.

We continued to press forward for change in both bodies of the legislature. As Leon Andersen put it, "our 1967 General Court is making history. Never before since we created our Constitutional state government in 1784 have we had men heading up our two legislative bodies with such a wealth of experience. Senate President Stewart Lamprey, a Moultonborough realtor, broke precedent by serving three terms as Speaker of the House. Now he's starting his second term as Senate President.

"His counterpart, Speaker Walter Peterson, is starting his second term in that high post, backed by two earlier terms as a House member. These are flattering records of achievement. To top it all, Prexy Lamprey is still only forty-five years old and Peterson is only a nifty forty-four.

"All this Lamprey/Peterson experience is expected to help the legislature immeasurably with the complexity of swinging back into annual sessions after ninety years of biennial customs. [Of course that was changed by the Monitor's own lawsuit.]

"It was ninety years ago, by the way, that we boosted the Senate size from fourteen to twenty-four. That was done because state business became so heavy and legislative chores had become so multiple that fourteen men could no longer handle the Senate's end of legislative deliberation. Now the time has come for us to go to thirty-six seats in the Senate. It has become physically impossible for twenty-four men and women to properly study and deliberate all the thousand measures, which regularly pour through the legislative hoppers each session.

"As it is, most senators now serve on two or more permanent committees and they often have to hold hearings at the same hour. This adds to plain stupidness to put it mildly," Andy concluded.

I was, of course, pushing for change faster than either Lamprey or Pete wanted to go, but we did make a good deal of progress. One of the proposals was toward more joint House/Senate public hearings, which was by far more efficient, particularly on noncontroversial legislation.

The status-quo obstructionists were saying that the distinction between House and Senate should be preserved and that separate hearings are better able to protect the public interest. We pointed out that a joint hearing would not prevent either committee from rehearing it if there was a necessity. Senator Nelson Howard, an opponent, said, "We're two separate branches of the legislature, and particularly the Finance Committee should hold separate hearings."

Pete tried to keep everybody happy: "We'd prefer to respect the prerogatives of each body and hold separate hearings except in a case where there is obvious inconvenience to the public or in an emergency situation where time is of the essence." He said, "Efficiency is not desired above all things in the legislature. Legislators should strive for reasonable efficiency, but you want to protect the public interest."

Pete said, "It can work in some cases, but I didn't want to be in the position of forcing it on the chairman." Lamprey had been encouraging joint public hearings to the extent of almost giving carte blanche to the committee chairman. In general, he said, "I think they're good, but major revisions are made in a bill in one branch. The second hearing is sometimes very desirable. Joint hearings do reduce the workload at the very end of the session. The sessions won't be shorter, but you will do more."

Pete and I continued to get harassed by the obstructionists. At one time, Emile Soucy was the motivating force behind a resolution to print out-of-state travel payments in the permanent House *Journal*. Soucy's motion was made by Dick Bradley, Republican, of Thornton, and Paul Keenan, a Democrat from Hudson.

Peterson took the floor and asked the House to postpone indefinitely the travel resolution and demanded a roll call. He told the House, "We've honestly tried to give you every bit of information. You have a right to know what's going on. I doubt this is a legitimate request, but more of a harassing action. If any member desires more information, we'll supply it fully and completely."

The House supported Pete 380 to 2 and that put them in their place for a bit.

Andy Andersen had this to say about the matter: "Rarely do men get tribute from their peers such as was heaped upon House Speaker Walter

Peterson by the House of Representatives Wednesday. He was given a sudden three hundred eighty to two roll call vote of confidence under possibly the most extraordinary circumstances we ever witnessed in our three dozen years of Statehouse reporting.

"Peterson took the floor in person to demand a showdown with a minority group of legislators, which had been challenging his leadership ever since the session opened five weeks ago. He said, 'The time has come for the showdown, because the continued harassment was impeding legislative business.' Making plain that he had become fed up to the ears with the situation, Peterson told the surprised House membership, 'A flat roll call showdown was needed to resolve the crises.'

"Peterson surely got it. Only Representative Bradley and Keenan of Hudson voted against Peterson. The Democrats joined the Republican majority to give GOPer Peterson the vote of confidence led by Larry Pickett, the Democratic minority leader. It was a rod-rammer. Peterson, generally mild-mannered and not given to bombast, laid it on the line. He spoke moderately and he weighed his words, but without mentioning names or mincing words, he lashed out at Representative Emile Soucy for his prolonged criticism of legislative operations.

"We had to grin. Soucy, who keeps referring to the Peterson regime as a so-called leadership, glumly listened. And then to the surprise of most, he voted to endorse the Peterson stand along with three hundred seventy-nine other solons who did the same thing.

"Peterson, a forty-four-year-old Navy veteran, threw a leadership gauntlet on the issue of a resolution calling for the disclosure of interim legislative mileage allowances. He said the information was available to any interested lawmaker or citizen, but Peterson emphasized that he was tired of the maneuvers and overnight ploys engineered by the Soucy/Bradley [bloc]. Peterson said they were plainly designed to embarrass his leadership. He also stressed the harassment had grown beyond further toleration.

"You could hear a pin drop as Speaker Peterson spent fifteen minutes defending his leadership. He disclosed the information demanded by the resolution filed by Bradley would be distributed as soon as compiled in the seats of everyone in the three hundred ninety-nine-member House. But he emphasized time and again that he's willing to supply anybody legislative information desired. He would no longer tolerate the manner in which it was demanded by the Soucy/Bradley minority.

"Representative Marshall Cobleigh of Nashua, Republican Majority Leader, presided over the unusual incident. Peterson was roundly applauded upon conclusion of his statement. Cobleigh was forced to rap for order against such forbidden legislative demonstrations.

"Representative Jim O'Neil, Republican of Chesterfield, put the question of voter confidence in; and then as a roll call was demanded, Representative Bradley tried to pull back his demand for reconsideration of the resolution, which had been killed by a one hundred eighty-one to one hundred fifty-eight voice vote the day before. But Peterson's dander was up. Bradley was refused his effort to duck the showdown. It went for this, three hundred-eight to two for the Speaker.

"The confidence vote for Peterson was a carefully planned pitch. It had been sponsored by the score of House Committee chairmen and Cobleigh and Pickett during a private morning huddle at the Speaker's office. They unanimously demanded that Speaker Peterson go for the showdown with no holds barred. We learned that the chairman particularly argued the unusual floor fight was necessary to put the rebel group in its place once and for all.

"Peterson emphasized this point; he said the time had come for the House members to decide once and for all whether they wish to operate amiably or in a posse of harassment. He added the showdown was necessary, because it was in the public interest to improve rather than impair the legislative image to the citizenry. We later suggested to Speaker Peterson the vote was one of the most inspiring endorsements we had ever seen any man get in our up-or-down political arena. We said it was an experience calling for humble gratefulness. He agreed and added he did not have the words to express his appreciation."

Three days later, Andy had another column about our leadership: "The 1967 General Court is booming along like never before, at least in our long experience. The Republican leadership appears dedicated to a determined drive to improve legislative process. This notable effort is already bearing fruit.

"The filing of bills is way ahead of anything we've ever seen after the first month of operation. The same goes for committee functions. It's all costing money for legislative personnel ranks have been augmented to produce efficiency and help the lawmakers do their duties, but as we said all along, our legislature should exert itself and become better equipped to make laws and create state government policies.

"So it is a pleasure to report this is coming to pass, however slow it must be, and worked out by trial and venture. As of the past weekend, a total of three hundred and sixty-two bills and resolutions have been processed and submitted to the solons by their Legislative Services Bureau. This represents a thirty percent increase over the same period in 1965.

"A record two hundred and forty-seven measures are already being processed through committees and hearings and some have been moved from one branch to another. This compares with one hundred and sixty-two years ago in the state."

Andy went on: "Marshall Cobleigh, the House Republican majority floor leader, is developing into quite an operator. He's applying business methods to House deliberations. He is, for example, providing a weekly work product list for all House committees distributed each Tuesday morning.

"It lists the status of all measures in each committee and reports what they accomplished in the past week. This is quite a stunt. It not only provides full information for each committee chairman, but lets committee members know what is going on and how their operations compare with other committees.

"These Cobleigh reports are useful in other ways. They capsule much information of aid to Speaker Peterson and his other aides to help expedite legislative processes."

Andy went on to tell how "Senate President Stewart Lamprey and his staff had launched a new public service with the cooperation of the House leadership. As a joint venture, the Republican and Democratic leaders of both branches are handing a daily summary of legislative happenings for some thirty radio stations throughout the state. This is made up of three daily five-minutes reports and then a fifteen-minute weekly summary, which hits the airways on Friday. Lamprey tells us Mrs. Polly Johnson, prominent Concord club woman and presently a Senate attaché, promoted the new service. She and Ray Burton of Bath, former educator and now Senate sergeant-at-arms, are in charge of the project. The legislative recap report is a good discussion of controversial bills.

"By mutual agreement, they would not include any political views partisans' opinions, we are informed. Speaker Peterson disclosed even more public relations are in the works. The legislative leadership on both sides of the political aisles set up monthly, or possibly semimonthly, news conferences. They will put themselves on the line for quizzing by newsroom, print, radio and television newscasters."

Frankly, both of these things were being done because we knew Pete might run for governor. We wanted to improve his image.

Reverend Peter Floyd, the first Episcopal chaplain, whom I had gotten elected by my clandestine efforts, continued to surprise us occasionally with his prayers. He asked God to "grant all the compassion and courage to love and follow the truth, save us from slipshod, phoney and dishonest thinking. Forbid that we should turn away from any question either because we are too lazy to learn or because we fear to give the answer. May we never regard as lesser human beings those who reach conclusions which differ from our own."

We were trying to set an election date for the Third District executive council election. We wanted to change it from late February to Town Meeting day on March 14. There was a vacancy because Councilor Emile Simard, who ran for the office and signed a declaration to protect the office, then applied for a federal post. He got the federal position and resigned as councilor. We said the date they set, February 28, showed disregard for the voters of the Third District.

It was late in the afternoon when we debated this. The election would be in a few days. Larry Pickett was fighting to have the date not on Town Meeting day, so he could get out the Democrats, not just Republicans. Recognizing the odds, he said, "It's snowing; it's a bad day for traveling. Let's vote now."

We won, and it passed to have the council election on Town Meeting day, but we expected John King to veto it. I got up and told Pickett that "the Republican leadership appreciated the great interest of Mr. Pickett in traffic safety," which drew heaps of laughter from the members of the House.

Carl Craft, an *Associated Press* reporter, had more to say about my efficiency statements to try and get the legislature up and moving fast. "It may sound more like a business firm's report than a statement on the second month's activities in the New Hampshire legislature, but it's a fact that business was up, production increased and efficiency improved. After the first third of the 1967 session, the record shows that the House passed sixty-three bills and resolutions in February compared with thirty-one during January, killed twenty measures in February against five in January and shipped three off to the governor for signing in February compared with none in February.

"The Senate passed fifty-seven bills and resolutions compared with ten in January, killed three in February, against two in January, and dispatched twenty-seven to the governor in February compared with four in January. All legislative machinery is spinning away."

The *Monitor* came up with the headline "Teeny-Bop Mafia" when twenty-one-year-old freshman legislator Peter Murphy (probably the youngest legislator in the nation) put together a staff of college students to help advise him and research matters.

Andy had this to say about Stew Lamprey: "Lamprey set another mark as he became president of the Senate side of our hundred and fortieth General Court. He read his six-page prepared speech setting guidelines for his new administration. This was novel. Never before, according to records, has a Senate President done this. Lamprey disclosed his plan to take the lead in making the legislature stronger.

"In doing so, he properly boasted about the substantial progress the General Court has already achieved in this area through the past eight years of his leadership. Prexy Lamprey said Legislative post audits of state agencies would be increased in tempo, so much so that within three years, he declared, every agency would be subject to a yearly check of its fiscal and business operations.

"We liked the manner in which Lamprey has pledged his regime to government improvement. He explained that all too long a legislature is dominated by governors. It now was striving to become its own master and live up to its Constitutional obligation to produce, rattle and bow to leadership.

"We smile at this one. Lamprey's on solid ground and makes overdue sense. We have repeatedly said that when New Hampshire elected a Democratic governor after forty long and weary years of Republican gubernatorial controls, the act would prove of lasting public value.

"Now as President Lamprey rolls up new records of achievement, he confirms our observation is correct. Lamprey stressed he would strive to get the legislature closer to state agencies by bypassing the governor's office as much as possible. So much so, he disclosed, he would sponsor a bill to allow legislative leaders to fill at least two seats on every major board and commission in the Executive Branch of our state government.

"We have an idea that this idea will die aborning. It shapes up as too radical a departure from our traditional form of divisional powers three way—Judicial, Legislative, and Executive Branch of government. In fairness, President Lamprey is not arbitrary about this unique proposal. He said it was but an idea. If a better means of getting state departments closer to and more responsible to the legislature could be devised, he would go along with it.

"It was pertinent, also, to hear Lamprey call for a broad reform of our state Constitution as the legislature convened. The following day Governor King said the same thing. Lamprey and King are completely correct.

"The legislature continues to be hamstrung when it comes to voting new tax laws to cope with changing times. We must abolish the word 'proportionate' relating to all state taxes. This was fine in the old days when most wealth was in land and buildings. Nowadays we have heaps of wealth and lucrative income sources which pay no state taxes at all and never will until we amend our state Constitution.

"This was not the only display of unity and purpose between King and Lamprey, in contrast to their personalized feuding during the 1965 session. Lamprey cited the proposed merger of the Retirement System and streamlined automation as major achievements of rejuvenated legislative vigor. The following day, Governor King said the same thing in his inaugural address.

"In his inaugural address today, Governor King asked the 1967 legislature to clear the way for a possible graduated tax in New Hampshire by removing constitutional restrictions on our power to levy taxes. King made it clear that he remains firmly opposed to any enactment of a sales or an income tax within the next two years.

"Gov. King went on to say, 'I said we won't need a broad-based tax during my term in office and I'll keep my word.' But in his speech, King said, 'The prohibition of graduated taxes could become a serious limitation to some future legislature. It would be prudent to remove the restriction now.'

"He urged the Republican-controlled legislature to 'join me in bipartisan efforts to restore what must be done in public interest. Progress, like all other things, carries a price tag and I'm not going to demean your intelligence by telling you we can accomplish our objectives merely by affecting economies in the operation of state government.'

"The legislature also proposed that the New Hampshire Senate would consider two special staff teams to help out with the pressure committee work during the coming session. Lamprey said that from one to four people would be on each team to assist key committees with field work and legal problems.

"He said the major committee affected would be Senate Finance, but other committees could request help: 'We are trying to upgrade the policy-making efficiency of these committees. We'll give particular emphasis to extra staff to go out into the field and investigate problems involved in various bills.'

"A full team would consist of an attorney, paid up to $237.50 a week, and an auditor from the state. A research assistant and a stenographer would be paid about twenty-five dollars a day. Lamprey said that while the price seemed high, the pay from the eight hundred thousand legislative appropriations would be dealt out only on the days the staff was actually working.

"House Speaker Walter Peterson said the House was also expected to provide adequate assistance to its nineteen standing committees, but would work on the pool basis."

One of the first battles I had in the session was the adoption of the rules, as I mentioned before. Veteran Representative Hilda C. F. Brungot, Republican, of Berlin, said about our rules proposals, "These rules mean a dictatorship. I don't like it." Peterson banged the gavel and said, "I take exception to that charge. Everything in the House will be decided in a democratic way."

Brungot hollered back, "The whole thing is a nigger in the woodpile. These rules will allow committees to meet while the rest of us chew our fingers. Then the committees will say, 'Okay, boys, come on down.' What about majority rule?" That's how the rule fight started.

I submitted another proposal for consideration before I became aware that I would be chosen for majority leadership. The bill was not a majority-sponsored bill but one I personally felt very strongly about.

As a substitute to school prayer, I was seeking introduction of a bill calling for classroom teachers in all grades in all public schools to hold a one-minute period of silence to be observed for meditation, during which time no activities would be engaged in.

I told the House that "the bill does not necessarily call for prayer, but [time that] can be used to pray for those who wish to pray. There is a place for prayer in schools. I don't agree with the U.S. Supreme Court decision in this area." I told them the meditation period could be used by the public school pupils any way they wanted to use it. "If it's useful to be thinking of things other than prayer such as work or country, then we haven't lost much. We will have given the people at least half a loaf."

Another quote from Andy Andersen: "It's nice to see dedicated public service honored. Representative H. Thomas Urie of New Hampton was given, perhaps, the most unusual Christmas cheer ever bestowed upon a New Hampshire man for his unflagging conservation efforts.

"He disclosed the other morning that he got the surprise of his life on Christmas Eve when the mailman delivered a registered letter from the National Wildlife Federation. It was notification he had been named National Conservation Legislator of 1966. Urie was also informed he was to receive a thousand-dollar check when the unique title was officially bestowed upon him on January 24th.

"Governor King wrote the National Wildlife Federation saying, 'I'm delighted that the National Wildlife Federation has chosen Representative Urie for this honor. We in New Hampshire have long recognized him as the champion of our natural resources. Thanks to Tom Urie and other public citizens, New Hampshire now ranks first among all fifty states in state aid to combat water pollution.'

"Representative Urie is a modest gent who wields persuasion more by personal friendliness than loud words. He told us with a chuckle that he also fell off his legislative seat when Governor King disclosed in his inaugural message that he would recommend tripling of state funds to fight pollution in the coming biennium.

"We know what Urie meant. We felt the same way. Because of the state anti-pollution drives, it is now tied to a $1 million biennial budget and hiking this by two million for the next two-year period is not peanuts."

Another major battle in the '67 session was when George "Pat" Angus said publically, "I am breaking away from the Republican leaders." He charged thievery of his amendments to his unemployment compensation bill. He said he was no longer going to sponsor HB435 and that he would do a hatchet job on the Department of Employment Security Advisory Council on the floor of the House.

"I've had it," said Angus. "The leadership stole my ideas and they're going to whitewash this bill and everything connected with it. The people in this state are disgusted with the unemployment compensation law. The leaders, including Speaker Walter Peterson, will get clobbered by the Republicans as well as the Democrats."

Angus charged that "a letter from House Speaker Walter Peterson to Department of Employment Security Commissioner Benjamin Adams yesterday contained his ideas for amendments to the unemployment compensation law. I told them my story and now Peterson is trying to beat me to the punch. One thing I held off on is the Advisory Council. The leaders are going to try to beat me in the committee hearing, but I'll take it to the House."

Angus said he wanted to sack the present Advisory Council, which he called "inequitable." Angus also said he wanted the search period for jobs to be changed from four to not more than eight weeks before taking a job at minimum wage. Angus told Peterson outside of the House of Representatives, "You are the weakest Speaker I've seen in twenty-six years. You have no guts." Peterson said to him, "Get back in there and make some more speeches."

My continuing fight for the Nashua Vocational Technical Bill ran into trouble in June when the House Public Works Committee chopped deeply into Governor King's proposal for a vocational institute in Nashua but gave the governor his capital improvements for the University of New Hampshire.

My public fight with Representative Cap Gay flared up in June during a debate on my legislation for state scholarship funds for New Hampshire students. Cap Gay was questioning me on the floor and said, "Mr. Cobleigh is the poorest floor leader we've ever had." Peterson interrupted Gay, slamming down his gavel. "The member will suspend. Mr. Gay, you're admonished. The chair will not tolerate that for one minute." Gay, who was against my scholarship money, then asked me why educators had given him the runaround. I replied that no one had.

Peterson told applauding House members, "I am serving notice on each and every member. The chair will tolerate no further excesses. The chair won't hesitate to call a member out of order and have him escorted out of the hall. Make no mistake about it. The chair will carry out his word."

Minority Leader Larry Pickett supported Peterson: "I compliment the chair. For a member to make public his private opinion of another member is disgraceful." Gay had left the House and was nowhere to be seen.

The Senate was having its contentious days too, and Democratic Minority Leader Harry Spanos and Senator Jack Chandler almost had a fistfight. Chandler, who opposed Spanos's legislation, threatened "to punch [you] in the nose. I'm too shook up to continue," and sat down. Senate President Lamprey ordered the exchange struck from the record.

Chandler had previously called Spanos's resolution "an instrument of the devil. It's a socialist measure. It's a soaking-the-rich deal. It would put a penalty on anybody who's worked hard and built up an estate. I don't want a sense of the voters taken, I don't want to see the doors open."

CHAPTER 33

Shaking Up the Establishment

When Peterson decided to move up from Speaker to campaign for governor, I decided to run for Speaker. I went door to door to every member of the House, calling on them personally in their homes all over the state: four hundred one-on-one sales calls in every community in New Hampshire.

As the 1967 session was ending, I announced my candidacy for Speaker of the 1969 House.

In a letter to House members I wrote, "Your support has made a difference in my plans. This is one of the most efficient and productive legislative sessions ever. I will be proud and honored if I am elected Speaker in 1969."

I had been told by both Peterson and Lamprey that the way to win the speakership was to "get in your car and drive to every member's house, talk to them, romance them, give them the pitch for your speakership, and don't leave until they say they will vote for you.

"Once they say they will vote for you," they told me, "thank them very much for saying they will vote for you against whoever runs against you. Once you have the order, thank them and get out the door. The minute you get home, you send them a letter thanking them for committing to you for Speaker no matter who runs against you."

According to Lamprey and Peterson: "Then you can count them if you don't get a reply saying I didn't say that in about a week after you've sent them the letter. People who run for Speaker and win almost always know within one or two votes out of the four hundred exactly how many they're going to get. The ones who lose, who didn't really pin down the commitment, are usually bitter, saying, "'They were a bunch of lying sacks of excrement.'"

Peterson was famous for not starting the House on time. Members would be waiting in their chairs at eleven o'clock for Peterson to come down to the floor and start the session. As they waited and fidgeted, he was upstairs in his office trying to find compromises for legislation before battles took place. I capitalized on the members' frustrations by promising to start every session in 1969 on time. If I had to be upstairs, I would send down my Deputy Speaker to start the House on time. Insignificant as it sounds, this was a key reason for my success.

The opposition forces tried a number of candidates to run against me. Once I got it established that I was better than Candidate A, Candidate B appeared. After about seven potential opponents, it was clear that I was ahead and was going to win, and I did. My final opponent was Bethlehem Representative Malcolm "Mac" Stevenson, chairman of the House Labor Committee and skid row host. I won easily; the vote was 163 to 68 in the Republican caucus. On opening day, after the Democrats nominated Bob Raiche, he withdrew his candidacy and moved that the clerk cast one unanimous vote for me.

As Speaker, I was determined to chart a course of major political reform to update the New Hampshire legislature and bring it into the twentieth century.

CHAPTER 34

1969 Inaugural Address

Here is what I told the members as I outlined the challenges facing the New Hampshire Legislature in the year 1968: I am honored to stand before you today as the duly elected Speaker of the New Hampshire House of Representatives. The warmth of your welcome increases my determination to conduct myself in this high office in a manner that will bring credit at all times to the office and to the legislature as a whole. I shall strive to rise above personal differences and consideration to the extent humanly possible so that we may together effectively serve the people of New Hampshire.

The federal-state system is on trial. State government is on trial. The New Hampshire General Court is on trial. The four-hundred-member House is on trial. And how we perform in solving the vital problems facing New Hampshire in the next ninety legislative days will determine in large measure whether or not these institutions will survive and remain a viable force of government.

I am distressed by the attitude of the public toward the New Hampshire legislature, and, in fact, against all legislatures across the country. Facing facts, to some degree the public's attitude is our own fault and is a product of the way our legislature is organized and the manner in which it functions. The need for respect and confidence in our legislative procedures has become more important as the impact of state legislation has become more widespread. Yet, certain of our procedures have resulted in the raising of questions as to whether all proposals before the legislature receive equally fair treatment. Where else would you see committee chairmen pocket-veto good bills and prevent them from being debated on the floor of this House? Where else would you find a 330-million-dollar business that did not even furnish each of its committees with a permanent room where they can meet when they choose and keep their records? Where else do you find policy-making bodies arriving at major decisions affecting hundreds of thousands of people without first receiving reports from qualified staff? Where else would you find a business that works only six months out of two years? A legislature slowed by archaic rules, underpaid, limited by time, and inadequately informed obviously has great difficulty in doing an effective job. Only the absence of quill pens and spittoons distinguishes the present-day General Court from the days when some of these rules and procedures I seek to change were adopted.

It is time we changed the structure of our legislature to utilize modern decision-making systems. It is no longer adequate to maintain a structure designed so the individual members can get home each night to tend their crops. It is no longer adequate to meet at a time of day that was set because of the train schedule when we no longer have any passenger trains in the state of New Hampshire.

David Broder told us, and wisely, I think, "The battle of Chicago was another warning—if one were needed—that unless the institutions of democratic decision-making are reformed, they are going to be destroyed in a bloody confrontation from within. This is not a partisan matter."

This is an important business with which we are entrusted. As former Massachusetts Senator John Powers said: "We draw the broad outlines, both financial and curricular, upon which your children's education is based. We create and maintain jurisdiction over the city and town governments that tax your homes, hire your teachers, provide police and fire protection, and collect garbage.

"We construct the highways on which you travel. We tax your gasoline, your cigarettes, your liquor. We license the doctors who treat you when you are ill, the nurses who care for you, and the men who bury you, as well as plumbers, electricians, pharmacists, engineers, and a hundred other professional and tradespeople with whom you deal every day of your life."

Yet the public does not respect us, and pays us only one hundred dollars a year and yet still complains about our caliber and our performance.

As the veteran members know, our legislature suffers from inadequate professional staff, from lack of comprehensive organization, and is handicapped by restrictions imposed by the state Constitution as to when it can meet. Generally speaking, the legislature lacks the tools for detailed analysis of the effectiveness of state programs.

I seek to change this because I feel it is the duty of the leader to propose ideas and to innovate. As Abraham Lincoln said so well: "The dogmas of the quiet past are inadequate to the stormy present. The occasion is piled high with difficulty, and we must rise to the occasion. As our case is new, so we must think anew, and act anew . . . and only then we shall save our country."

The Newport, New Hampshire, *Argus Champion* recently said: "New Hampshire hungers for leaders with the understanding, the vision, the courage, and the intellect to bring forth bold, new, bright, practical ideas . . . to show us how New Hampshire can achieve the greatness of which it is capable."

I certainly don't claim to have that type of leadership ability, but neither do I subscribe to the credo of Boston's notorious mayor James Michael Curley, who used to love to say, "There go my people, I must follow them because I am their leader."

I feel that it is my duty as Speaker of the House to propose new methods of reaching major decisions. It is, of course, your duty to examine these methods and determine whether or not they are effective tools to utilize in solving our problems.

In putting the New Hampshire legislature's problems in perspective, I think it is fair to state that, while we have many outdated practices, we are actually much further advanced than many of our sister states, and credit for this, of course, must go to my predecessors in this office, and particularly to Stewart Lamprey, who in his ten years at the helm of one or the other branches of this legislature has innovated many reforms in a quiet way. As Jefferson said:

"Laws and institutions must go hand in hand with the progress of the human mind. As that becomes more developed, more enlightened, as new discoveries are made, new truths disclosed, and manners and opinions change with the change of circumstances, institutions must advance also, and keep pace with the times."

I believe state governments must be modernized before they can expect to reverse the trend toward federal assumption of the state's traditional responsibilities. It is clear the drafters of our Constitution envisioned three branches of government with a system of checks and balances. While the Constitution provides the framework, it is necessary that each branch assumes its responsibility by operating efficiently.

If we do not modernize our procedures to solve New Hampshire's problems in New Hampshire, then the slow erosion by the federal process will become an avalanche of unbelievable proportions. It is when the states are not responsive to the people and their problems that the federal government moves into the vacuum.

I consider myself a fiscal conservative. I do not intend to make the mistake many conservatives make in that they are so conservative on a national level that it carries down to the state and local level, and their very conservatism on the state level creates a vacuum that the liberals from the federal level are very eager to fill. While I am a fiscal conservative, I do not believe one should have a closed mind. It shall be my intention to evaluate every process in this legislative branch to determine why we do the thing that way and consider whether or not there is a better method available using modern techniques.

Every method will be evaluated with the end in sight of how we might most effectively utilize the time and service of the four hundred men and women in this legislature to best serve the people of New Hampshire.

The issue is not states' rights, but states' responsibilities. The challenge is to develop a legislature capable of acting on problems rather than belatedly reacting under pressure from other units of government. At stake is the future of representative democracy in a complex technological era. The rewards of legislative reform can mean better use of tax money, revenue raised by the states as well as that raised by the federal government. The rewards of legislative reform can mean improved human welfare and a safeguarding of individual liberty.

The important first step is a strong, efficient, and effective state legislature.

I have already, in my capacity as majority leader of the 1967-68 legislature, initiated some steps to improve the efficiency, and thus the professional quality, of our legislature. In September we formulated eight task forces to study our current procedures, and it's my pleasure to announce that as a result of their activity and dedicated service, we can unveil today a legislative intern program that has been arranged through the cooperation of the University of New Hampshire and Dartmouth College as a pilot program to make available twelve students to the legislative branch of government for research and staff assistance. I might further add that this will be done at no cost whatsoever to the legislature during this session.

As a result of this move, I can announce to you that I have been able to eliminate ten untrained positions on our legislative staff at a savings of close to $20,000. This was done not by firing veteran employees, but by not replacing unskilled employees with additional unskilled employees. I can further announce that we have set a policy of hiring no defeated legislators as legislative attachés, and that we have adopted a policy of using personnel tests in the selection of any new legislative employees.

As you know, we will be voting later on today on proposals developed by my task force to consider revisions of the legislative rules and procedures, directed toward increasing the efficiency of our operation without injury to the democratic method.

In these proposals we are seeking to replace one major deadline—the July 1 deadline—with a series of smaller deadlines so that we can more equally distribute the legislative workload. We are also proposing for your approval a realignment of our committee structure for the same reasons. We have prepared the first orientation manual for new members, and while it is a modest effort, at least it is a step in the right direction. I will propose a Constitutional amendment to call for the legislature to take office upon election and to organize in November so we will not again be delayed by division of authority. We are making a comprehensive study of the legislature's duplicating and printing facilities with the hope of reducing our substantial expenditure in this area without decreasing our efficiency.

For the first time in the history of the New Hampshire legislature, every committee will have a permanent room so that it may better schedule its activities and so that they can meet longer each day and thus generate more business for floor activity early in the session.

It is imperative that committees have a room of their own, have adequate meeting time, and that they meet every day until all bills have been cleared from the committee. We can no longer afford the luxury of one-hour-a-day committee hearings. We must redistribute the committee workload and we must work the committees longer and harder. For this reason I propose a change in the starting time of the daily session. I will not prejudge whether a change to morning sessions or afternoon sessions would be more effective. I therefore propose that next week we try afternoon sessions with the committee meetings in the morning. That the week after we try morning sessions with the committee meetings in the afternoon. The third week we go back to the old system of eleven o'clock meeting. On the fourth week I would propose a referendum to determine the best meeting time after the entire House has had a week's try of each procedure.

I consider it essential that we implement the recommendations of the various committees that are proposing rules changes, especially those rules that would establish deadlines (1) for the introduction of bills; (2) for the early consideration of bills by committee and the elimination of the pocket veto; (3) for the completion of action by the originating house; and (4) for the completion of final legislative action. I think we can all agree that the idea of working a few hours each day for the first month or two of each session and then working around the clock for the last month of the session can only have a serious detrimental effect for the entire state and legislative process.

As I'm sure you can see by now, I love this House of Representatives. I believe strongly in it. I seek to make it more effective. I am going to propose for your consideration under Constitutional Amendment No. 1 a proposal to take the antiquated pay provision for the legislature out of our Constitution and seek to amend the Constitution by having the pay and expense allowance for legislators set a year before each session by a Blue Ribbon Commission—one half of whom will be appointed by the governor and one half of whom will be appointed by the Supreme Court of our state. I think that this proposal will meet the objections of the citizens who have feared allowing us to set our own pay and will establish a vehicle for eliminating a problem that makes it a real sacrifice for many of us to serve in this body.

Regarding the size of the House, I do not propose to support any reduction in the size of our House. I do not think that four hundred is a magic number but I support the citizen-legislator concept. I recognize there are those who differ with me on this issue. I know that government is the art of the possible. I am convinced that it is impossible to reduce the size of the legislature except at a Constitutional Convention; therefore, I will exert my energies in making those changes that are attainable. I would point out, however, to those of you who support keeping the legislature at its present size that you have a responsibility to make this legislature effective. I'm convinced that to make it effective, we must adopt the rule changes that will be proposed later on today. Because there has been a problem of communication between the leadership and the membership, I will today institute a system of utilizing three assistant majority leaders, a party whip, and six section leaders so that we can more effectively communicate and have a meaningful discussion of our proposals.

> Majority Leader: Harlan Logan
>
> Assistant Majority Leaders: Webster Bridges, Lawrence MacKenzie, David Sterling
>
> Section Leaders: Donald Hayes, Donald Welch, William Andrews, Maurice MacDonald, Theodore Aucella, Jeannette Gelt

We will propose making the legislature a continuing body during the biennium for which it is elected; we will support annual sessions or at least allow the legislature to spread the number of legislative days over the biennium.

We will make the functions and interrelationships of the Legislative Council, the Judicial Council, the Fiscal Committee, the Office of Legislative Services, and other such groups the subject of a comprehensive study.

It is hoped that such moves would place the legislature in a position in the formulation of public policy rather than in the position of merely reacting to expanding federal legislation and the many competing pressures of citizens for more services.

Staff and facilities are necessary to improve the information available and expedite other aspects of the legislative process. The cost of an inefficient legislature is difficult to determine but should be estimated in relation to the cost of these improvements.

Because I am concerned about the survival of the legislative branch of government and in fact state government itself, I am today appointing a Blue Ribbon Legislative Advisory Committee whose responsibility will be to make a broad and comprehensive study of the organization, facilities, functions, and needs of the General Court—with the goal of discovering and recommending ways and means of improving and strengthening the ability of the General Court to fulfill its responsibilities in our representative democracy.

The following leading citizens of our state have agreed already to serve on this advisory committee, which will be staffed partially by our interns and partially by industry at no cost to the legislative branch of government:

> Winthrop Carter Jr., Hollis, vice president of Nashua Corporation
>
> Lane Dwinnell, Lebanon, former governor of New Hampshire
>
> W. Douglas Scamman, Stratham, former Speaker of the House

> Norman A. McMeekin, Haverhill, Representative, former Speaker of the House
>
> Dr. Raymond Danforth, Henniker, president of New England College
>
> Lawrence Spellman, Concord, attorney
>
> William S. Green, Manchester, attorney
>
> Stephen H. Taylor, managing editor *Lebanon Valley News*
>
> Richard Noyes, publisher *Monadnock Ledger,* Jaffrey
>
> Raymond Hall, Amherst, director of public relations, Sanders Associates

Finally, I would like to end on a personal note, if you will permit me. My route to this position has not been an easy one. After a tough election, two strong temptations present themselves immediately. The first is to strike out, to punish, to hurt those who have opposed you. I shall resist and defeat this temptation. The problems confronting our people are far too important to permit the luxury of personal vendetta, even if I were so inclined. To those who for reasons good or bad sought my defeat I offer the right hand of friendship—and my pledge to disregard personal animosity for the sake of public progress.

The second temptation that confronts a strongly opposed winner is to walk on eggshells, to conciliate, waver, take no firm stands, antagonize no one—in sum, to drift with the currents of consensus. I shall also resist and defeat this temptation. The problems confronting us require well-considered, vigorous, bold, and progressive action. They shall receive it, to the extent I can provide it.

My credo has always been: I am only one, but I am one; I cannot do everything, but I can do something; and what I can do by the grace of God I will do. Let us conduct ourselves as to do credit to the government we serve, and the people we represent. Finally, let us so conduct ourselves that we may look back in the years to come and say with quiet pride, "I'm proud to have served in the 1969 legislature."

There you have it. Those are my goals. Those are my aspirations for this body. And that is the challenge I leave with you.

CHAPTER 35

Greta Ainley

The first time Peterson let me preside over the legislature was because he was up in his office. The session started out with two death resolutions. The procedure is for the clerk to read the resolution, then the Speaker says, "The House will now arise in a moment of silent prayer for the dearly departed member."

Nervously I uttered those words. Just before I bowed my head, I looked out at the congregation of the legislature. I saw that Greta Ainley had finally gotten her new front-row seat.

Front-row seats were narrower and smaller than the other seats in the hall. Greta Ainley was a large, corpulent woman. As Greta rose for the moment of silent prayer, she got stuck between the arms of the chair. There she was, hung up between the two arms of the chair. She couldn't sit down, she couldn't stand up.

Unfortunately, on this particular day there were two death resolutions, so when I banged the gavel for everybody to sit after the first one, there Greta was still hung up between the arms of the chair.

The clerk started reading the second resolution for another dearly departed member. Two thirds of the way through it, Greta finally freed herself. She landed in the seat of the chair with a tremendous *whoof.*

I was overcome with laughter. The members, looking down at the podium, couldn't figure out why the young acting Speaker was in hysterics when we were doing a death resolution.

Greta had a history of choosing the right person for Speaker. She ran a coffee at her house in Manchester for her favorite candidate every two years. She had something like sixteen years of consecutive winners. She always jumped with the one she was sure was going to win. She didn't jump too early.

Greta decided I was going to win the speakership, so she hosted a coffee on my behalf. Being my usual high-strung, aggressive self, I was quite nervous at the occasion because it was the biggest group of delegates to vote in the election. I was waiting to give my speech telling the members how I was going to start the House on time and why they should vote for me for Speaker.

143

Greta finished her flowery introduction of her history of picking winners. She announced that I was her pick this time, and closed with how pleased she was to support me. Greta started to waddle back to her chair, only to trip over the rug. She fell flat on her face.

About ten other members and I tried to lift her. Finally we got her back on her feet again. By then, any momentum in my speech had been greatly diminished.

Once I was coming back from a business trip to the West Coast in time to attend the funeral of D. Frank O'Neil, revered columnist for the *Manchester Union Leader*, who had just died at an early age. I got into the church about a minute before the ceremony was to start. I was looking for a friendly face to sit with when I heard a pseudo-whisper: "Mr. Speaker, sit here with me!"

I looked over and there was my friend Greta Ainley. I scooted in beside her in the pew. The church was full of the employees of the *Manchester Union Leader* because D. Frank O'Neil was widely respected by his coworkers. As the service started, the first people down the aisle were the honorable pallbearers Governor Wesley Powell, former governor Mel Thomson, and publisher William Loeb.

Greta, in a whisper that you could hear throughout the church, said, "There go the three most hated men in New Hampshire."

I tried to duck down as everybody turned to see who had uttered those immortal words.

Creating a Monster

Ihad been instrumental in creating the monster that became Chris Spirou. The first time we met was the day before Christmas, when my friend and judiciary chairman Kim Zachos brought the young newly elected Greek-American state representative to Concord to meet the Speaker and talk about committee assignments.

I was in a quandary when Zachos and Spirou arrived. I had just been informed by the warden that the prisoners at the state facility were about to revolt. They were demanding that the Speaker come to the prison that night (Christmas Eve) and hear their grievances.

I was married at the time and had children, ages two and five. There was no way I was going to spend Christmas Eve at the state prison. I was going to be home with my wife and kids as they got ready for Christmas. While I was discussing the matter with my friend and adviser, Zachos, Spirou was sitting there. He said, "Mr. Speaker, maybe I can help you. I will go to the state prison tonight. I know most of those guys. A lot of them come from the neighborhood. Maybe I can help you calm the waters."

I said, "I'll tell you what. If you go up to the prison and represent me tonight and can calm the waters, I'll talk to Bill Loeb and see if we can get a picture of you on the front page of the paper."

Spirou said, "On the front page of the *Manchester Union Leader?* Oh, Mr. Speaker, if you could do that, I would love it!" So I called the editor of the paper and asked him to send a reporter to cover the meeting at the prison, saying that Chris Spirou was going to represent the Speaker.

The meeting took place. Spirou really did know a lot of the prisoners. He was effective in listening to their grievances. The next day, there was Chris's picture on the front page of the paper. From that day forward Spirou became a publicity hound. I had, in essence, created a publicity-seeking monster in Chris Spirou.

145

CHAPTER 37
He's Going to Shoot You

There are a couple of other stories about my speakership that demonstrate my flamboyance. One of the society ladies from Concord who was a big Republican Women's Club member and very fancy country-club-type lady was a member of the House. She didn't like my style and she didn't vote for me for Speaker.

When it came to seat the members, I placed her next to Ira Allen, who was a street kind of person who operated the sewage treatment plant in his hometown of Littleton. Ira was often surrounded by the aroma of his workplace! I figured that if I had a country club lady, I should put her next to the sewage treatment man as an appropriate reward for voting against me, and I did.

A woman who was the girlfriend of one of my opponents voted, of course, for her friend and not for me. I removed her from the committee she'd been on for a number of years. She was very upset, so she came to my office and begged to get back her old committee. She declared, "All is forgiven now that you have won."

I said, "All isn't forgiven because I didn't win with your help. I won despite you because you didn't vote for me. So you're not going to get the committee of your choice."

She then proceeded to cry. I was adamant and would not give her back her committee. The next day she told the *Manchester Union Leader*, "That SOB didn't even offer me a handkerchief when I was crying in his office!"

The person most upset at me for the tactic of rewarding my friends and remembering my enemies was a World War I veteran who was a heavy drinker. He had a prized aisle seat in the New Hampshire Legislature. I took his back-row aisle seat away from him because he had opposed my Speaker candidacy.

The man showed up in the legislature with a gun one day—a pistol. Minority Leader Bill Craig came down to the podium and said, "I don't want to alarm you, Marshall, but Cap Gay's in the back of the hall with a pistol. He says he's going to shoot you."

I was a little nonplused by that. I started clearing out the material on the podium floor so that I could dive down and duck if he started shooting. The debate in the House was proceeding as usual. The cantankerous

Mr. Bednar was questioning my parliamentary rulings. In this particular case, the members noticed that usually when I was questioned about parliamentary rulings I just recited the answers off the top of my head. Today the members noticed I was perusing the rule books feverishly.

The members figured Bednar must really have gotten me today because I was going into the books to find out what the rule actually was. I wasn't worrying about Bednar and his parliamentary procedure. I was worried about how you take a gun away from a member of the House who wants to shoot you, particularly when your inherited sergeant-at-arms, Lloyd Fogg, was eighty-six years old and wasn't going to be much help in a confrontation!

Unsure of how to proceed, I called the governor's office. I asked to speak to Peterson. "It's an emergency," I told the governor's secretary. "I've got to speak with him right now!"

I said, "Pete, this is Marshall. Is there anything in the rules that says you can't carry a gun onto the floor of the House? I can't seem to find out where it is in the rules. Cap Gay is in the back of the hall with a pistol. He says he's going to shoot me!"

Peterson said, "Marshall, have you been drinking?" (This was at 11:15 in the morning.)

Peterson called Attorney General Rudman. He sent State Police Colonel Joe Regan to the House, and Regan disarmed Cap Gay. We tried to pass a rule banning guns from the floor of the House, but the gun advocates got their backs up. We ended up with a new rule that you cannot carry guns on the floor of the House, but no one can search you. I believe that is still the rule today.

An interesting episode occurred during the debate on whether to increase welfare funding. A black activist had been hiding in the unused stairwell between the House floor and the House gallery. He appeared in the first row of the balcony, brandishing and shooting what turned out to be a cap pistol. He was shouting welfare slogans and throwing leaflets all around the House floor. He continued to fire his cap pistol. He scared the hell out of me and the other House members.

It then became a big issue about whether I should press charges against the gun-wielding activist. I decided to press charges because the median age of House members was sixty-nine. One member had died that year of a heart attack during the debate on a bill he was advocating.

CHAPTER 38

My Biggest Regret

The biggest single regret of my state legislative career was the repeal of the law that I had sponsored calling for and funding an east–west highway from the Maine border to connect with highways leading to Albany, New York, past Keene, New Hampshire.

The bill passed the House on June 13, 1969, and the Senate on June 24, during my first term as Speaker of the House.

Imagine how much less expensive the construction costs were back then compared to what they will be when New Hampshire finally gets around to building the badly needed cross-state east–west highway.

Think of the economic development that would have occurred if the road had been finished in the early 1970s.

Think of how much easier it would have been to get the necessary environmental approvals back then compared to today's convoluted processes to build anything, never mind a cross-state superhighway.

Two legislators who were friends of mine led the effort to repeal the law for local political reasons. I did not take their efforts seriously. I thought they were just demagoging for local consumption. I could not let myself believe that serious, competent legislators really wanted to kill this badly needed law.

Doug Scammon didn't want his constituents to have to pay a twenty-five-cent toll. Rob Trowbridge didn't want a road to go through his hometown, pristine Dublin. I did not take their repeal efforts seriously.

When the roll call started in Rockingham County, it was soon fifty-two to nothing. Then the snowball effect took over. They had momentum. The repeal of this vital legislation was under way. The people of New Hampshire were the big losers, victims of my failure to realize that these two clever legislators were serious. It was the biggest regret that I have about my legislative service. It really hurt the state of New Hampshire.

CHAPTER 39

Biting the Bullet on Broad-Based Taxes

The state was broke. What I thought was a bare-bones budget from the Appropriations Committee was at least seventeen million dollars short on the revenue side. I had always been a vociferous opponent of broad-based taxes of any kind. Yet something had to be done. I agonized over this dilemma. Finally I decided that I had to bite the bullet. I called a press conference to announce my decision.

It turned out to be the strangest press conference I ever participated in. My staff handed out my carefully prepared statement. It said that I was "abandoning my opposition to broad-based taxes and would support a flat 5 percent income tax bill." I looked up and saw that the previously crowded room was empty. The entire press corps had run to their phones to call in this major breaking story. The press conference had lasted less than three minutes. In retrospect, that is how you know that you have really made news. My statement was a front-page right-hand-column lead in the *Concord Monitor* and most other papers in the state that day.

Under the headline: "Income Tax Measure Gets Cobleigh Blessing," the *Monitor* reported that I was abandoning my stance against a broad-based tax because of the state's pressing needs, and that I specifically made note of the needs of the University of New Hampshire and needs of retarded and crippled children. The paper quoted me: "'I must, however, take this action, because I feel it is the responsible position. I have an obligation to support my governor. I have an obligation to support the hard-working Appropriations Committee I appointed. But I have a more compelling obligation to do what is right for the people of New Hampshire. New Hampshire is the only state in the nation that has neither an income tax nor a sales tax.

"'We must, with a budget this tight, have a surplus of at least $1 million. This means we must raise ... $17 million in additional taxes.

"'The Appropriations Committee has told you this $17 million figure represents a workable but tight budget. I salute them for following the governor's hold-the-line concept."

"'Yet, I submit that despite the governor's and the Appropriations Committee's high motives, there are certain areas of their respective budgets where we cannot hold the line.'

"Cobleigh further stated, 'And thus I take this action because I believe whatever happens to each of us in this state does indeed make a great deal of difference to all of us. Therefore, I will submit on behalf of all of us this supplemental budget. I have opposed broad-based taxes on numerous occasions in the past years in the halls of this House, before the Constitutional Convention and at my party's convention. I have tried to follow the dictates of this year's convention. I have resisted new taxes as best I know how. But I find today, I cannot resist the vital needs of the people of my state. I shall next week support HB405 so that together we can meet the real needs of our people. If this be political suicide: so be it. I believe we, in good conscience, can no longer hold the line and take away the opportunity to lead normal lives for so many of the people of the state of New Hampshire. I urge you to examine the fiscal facts as I have examined them and do what you think is right for the people of the state.'"

The liberal press support was kind. The *Monitor* said, "Cobleigh Backs Broad-Based Tax: House Speaker Marshall Cobleigh, R-Nashua, finally has supported a broad-base tax for New Hampshire."

The article went on: "He delivered an impassioned address in the House yesterday announcing his switch. It was an act of statesmanship and courage, for he can expect to be deluged by snide, vitriolic and unprincipled attacks from the far-right fringe. 'If this be political suicide, so be it,' he said.

"But we doubt it. Cobleigh did what was necessary. Political constituencies seldom punish a man of high principle who has the grit to do what is right, as distasteful as it may seem.

"New Hampshire simply cannot continue to trample on the poor, the unfortunate, the physically and mentally handicapped, its pathetic children and the aged under the pretext of 'economy.'

"The state has been doing this—for years, and Cobleigh saw it. At the same time, it has been building beautiful roads, constructing more and more liquor stores, building parks and buying mountaintops while its people took the whacks of the economy axe.

"Cobleigh threw his considerable support behind HB405, a five percent personal and corporate income tax bill with generous exemptions designed to produce about $104 million per biennium. The bulk of these funds would be returned to cities and towns.

"At the same time, the measure would repeal many of the state's antiquated and discriminatory taxes.

"The bill is due on the House floor Thursday. It is gaining support.

Whether it now has sufficient backing to pass is questionable, but Cobleigh's endorsement well could put it across.

"Cobleigh did what an honest and dedicated representative of the people must do. He marshaled the facts of New Hampshire's fiscal plight and made a decision in accordance with his best judgment.

"He could not in conscience simply parrot the wishes of his constituency, for nobody favors additional taxation. He did what he had to do, and hopefully others will join him.

"Simultaneously, Cobleigh said he would introduce a $5 million supplemental appropriations bill to bring nine state programs that affect the state's human resources up to reasonable levels.

"It included, for the 1970–71 fiscal years, an additional $2.4 million for the University of New Hampshire. The $2.6 million balance would be channeled to such programs as help for physically and emotionally handicapped children, Laconia State School, Community Mental Health Clinics, etc.

"Cobleigh said the state would have to raise an additional $17 million in revenue to balance the budget. This is precisely the figure the *Monitor* cited last Nov. 8.

"Cobleigh emphasized in his House speech that even if the $17 million in additional revenue were provided, the state budget still would be 'very tight.' He said it would be in keeping with Gov. Peterson's 'hold-the-line' concept.

"Thus Cobleigh's switch to endorsement of HB 405 represents a dramatic change in concept, but only a minimum recognition of the state's total needs.

"Some credit for the Cobleigh stand must be given to the astute and persuasive House majority leader, Harlan Logan, R-Plainfield, who has been leading the House battle for enactment of a revenue measure that would help the state fulfill its obligations.

"A skirmish has been won in the war to serve the people of New Hampshire adequately. But the decisive battle is still ahead."

My dramatic announcement gave the tax fight some short-lived momentum. Then we made a major mistake. A group of well-meaning allies in the state, including: Manufacturers Association, Retail Merchants, Farm Bureau Federation, Auto Dealers Association, League of Women Voters, State Chapter of the American Association of University Women, Rural Area Development Committee, Education Association, School

Board Association, Council for Better Schools, Committee for Better Water, PTA, and Municipal Association, along with many other organizations and individuals, ran a full-page advertisement in every daily and all the big weekly newspapers explaining "how much state income tax you will pay if HB405 were enacted." It showed that a couple earning $25,000 would also pay $1,000 in state income tax. It included a scale for all different income levels. This scared the hell out of middle-class taxpayers. Chances for passage of HB405 went downhill fast, because our well-intentioned allies had run a factual advertisement outlining what it would cost.

We did not immediately sense the problem. The *Monitor* reported "breakdowns of the amount that would be paid in taxes by wage earners, gave many of the public and legislators second thoughts on the matter."

"There's some sentiment in favor of the sales tax in place of the income tax," said income tax proponents.

The media reported, "The possibility of an income tax in New Hampshire gaining House approval dimmed today in the face of strong opposition.

"Instead, supporters of House Bill 405 shifted their sights to hopes that a special session of the legislature in the summer would solve the state's money woes.

"Where mounting support of the flat 5 per cent income tax was evident during the weekend, it rapidly dwindled and lost necessary ground to pass the bill today.

"Many would-be supporters, shifting from support to opposition, explained the move this way: 'When the people of my constituency looked at the figures on what they would have to pay and the amount the towns and cities would get, they didn't like the bill—not one bit!'"

"Just as we now require first-class highways throughout the state to help solve our transportation problems, we must have basically sound and adequate taxes to help us solve our fiscal problems.

"I have rejected the idea that these problems can be solved by a campaign to induce every adult resident of New Hampshire and every visitor to the state to drink twice as much liquor, smoke twice as many cigarettes, and place twice as many bets on horses or dogs as they now place," Majority Leader Logan told the House.

Logan added in his junk heap of rejected proposals "a special variety of money tree . . . which would grow only in New Hampshire."

He added, "Finally, I have rejected the idea that the solution to our problems is to convert New Hampshire into a kind of statewide gambling casino—a three-way cross between Las Vegas, Reno, and Monte Carlo. Having rejected these popular pipe dreams, I came back to HB405."

The Majority Leader said the House was divided into two camps, those who "have opened their eyes and their minds to the urgent needs of the state . . . and those members still avoiding the central issue."

We put up an impassioned fight when the bill came up. Leading off the debate was Rep. David Nixon, R-New Boston, chairman of the House Ways and Means Taxation Subcommittee, which put the bill through the full committee and sent it on to the House.

He gave a forty-minute talk, covering the wide range of the existing tax structure in the state and the alternative that he said HB405 offered.

Nixon reviewed the looming seventeen-million-dollar deficit facing New Hampshire and asked bluntly what the legislators proposed to do about it.

Nixon asked, "Tell me which state troopers or state employees you intend to dismiss, if we don't pass some new taxes."

He repeatedly called on the lawmakers "to show your guts and vote for this bill.

"I know you're under tremendous pressure," he went on, " but you have a chance to go home and say you were a member of the 1969 legislature that did something—that had the guts, the guts to vote for a tax to supply the money this state has to have."

Among chief opponents of the bill was Robert Lawton, R-Meredith, the owner of a bowling alley and pool parlor.

Lawton blasted the leadership of both parties, accusing Cobleigh and House Majority Leader Harlan Logan, R-Plainfield, of waging "a completely unfair campaign to ram taxes down our throats."

He reminded the lawmakers, particularly Republicans, that the GOP party platform in New Hampshire called for resistance to new taxes.

Majority Leader Logan, recognized as the most articulate spokesman for the proponents of the bill, made an eloquent plea for the levy.

He based his talk on the issue, "It's the only thing New Hampshire can do to meet clear demanding needs."

Logan talked of several "hiding spots" where opponents were lodged, using the hiding spots "as an excuse to vote against this income tax."

He said he rejected waiting for the task force, waiting for federal tax sharing, waiting for a graduated income tax; hiding behind the excuse "the state's needs were properly being met; rumors the governor would not sign the bill; the possible implementation of a sales tax; and the excuse the poor would be hit hardest by the income tax.

"'I see people, particularly women, who would not turn away a hungry dog, but who are hesitating about helping a crippled or a spastic child, a mentally retarded teenager, or a helpless old lady," he said.

"These things cost money.

"You are not living in Lower Slobovia. You are living in New Hampshire, a state which is growing, changing, and which, despite you, will move forward."

The questions and answers and the speeches of twenty-three legislators all lasted more than six hours.

We made a valiant but losing effort. The people did not want New Hampshire to have an income tax. Thirty-four years later we still live without an income tax.

Without the income tax, we still had a seventeen-million-dollar budget gap. We had to pass something before adjournment or come back in a special session to solve the problem. We looked at legalized gambling, doubling corporate filing fees, a 10 percent amusement tax, an expansion of the room and meals tax, increasing the legacy tax, an increase in the insurance premium tax, a real estate transfer tax, a plain sales tax, and a combined sales and income tax.

The day before the tax vote, I stopped at the Highway Hotel and found a representative from Durham, who was a heavy drinker, quite drunk and incoherent. I proceeded to chew him out: "Look, the people of Durham are the biggest supporters of a broad-based tax. They sent you up here to pass the tax. That vote is going to be at eleven o'clock tomorrow morning. I want you in my office at five minutes of eleven, sober and prepared to vote for what the people of your town want you to vote for! Now, you get yourself to bed. Get your ass over to my office at five minutes to eleven tomorrow morning."

Sure enough, the next day, he showed up at the Speaker's office at five minutes of eleven, chastised, utterly hung over, shoes on but no socks, looking like death warmed over, but ready to do his duty and vote for the income tax!

One veteran observer said, "Today they voted to tax the sale of a hot dog but not to tax the sale of a house."

We eventually put together a patchwork revenue package to solve the problem, but only for the short term.

CHAPTER 40

1971 Reelection as Speaker

In my second run for Speaker, the *Union Leader* was wildly against me because I had passed an abortion bill in the previous session. Even though it languished in the Senate, I was, to them, a liberal moderate.

They decided to run a conservative against me for Speaker of the House in the runoff after I had won the Republican caucus. So there was a race among me as the Republican nominee; Joe Eaton, a conservative; and Bob Raiche, the Democratic leader.

The problem was that under the House rules, you need a majority vote to be Speaker. There were 385 members present on the election day for Speaker. I needed half plus one, or 193, votes to win. On the first ballot I got 189; Joe Eaton came in second with 112; and Bob Raiche, the minority leader, had 87.

The *Manchester Union Leader* said: "It took six and one half hours, two secret ballots and dozens of speeches before New Hampshire's House of Representatives elected Marshall Cobleigh to a second term as speaker yesterday. The final tally showed Cobleigh the winner with 216 votes to 118 for Hillsborough conservative Joseph Eaton and only 48 for Minority Leader Robert Raiche.

"Cobleigh needed to get 193 of the 385 ballots cast to win the second vote.

"The Nashua Republican had fallen a scant four votes short of a majority in the legislators' first attempt to elect a speaker.

"The all-day opening session of the 1971–73 legislature was predictable only in its unpredictability. Backers of Raiche and Eaton surprisingly won their fight for a secret ballot election. Both camps had said the secret ballot would favor their man but even more surprisingly it favored Cobleigh."

Thus, I had to get four additional votes in the second ballot.

There was a recess while they counted the ballots. We had gone up to the Speaker's office to organize to go out and get the four votes we needed.

Pretty soon, one lieutenant came back and said, "I can get you the Dover delegation if you will make John McGlaras chairman of the Military and Veterans Committee."

Another aide said, "I can get the Berlin delegation if we put two of them on Liquor Laws." A third came in and said, "I can get the Claremont delegation if we make Pat Angus chairman of Ways and Means."

I was unaware that the office door was open. Rod Paul, a reporter for the *Concord Monitor*, was sitting outside the room. I hollered out, "For Christ's sake, don't buy a landslide!" Paul scooted out of the chair. I was scared stiff that the next day there would be a headline in the *Concord Monitor*, "Cobleigh Says, 'Don't Buy a Landslide!' "

The final tally showed me the winner with 216 votes to 118 for Joe Eaton and 48 for Minority Leader Robert Raiche.

CHAPTER 41

The New Look

After that emotional victory, I was escorted to the podium, where I told the assembled members:

> A fiscal crisis.
> Many unmet needs.
> A bill passed.
> Many problems unsolved.
> A goal not achieved.
> Many hopes not attained.
> An injustice unrectified.
> Many people concerned.
> These are the seeds of our problem.

Yet I might have faced these problems differently if this talk had been given the previous week.

I had written a concession speech for the first time in my life.

My family had rallied because I was in trouble for standing up for what I believed in. My friends too had pulled together. Even with a secret ballot, the members who might or might not agree with me on issues had decided that my leadership qualities were needed by this House. Even so, many friends said after I won, "Maybe he has finally learned a lesson to moderate his strong convictions."

Many advised me, "You're going at it all wrong" to win an election. "A candidate should always talk in generalities; he should sound like he is saying something but actually say nothing at all. A strong position on an issue will only turn off some voters."

I had always rejected this theory, but I was wavering. Nevertheless, despite all this friendly advice, my concession speech would have ended with the words "I did it my way." Strong as these words were, the conviction behind them was shaky due to the personal abuse to which I had been subjected during the campaign from sources outside the House.

But within a week after my election, for which I remain truly grateful, a major event occurred that changed everything.

CHAPTER 42

Reelection Speech

O*ur deficit was ten million dollars more than I knew. This is what I told the legislature:*

As your Speaker during the last session I must accept the blame for this mistake.

Sure, I can rationalize by saying that we were so busy selling a program in the busy fifteen-day special session that I didn't have time to adequately review the figures submitted by the executive branch.

When a situation arises whereby there is a ten-million-dollar deficit or error, it shows the lack of our ability to sufficiently audit the offices of the comptroller and the state treasurer. Such a situation should and must no longer be tolerated.

Sure, I can make other excuses, but I knew in my heart that while I talked of a full-time professional research staff for the legislature, I did not have the guts last year to propose to you the hiring of a trained political scientist for my staff because the best qualified person was a woman who was making $12,000 a year where she was. I also knew I didn't have the guts this year to hire the best candidate for my staff assistant, because she, another talented woman, was receiving a current salary of $10,000 a year and I didn't think you'd buy it.

I knew you'd rejected a reform of the executive branch for professional assistance, and I didn't dare to try for the same kind of professional help for the legislative leadership.

When a lack of foresight and courage to equip ourselves with the tools to do the job causes clerical errors, that is one thing, but when it causes a ten-million-dollar deficit, then something must be done. I cannot, in good conscience, be quiet any longer. I feel it is time for us to take a new look at ourselves and our structure.

The late President John F. Kennedy once pointed out: "When written in Chinese, the word 'crisis' is composed of two characters: one represents danger and one represents opportunity." The opportunity to join together and take a new look at how our government and our Constitution help or hinder us in solving the problems now facing the state.

The time is now!

Time for us as representatives of the people of New Hampshire to mount a disciplined attack upon our common problems, to band together in a united effort that will result in positive action.

It is time for us to take a new look at the staff competence and training of both the legislative and executive branch.

It is time for us to take a new look at the problems of our people that we have too long ignored.

It is time for us to take a new look at our tax structure.

As my Blue Ribbon Committee has said so eloquently, ". . . the first basic obligation of the legislature is to consider how the legislature may best serve the people of the State of New Hampshire and then proceed to operate so that it may effectively fulfill this obligation . . . that New Hampshire government should move forward from its present position of a government acting on crises to a position of leadership based on adequate pre-planning developed from sound forecasting of future requirements."

A very wise man once said, "Progress begins with getting a clear look at the obstacles."

With those words of wisdom in mind, I ask all of you to consider the needs of our New Hampshire.

We must bring a businesslike, problem-solving attitude to state government. At the present time our state does not know and has never set forth exactly what its goals, priorities, and needs are. For too long we have passed and killed bills on a hit-or-miss, happy-go-lucky basis. We must start to plan, we must look ahead, we must set priorities, and we must allocate resources. For too long the end product of our system is a failure to perform, a failure to set forth priorities and to allocate the resources to do the job. I have today sent a letter to each of our seventy-six state departments requesting them to list their goals and programs for their department and their priorities and have asked them to furnish this information to the legislature by March first. It will be my intention, through an expanded performance audit program, for the legislature to see how well they are working toward reaching these goals and fulfilling these priorities.

It is later than you think for our state government. It is not enough to be against pollution, against drug abuse, or concerned about our campuses. We must be organized to get at the basic roots of these and other problems and come forth with constructive solutions.

In time of war, when the enemy threatens our shores, the people of America put aside their differences and get the job done. Our enemy is the incompetence of our government to meet the needs of our people and, make no mistake, meeting needs costs money.

It is not enough to scold our young people and condemn our university. We must take a new look at how relevant our government is and how it is organized to solve problems.

Modernizing state government is not a partisan issue. Good government is everybody's business and we must work together to support needed changes. There are those who will say that the program I am about to outline is too radical a departure for you to adopt, but I would point out that whether you accept this program or not, the legislature and the legislature alone is the only one who can solve these problems. The legislature is where solutions are supposed to happen.

If we do not accept this challenge, then we must share the responsibility of the failure of state government to perform.

It has been said that the legislature is the funnel or the bottleneck through which the future must flow.

If every dollar spent on patchwork repairs were spent on rebuilding the foundation, how much better off we would be. I think we can meet this challenge. To help us to do so, I would propose the following changes:

That we resubmit Annual Sessions to the voters next March as the only question on the ballot at that election and that in November 1972, we submit to the voters a reduction in the size of our House to 250 members and an increase in the size of our Senate to forty, including a Legislative Compensation Commission.

I believe in a citizen legislature.

I believe in a large legislature.

But I do not believe that 400 is a magic number.

I would propose that we abolish the Legislative Council or Study Committee and place all committees of the House on a permanent, continuing basis.

I would propose that we furnish the Constitutional Revision Committee with staff that will enable them to prepare a redraft of our Constitution for presentation to the next Constitutional Convention.

I propose the reintroduction of the early organization of the legislature, the Constitutional amendment that failed by only one vote in the 1969 session.

I propose that we make the right-to-know law apply to all actions of this legislature and its committees.

I support absentee voting in our primaries, where so many final decisions are really made, and I propose that before each election we mail to every registered voter a sample ballot and an explanation of the Constitutional changes.

I propose the establishment of a pilot program to establish a regional government center in Cheshire County. This project would allow the various departments of the state, county, and federal government to be located under one roof, resulting in a saving to the taxpayer and a great convenience to the public who utilize their facilities.

I support the creation of a revenue department to replace our outdated Tax Commission, whose training and responsibility have been primarily to collect taxes from municipalities rather than to be a real revenue arm of state government.

I propose a study committee to redraw our antiquated county lines to reflect today's population trends rather than have one of our counties have a population of 18,548 and another have a population of 223,941 in an attempt to truly utilize the regional government concept to solve problems such as law enforcement and sewage disposal.

I believe we can no longer afford the petty bickering among the various law enforcement agencies in our state and we must have reorganization under the Attorney General's office.

I believe we must restructure our foundation aid formula to help our hard-pressed communities meet quality education standards and then set the actual payment at a level where we can carry out this commitment with a portion of our resources.

We must integrate our various toll road systems and start immediately to undertake the east-west toll road from Manchester to Portsmouth, which has been proved feasible by the study authorized by this legislature last session.

We must reinstitute the Concord Area Planning Commission so the state can settle now whether our government center is going to be on one side of the river or the other.

We should study a centralized printing system for state government.

We must take a new look at the needs of our people that are not being met.

It is obvious we must improve our parole and pardon system.

It is obvious we need full-time psychiatrists at the prison and the industrial school as well as our county jails.

It is obvious we need an integrated prison system if we are to rehabilitate rather than simply incarcerate.

I propose a well-funded, in-depth study of hospital costs in the state of New Hampshire, which have skyrocketed tremendously. At the same time we cannot fail to also study how well we are caring for our elderly and our ill in nursing homes.

We need a redrafting of our laws dealing with credit information so that our citizens can be protected from false reports.

We need an examination into the practice of landlord and utility deposits, which are penalizing our young people at the expense of big business and monopolies.

We must greatly increase our funding for community mental health centers.

We must increase our funding for heart rehabilitation.

We must greatly increase our funding for the deaf, handicapped, retarded, and emotionally disturbed children, and

We must bring the fringe benefit package of our state employees into the twentieth century.

To achieve even a portion of this far-reaching program, we must provide ourselves with the tools. I shall propose a supplemental legislative budget in the amount of $50,000. While this may seem like a lot of money, and it is, it is insignificant compared to the ten-million-dollar error we caused last session because we failed to do our job properly. This appropriation will include research staff for committees as needed during the session and on an interim basis. It will include a management consultant to serve as an assistant to the legislative budget assistant. It will include an increased secretarial pool for the use of our membership and it will include a program whereby ten graduate students from Harvard Business School will, utilizing zero budgeting techniques, look into the effectiveness of ten of our state or regional offices. Their studies will include a comparison of what the agency was set up to do and what it actually does; what are its goals and whether modern business techniques are utilized by the agency; should the agency continue to exist at all; and how do the accomplishments in these agencies in our state compare with our sister states of Maine and Vermont.

Management studies of individual state departments are necessary and beneficial as shown by the excellent results of such a study in the governor's office.

We should contract immediately for a significant study of one department of our state government to be completed in time for analysis by our fiscal committees and to be considered as a model for future management evaluation.

All of this, of course, will take additional funding, a greater allocation of our resources. I believe the people of New Hampshire are willing to increase their commitment to state government if we increase its commitment to excellence of performance.

I shall, of course, continue my support of a broad-based tax as the best way to meet our tremendous fiscal dilemma.

I have arranged to have the proponents of the various approaches to broad-based taxation get together and see if we can't combine the best ideas from all of the plans.

I am setting up a series of meetings with economists, political scientists, labor leaders, businessmen, and ordinary citizens to try and reach agreement on the fairest form of taxation based upon ability to pay, a method that would not hurt those who exist on limited incomes. I have no pride of authorship in this study.

I will remind those of you who support broad-based taxation that we can no longer afford the luxury of choosing which broad-based tax we wish to support. I would ask any of you who have strong feelings in this area to communicate them to Ways and Means Chairman Samuel Reddy, who is coordinating these studies.

We must raise substantial revenue in this session. Let us work together to do it in the fairest manner.

Because many of these problems cannot be solved in six months and because over 66 percent of our voters have on two occasions supported annual legislative sessions and because the remarkable productivity of a well-organized special session has been demonstrated, I would plan to seek a Special Session next April to finish our work on these programs.

These are my goals.

These are my aspirations.

I recognize that probably no person in this hall supports all of these programs. I would hope that everybody in the hall could support some of them.

I would ask each of you not to instantly react against any of these ideas because "We always have been against them," or because conservatives or liberals or this lobby or that lobby has always opposed them.

Abraham Lincoln once told the Congress of the United States (and I quote), "The dogmas of the past are inadequate for the stormy present. We must think anew, we must act anew . . ."

As your Speaker, today I stand before you—the New Hampshire House of Representatives—and I say that our state needs a new look . . . a positive approach more in the direction of our time and our economy.

I ask you to take a new look at each of the problems facing our state. I ask you to take a new look at how state government can be more effective in solving problems.

Somebody once said, "We must accept responsibility for what we leave here."

So, then, let us take this responsibility . . . acting together as a legislative body seeking to make New Hampshire not only a nice place to visit, but also a better place to live . . . and I ask you all to join with me, as a House united in our common effort.

I thank you.

CHAPTER 43

Enacting the Reforms

My speech set forth my agenda for reforming the New Hampshire legislature. I was determined to prove that, yes, young men could change the world and I was the man who could lead. I went at it with energy and enthusiasm.

I was determined to implement each and every one of my proposed changes. In my mind, nothing could stop me.

It is axiomatic, however, that it is normal to resist change. People are afraid of new ideas and reluctant to change the pattern of business they have been used to. The New Hampshire Legislature was no exception. The median age of the members of the legislature in my first term was sixty-nine years. The Russ Carter's motel poker crowd were determined to continue their ways despite the efforts of this young whippersnapper! They were already upset with me because they were the ones who had put together the sneaky petes whom I had exposed at Stewart Lamprey's instigation in an earlier session. They were eager to get back at me in any way they could.

I was determined to prove that I was the kind of leader who could accomplish these lofty goals. I set forth, on dozens of fronts, to reform and modernize the New Hampshire legislature.

One of the most interesting battles was my effort to elect an Episcopal priest as the chaplain of the New Hampshire Legislature. New Hampshire, being a traditional old-line Yankee state, had never had a chaplain of the legislature who was not a Protestant. It was just tradition. I came up with a candidate who was young, crew-cut, and Episcopalian. This shook the pillars of the various other churches of the state.

I was confident he could win. I suspected that I could get the help behind the scenes of the Catholic and Jewish gentry who had never had a House chaplain. The way to break the long-term Protestant hold on the chaplainship was with an Episcopalian.

The way the election worked was each county had one member on the selection committee to choose the new chaplain. I had five votes for the Episcopalian, but I couldn't break the hold of the other five counties.

Finally, the night before the chaplain election, I came up with the idea of suggesting that my chaplain nominee meet me at the bar at the

Highway Hotel. I told him to make certain to come wearing his priest's collar. The priest was young, flamboyant, and idealistic—a typical clergyman of the 1960s.

I had seen to it that the Coos County delegate on the selection committee, a Berlin employee of the Brown Company and a Roman Catholic, was fed a number of free beverages by one of the lobbyists, Emile Soucy.

The Berlin delegation was famous for its ability to smell a free drink five miles off. Emile, who represented the liquor industry, used to host them quite regularly. He would even get them to sponsor bills for him. He would later get the Berliners to withdraw the bad bills he had asked them to introduce. This proved to his wholesalers how much influence he had in the legislature.

Anyway, he got the Berlin delegate drunk. Then Emile brought him in to sit down with me and the Episcopal candidate dressed for the chaplaincy in his Episcopal collar. I told the young Berlin representative what a great opportunity he had in supporting Father Floyd. I told him that the Protestants had controlled the election for years. There had never been a young leader like Father Floyd serving the New Hampshire Legislature. If he would vote for Father Floyd, it could really strike a blow for the forces of freedom of religion in New Hampshire. It would be deeply appreciated by the Catholics in Berlin.

I never told the Berlin delegate that Father Floyd was a Catholic. In fact, Floyd was used to being called by his first name, not by his title. However, I kept referring to him as Father Floyd. The collar plus the title conveyed the impression to the Berlin delegate that this young priest was a Roman Catholic. In reality, Peter Floyd was an Episcopalian and I knew it.

Without ever saying he was Catholic, I did everything I could that night to convey the impression that the Berlin delegate would be voting for a Catholic. After several beverages, the delegate made his commitment. I had made history with the first non-Protestant chaplain in the history of the New Hampshire Legislature. I had not done it in a way that would get much approval by the religious community, but I accomplished my goal.

CHAPTER 44

"This Is the Day the Lord Hath Made, Let Us Rejoice and Enjoy It"

The legislative chaplain became famous for his prayers, which he ended every day with the same words, "This is the day the Lord hath made, let us rejoice and enjoy it." That soon became a standing joke. Anytime anybody got a piece of legislation passed or achieved any other accomplishment, the members would come out with the slogan "This is the day the Lord hath made, let us rejoice and enjoy it." It became almost the motto of that session of the legislature.

When the tax fight came to the floor, there was tremendous pressure on the Speaker to allow it to be televised. I did allow this because it was a momentous date in New Hampshire's history.

The only time there had been a chance to pass a so-called broad-based tax in the past was in the early 1950s when Sherman Adams was governor and Dick Upton was Speaker. They had decided the state couldn't go another year without the passage of a broad-based tax.

Now, some twenty years later, I had made the same decision. I had advocated the position of a broad-based tax. It was to be debated on the floor that day. Almost every member wanted to speak on this historic occasion. There were those who wanted to go on record as being for a new tax structure for the state in the interest of equity, fairness, and need.

The majority, however, did not want the new tax. They did not want to violate the pledge. They wanted to maintain the status quo. They wanted to be on television to make a speech so the folks back home would know that they had stayed firm and resolute.

The debate went on for hours, with every member getting up and pontificating on one side or the other. Finally, to everybody's relief, the last speaker had his say. The vote was held. The tax was badly defeated.

D. Frank O'Neil, of the *Union Leader*, asked me, "Doesn't this mean that you're in political trouble because the tax you advocated was roundly defeated?" To my later regret, I said, "Frank, if the election was being held tomorrow, yes, I would be in trouble. But the election is a year and a half away. By then the people will have forgotten. I don't believe I'm going to end up in any political trouble."

This was probably an accurate statement and a good analysis of the facts—except for one thing. Every month from then on, the *Union Leader* reprinted that story under the headline, "Cobleigh Thinks the Voters Will Forget." The *Union Leader* kept reminding the voters that I advocated a broad-based tax. I was depending on the voters to forget. The paper would continue to bring it to the voters' attention so that they would not forget.

The night of the vote there were many parties in various cocktail rooms. One side spent the rest of the day filled with joy and enthusiasm on the behalf of the anti-taxers. Heartbreak and sadness and sorrow weighed heavily on the side of the reformers, who thought it was terrible that the so-called good guys had not prevailed.

The television station had decided to rebroadcast the entire debate. In each of the cocktail rooms, the TV was on, and clusters of members would gather to watch. If a friend was speaking, and someone could re-member the chronology . . . Everyone had an idea of when his speech was coming up and when his friend's speech was coming up—so the crowds around the TV changed according to who was due to speak next and who that person's friends were.

Eventually the parties died down. My friends and I went up to my massive bedroom on the third floor of the Highway Hotel. The door, as al-ways, was open. We were relaxing and having a few more beers as we watched the replay of our defeat.

I lay on my bed and decided to call my wife down in Nashua to tell her about the defeat. She, of course, was aware that we had lost because it was the big news of the day. I wanted to talk to her about what had gone on and bring her up to date on all the happenings that day. As we con-versed, with me lying on the bed and talking on the phone, my leadership team gathered around the television set. A woman ambled into the room wearing a see-through negligee and nothing else.

This immediately got everybody's attention. I said to my wife, "You wouldn't believe what's happening, but a woman just came in here with practically no clothes on. You can see everything. The guys are getting all excited." It turned out that the lady had rented the room across the hall. She couldn't quite understand why all the guys were so interested in the TV when she was standing there displaying her wares.

She mesmerized the troops. Two or three of them tried to take her back into her room and convince her of their manly prowess. About that time, I appeared on the television screen myself. I said to my wife, "My speech is on now, why don't you watch it?" I rushed over to the TV set to get a better view.

The woman looked at the guy on TV. Then she looked at me. She said, "That guy looks just like you." She couldn't comprehend the fact that this was a replay of the debate and that it was me. She couldn't understand how I could be in the bedroom and on the TV screen at the same time. One of the other legislators said to her, "Come on, you're interrupting the show. Let's go down to my room." He took her out of the room. He succeeded in talking her into going down to visit his room on the first floor.

Shortly after the two of them left, a couple of Concord policemen appeared at the door. The cops, of course, recognized me. They asked me if I had seen this lady roaming around the halls. I was forthright, to a point. I said, "Yeah, she apparently lives across the hall. She came in here, but we kicked her out. I don't know where she is now." The police said, "Well, if you see her again, call the front desk. We're looking for her. She's an escapee from the Concord State Mental Hospital."

I had one of my allies surreptitiously check down the hall to make sure the police were gone. As soon as I was sure the corridor was clear, I got on the telephone and called the representative who had taken the woman to his room. According to him, this is the way the story proceeded. He had convinced the woman to make love with him. They had gotten into bed. He was just about to assume the position when the phone rang. It was the call from me. I told him to get that woman out of his room immediately. "The cops are looking for her," I told him. "We don't want them to catch her in your room because it will be all over the papers. So get her out of the room immediately." The plaintive lawmaker looked at the naked lady in front of him and said to me, "Can't I have ten minutes?" I told him, "Hell no! Get her out of the room or it will be all over the papers not only in Concord, but in your hometown as well. You don't want that to happen."

Reluctantly, he sent the woman out of his room. Apparently the police found her a few moments later out in the motel parking lot in her negligee, and they brought her back to the state hospital.

Because I was the last speaker in the tax debate, the program soon ended. After a few farewell drinks, the guests left my room and returned to their rooms.

About two o'clock in the morning, I was awakened by a telephone call. It was the commissioner of safety, Dick Flynn, saying, "Marshall, I hate to tell this to you, but there's bad news. Your assistant majority leader, Dave Sterling, has been killed in a car accident."

I said, "Are you sure it's him?"

"Yes."

I asked, "Was he drunk?"

He said, "No. He had been on a date with his girlfriend. They had gone to a movie. He was extremely tired and apparently fell asleep at the wheel and crashed into a big rock."

I said, "Oh my God. Thanks for alerting me. Has his family been notified?"

Flynn said, "Yes, we have taken care of that."

I told them, "Good. I'm glad you did that—and I don't have to."

My roommates and I got up and talked about the tragedy and what we would have to do. We determined that it would make sense to have a memorial service in the legislative hall the next day. We set about making the preliminary arrangements that night. We finally got back to bed about three in the morning. At about 3:15 I got an amazing call from Dave Sterling's mother.

I expressed my sympathy and told her what a wonderful young man Dave was and how much we would miss him here.

She said, "That's what I'm calling about. His brother in Washington has agreed to come home and run for his seat. Will you make his brother an assistant majority leader to take Dave's place?" I was shocked and appalled that Mrs. Sterling could be so much of a stage mother. She was calling to ask for a title for a son who didn't even live in the state less than two hours after her other son had died.

It was difficult to believe what I was hearing. I told her that I would look into the legalities of it and get back to her.

When I hung up the phone, I explained to the rest of the troops, who had been awakened by the call, what had transpired. They knew she was a stage mother. They knew she was proud as heck of Dave's accomplishments. But they couldn't comprehend that she would try to fill her dead son's job before his body had even arrived at the funeral home.

We started the session that morning with a hastily arranged memorial service that my other assistant majority leaders and the chaplain had put together. It was a most impressive service for a shocked New Hampshire legislature. Dave was only twenty-nine years old and a leader of tremendous promise.

The thing that bothered me the most during the service was that one of my assistant majority leaders, Larry MacKenzie, had placed a rose in Dave Sterling's front-row seat. All through the service, the members couldn't see it, but I had to preside staring at that empty seat where Dave had sat and look at that lone rose. It really got to me emotionally.

Carl Craft, of the Associated Press, put it nicely: "David A. Sterling was a flame growing brighter. This strikingly handsome young country lawyer from Hillsboro ignited new Republican interest in Richard M. Nixon. Sterling helped light Nixon's path to the presidency.

"Sterling was 30.

"Yet, he already was the youngest ever to serve on the Republican National Committee, already the skilled leader of the New Hampshire campaign of a man who eventually won the White House, already in a second term in the state House of Representatives, already an assistant majority leader of the 400-member lower legislative chamber.

"Today, his flame was extinguished—he died, alone in his overturned auto, along a roadside in nearby Antrim.

"State Police said Sterling's northbound car ran off Route 202 about 2 A.M., rammed a rock, flipped and skidded. He was pronounced dead at a hospital in Concord—the 51st person to die this year in New Hampshire traffic accidents.

"Sterling's future 'as a friend and confidant of President Nixon was unlimited,' said House Speaker Marshall Cobleigh, of Nashua, expressing the grief of the Republican legislative leadership.

The service was over. The House had to resume its normal business. Because the combined sales and income tax bill had failed the day before, we had to pass some patchwork tax bills to meet the needs of the state.

After extensive debate, parts of the substitute package was agreed to but there were still some twenty-odd bills waiting to be disposed of. Jim O'Neil, my deputy speaker, came up to the podium and said to me, "Why don't you take a break and go upstairs? You had a short night and you've had a tremendous burden to preside over this memorial service and the tax debate. Why don't you take a rest a little bit and put someone else in the chair? I'll be glad to do it if you'd like."

I resisted, but I finally realized it made sense. I was emotionally drained and extremely tired. I had had very little sleep during the night between the various phone calls and the planning of the memorial service. I put the deputy speaker in the chair and went up into the Speaker's office.

I had no sooner walked into the office when I received a call from Mrs. Don Welch, who wondered if I knew where Don was. He had not been home last night. She had no idea where he was. I said, "I don't know, but I'll find out. Where are you?" She said she was in the Concord Hospital, where she had just had a hysterectomy. She was very upset that she hadn't heard from her husband all night. I assured her I would check into it.

She asked, "Is he all right? Is there something wrong?"

I said, "No, I don't believe so. Let me see what I can find out. I'll get back to you as soon as I can." As I was finishing the call with Shirley Welch, a legislator rushed into the room and said he just heard over the radio that Don Welch's car had been found in the river and a dead body had been found in the car. The body had not been identified, but the license plate was a legislative license plate. It was Don Welch's.

I called the radio station to find out what information they had. I gave them hell for putting it over the air before the family had been notified. I tried to verify the identity of the body, which the radio station could not do. I then called the commissioner of safety again and asked him what the situation was. I found out that they thought it was Don Welch but they hadn't found anybody up there to identify him.

Meanwhile, Shirley Welch called back and she said she heard that Don had been killed in a car accident. "Is it true?" she asked.

The body had not been identified yet. I said, "I don't know. I'm checking on it. I will get back to you shortly." I told her just to take it easy. She said, "No, I'm going to check out of the hospital and come there to the statehouse."

I got off the phone with her and immediately called the hospital. I told them that she was trying to leave and that she'd better stay where she was because it was probably true about her husband. Shortly thereafter, I received another call from the commissioner of safety, who informed me that the body had been identified. It was that of Don Welch.

This caused a tremendous strain on me and the rest of the leadership. I had to call the hospital and tell Shirley Welch that it was true that her husband had been killed. I promised her that we would have a memorial service similar to the one we had held that day for Dave Sterling.

The next day, there was a second memorial service, this time for Don Welch. We had wakes and funerals of both these leaders to attend.

An ironic twist is that Sterling and Welch had been the co-chairmen of the Speaker's Testimonial and all the checks and ticket purchases had been made in their names. A further irony was when the Episcopal chaplain, Peter Floyd, whom they had helped engineer into office, started the prayer before the session. He said, as usual, "This is the day the Lord hath made, let us rejoice and enjoy it."

I thought, I have lost tax reform and two dear friends and members of my leadership team. He wants me to rejoice and enjoy it?

CHAPTER 45

Riding for a Fall

My heady ride on the road to success came crashing down at the time of the Annual Speaker's Testimonial.

At the completion of every speaker's term, it is customary to honor him (or now her) with a testimonial at which he is praised for his accomplishments, both real and imaginary.

My wife Carolyn ran my business. That was how I was able to take the time off to serve in the legislature. When it came time for my testimonial, she jumped in feet first and helped pull it together. She made it into a spectacular recitation of my accomplishments in changing the New Hampshire Legislature.

Yes, I was a young man. Yes, I was less than thirty-five. I had now been House majority leader, House Speaker, and vice president of the Jaycees, the organization that had run the original "Ten Outstanding Young Men" program that had inspired me into this world of service.

Carolyn organized a superb testimonial. She had speakers from the insurance world, where I made my living—national figures from those organizations. She had, of course, the governor, and the senate president and other legislative leaders who were proud to praise all the changes I had made to reform the legislature. It was, indeed, a night of celebration. I concluded the evening with a touching and emotional speech. I said none of these accomplishments would have been possible without the work and assistance of my wife, and helpmate, Carolyn. The audience was touched by my emotion and by my obvious devotion to my wife.

A week later, as the session was winding down, my wife, who had been staying with me at the Highway Hotel, met me at the bar. It was obvious at once that she was drunk. I sat down at the bar to join her. She told me that she was in love with my chauffeur and aide, Bill Woodward, and she wanted a divorce. I was stunned. I had not had any inkling of this development. It caught me by complete surprise.

I asked her, Couldn't you wait to make this announcement until after the legislature had adjourned for the session in another week? She said, No, we've already told some of our friends and some of yours. I want you to get a room of your own for tonight because I'm not going to sleep with you anymore.

I was devastated. I convened a quick meeting of my key advisers, whom I kiddingly called "the seventy-two club" because I said they were all going to run against me for Speaker in 1972 if I didn't get out and go someplace else.

I told them the problem. They, too, were stunned. Nobody had seen it coming. They talked about the ramifications for my career, how best to handle it from the public standpoint. Then it came time for the bar to close. They said, Well, we'll talk about it some more tomorrow.

I went back to the room that I shared with Carolyn only to find the door locked. The security chain had been installed so that I could not get in. I sent one of my aides down to the desk to try to rent me another room, only to discover that the hotel was sold out for the night due to the activities of the closing of the session.

Finally, one of my key supporters and a senate aide, "Landslide" Turner, said he had a hacksaw in his car. We could saw the chain. I could use the other bed in the bedroom because there was no other place to stay.

By now, I had enough to drink that I didn't want to drive anyplace, either. Landslide went down to his car. He couldn't find his hacksaw. As he always did, Senate President Jack Bradshaw came to my assistance. He went and got his hacksaw. Three or four of my aides and allies were gathered around as they tried to saw through the chain that was barring me from entry into the room that for the session had been my bedroom.

It was noisy work at best and pretty soon somebody said, "Watch out, here comes Creeping Jesus."

"Creeping Jesus" was the name they had given the unfortunate night watchman, who had some sort of palsy. His feet shuffled and his head was down as he made his appointed rounds to make sure the building wasn't on fire and no parties were going on after hours. They put away the hacksaw until Creeping Jesus got beyond them. Then they resumed sawing through the chain. Finally, I was able to return to the other bed.

CHAPTER 46

Terrible Times

Iwas devastated. Despite several efforts to try and resurrect the marriage, it was clear that Carolyn was going to cast her lot with Bill Woodward. My friend Russ Howard wrote a magnificent letter to Carolyn trying to show her the errors of her ways. Russ reminded her how much she and I had struggled together to build a career that had reached such a high note and how she was tossing it all away, but to no avail. She was adamant and the divorce proceedings went on.

I eventually became reconciled to the loss of my wife. I couldn't cope with the fact that my two daughters, ages five and two, were no longer living with me. The kids were, in fact, being used as a tool in the divorce proceedings by Bill and Carolyn. If I wanted visitation rights on Friday, they said Saturday. If I said Saturday, they said Friday. If I wanted them in the daytime, they said night. If I wanted them at night, they said daytime. They knew my schedule was complex. They did the best to withdraw the kids from me or make me change my schedule in ways that I had real trouble conforming to.

Their refusal to be at all flexible in the area of the children's visitation devastated me. I had great emotional difficulty handling the situation. The *Manchester Union Leader*, of course, publicized every aspect of the divorce trial in as inflammatory and sensational a way as it possibly could. This made it even more difficult for me to deal with.

CHAPTER 47

Protecting the President

The session was in the midst of the Vietnam War. All of the unpopular political ramifications of the war dominated the agenda as the New Hampshire presidential primary loomed on the horizon. The antiwar activists came up with the idea that they would put on the New Hampshire presidential primary ballot a question: "Do you support the Vietnam War or would you prefer that America got out of the war?"

This would have been a disastrous referendum question for President Richard Nixon to have to deal with as he sought reelection. His operatives called on me to kill the legislation. I knew that if the bill got to the floor of the House, it would probably pass. I determined that the only way to protect the president was to pocket-veto the bill myself.

The Speaker of the New Hampshire House does not have the power to pocket the bill. I took the position that the Speaker can do anything that isn't expressly prohibited in the rules of the House. I stuck the bill in my desk drawer. I vowed never to let it get into the legislative process.

A bunch of the Vietnam vets demanded an appointment with me and my leadership to discuss the situation. These protesters arrived in my office. They went on at great length about the problems in Vietnam. They weren't being respected when they got back home. They recited the litany of other complaints that were being heard around the world at that time by America's returning veterans.

They made the mistake of telling me that my team and I did not understand what they had gone through and what war was like. This set me off. I told them that I had served four years of active duty in the U.S. Navy. I had seen my friends die. That a lot fewer people were dead from the Vietnam War than there were from the other wars. I quoted the following statistics of the number of people who died in each of our wars: Korean War 33,651 in three years; Vietnam War 47,369 in eleven years; World War I 53,513 in two years; World War II 242,131 in four years.

I also told them that when my friends and I were in the war, we didn't end up stoned on drugs. We didn't come back all screwed up, because we had the courage not to use drugs. Seeing our friends die wasn't any easier on us than it was on the people in this room.

They told me, "You don't understand how bad it was. You don't know what problems we have seen." I told them, "Don't lecture me. You don't know the problems the people in this room have seen! The man over there, my deputy speaker, his son was killed in the Vietnam War. He didn't come home drugged up. He made the supreme sacrifice. He lost his life.

"My majority leader's daughter was a Vietnam protester. You folks would know her name. She was in the brownstone in New York when the building blew up. She and her friends were last seen in the rubble of the building with their clothes blown off their bodies. She has disappeared off the face of the earth. He would love to know where she is. Is she alive or is she dead? Yes, he's suffering through that.

"I just suffered the loss of my two children through a divorce. All three of us are going through our own hell on earth. The hell you guys went through is not any worse than hell we've gone through. So don't be lecturing me, you drugged-up veterans, about what the horrors of war are like. We have lived through horrors too. We've kept control of our emotions and our bodies and our faculties, unlike you guys."

With that, I threw them out of the office. I renewed my vows not to bring the legislation to the floor.

The liberal newspapers in the state editorialized against me and pointed out that I didn't have the authority to do what I was doing. I held fast. Nobody challenged me and took it to the floor, so I got away with it. The president didn't have to deal with the Vietnam War resolution as he sought reelection in the New Hampshire presidential primary.

My pocketing of the proposed Vietnam War referendum on behalf of the Nixon administration almost cost us the New Hampshire first-in-the-nation presidential primary. On two different occasions, Florida and Nevada were seeking to advance their primary before ours. I called then Nevada governor Paul Laxalt, whom I did not know at that time but later became fast friends with, and told him our legislature would be in session until July 1 and his would be home by April 1. Whatever date they moved the primary to, I would move ours earlier after they had adjourned. It was a poker bluff of the highest order, but he bought it. I convinced him to veto the legislation and leave New Hampshire first. Later, Florida tried the same thing and I called Speaker Dick Pettigrew, whom I knew, and pulled the same bluff on him. That was also successful.

But Democrat Harry Spanos was livid at me for pocket-vetoing the Vietnam resolution and he decided to kill all bills I had sponsored in the

Senate. One of these bills was to save the New Hampshire presidential primary. My name was listed first as sponsor and Spanos decided to kill the bill. We had a major war between the House and Senate, but the Senate eventually agreed to let the bill pass, saving the New Hampshire primary by one vote.

CHAPTER 48

Washington Bound?

I decided that despite the tremendous bad publicity I'd received over the most highly publicized divorce in the history of this state, I would run for the U.S. Senate. I sensed the fact that the incumbent senator, Tom McIntyre, who really resided in Florida, was out of touch with the people and could be beaten.

I felt that if I'd been a conservative at that time, the chances of my running successfully for the Senate were small because of the divorce. But being a liberal moderate, well, the liberals were accustomed to divorcing. They wouldn't hold it against me. I decided that I would plunge forward and make the effort to achieve my lifetime ambition.

I had decided the way to run for the Senate was to put together a great direct-mail list and a strong letter seeking support and funds. We worked long and hard on the list and long and hard on the letter. Finally they were complete. The letters that I hoped would be the linchpins of the campaign were sent to the post office with my aide (who had replaced Woodward) and the aide's friend, who was a Democrat.

They were supposed to take the mail in their car to the post office along with my check to cover the costs of sending out the 40,000 letters to potential supporters, including all the members of the House and all the people whom I had helped during my five terms in the legislature.

The returns on the letter were extremely disappointing. Only a few people sent back the envelopes asking for bumper stickers or volunteering to hold a coffee, put a sign on their house, or send me money. I couldn't understand why. I had made a living by my direct-mail expertise.

Six months after the election, when trying to balance my checkbook and file the necessary campaign finance reports that were required even though I lost, I found that the check for the postage on the letter was missing and had never cleared the bank.

Then I started questioning my aide. He eventually admitted that they had never mailed the letters. They threw them in the dump because they were both really, truly Democrats. The whole key to my campaign effort never reached the voters. They mailed one very small bag of letters to people. That's how I got a few back. The great majority of the letters were deposited in the dump—not the post office! My campaign never really got off the ground.

Another key factor was that I disproved the old adage that any publicity is good as long as they spell your name correctly. I had received mammoth publicity for my activities in the legislature, but a lot of it was negative.

The Senate loss was a major disappointment and I had trouble adjusting to it as well as to the divorce. When the first Christmas alone came, I wanted the kids to visit me. Carolyn insisted that the kids would spend Christmas with her. They could spend the day after Christmas with me.

Christmas happened to be on a Friday that year, so Friday the kids spent with Carolyn. Then I had a Christmas for the kids, aided and abetted by my family, on Saturday. Carolyn's visitation rules were that I had to have the kids back by seven at night. So, after I brought the kids back to Carolyn's, I went to my neighborhood bar to drown my sorrows.

I sat there in utter misery. The regular bartender wasn't on. The new guy didn't talk to me. At about a quarter past twelve, I looked up to see an attractive woman about three stools over, who had just appeared out of nowhere. The band was playing and I asked her to dance. The dance was the last dance of the night. It was one of these apart dances that I didn't really know how to do.

I was up there dancing with a lady. When the song ended, I didn't even know her name. We hadn't had any conversation while dancing to loud music. I stammered out, "Would you like to come over to my house for a drink?"

To my utter surprise, she said, "Yes, on one condition."

I said, "What is that?"

She said, "You've got to get me out of there by three o'clock tomorrow afternoon."

I said that's very reasonable and proceeded to take the woman to my house. We had a number of drinks. It turned out she was in love with a married guy. He had told her that he had to spend the holiday with his wife but after the holiday, he was going to divorce his wife and marry this lady. She only told me her first name. I tried to get the last name out of her. We had a very enjoyable evening. I did get her back to her car by three o'clock the next afternoon.

I said, "Will I see you again?"

"If he stays with his wife," she said, "I'll call you because I had a wonderful time. But if he doesn't, you'll never hear from me again. If he comes with me, I'm going to marry him and that'll be it."

I never heard from her again.

A year and a half later, I was speaking to a local bar association when a lawyer came up to me and said, "Marshall, I hear that you're a very nice guy and very good in bed."

I said, "Where in the world did you hear that?"

He said, "Do you remember the day after Christmas, the woman you took to your house? Well, I was her lawyer. The husband did divorce his wife. I represented him in the divorce. They told me the story about her night with you. They wanted me to tell you that they're happily married. I can't tell you their name because I promised them I wouldn't."

So I never did hear from her again, but I was glad to hear at least that her life had turned out better than mine.

CHAPTER 49
Prorogue Address

As my final year as Speaker came to an end, I put all efforts into developing a prorogue speech to the members and the public summing up our accomplishments. This is what I told them:

PROROGUE ADDRESS: 1972 Special Session of the Legislature

As this Special Session draws to a close, one realizes as we look around this chamber that we will never all be here together again. As my second term as Speaker draws to a close, I am reminded of President James Garfield's memorable remark, "My God! What is there in this place that a man should ever want to get into?"

This closing has a special significance to me personally, for, unless we are called back again in special session, it marks the conclusion of ten years of legislative service to the people of New Hampshire.

In looking back, I have enjoyed the challenge of being Speaker of the House but I would be less than frank if I didn't make it clear to you that I am considering challenges in other areas.

After ten years of service, it is a time for reminiscing. It is a time to look at accomplishments. It is a time to review unmet needs. It is a time to diagnose this institution we all love, for diagnosis precedes cure and we cannot help this House until we become sensitive to its problems.

What was it like back in 1963? In that session we considered eight hundred and forty-eight bills as compared with one thousand four hundred and forty-seven in the 1971 regular session.

It was, as you might expect, an unhurried atmosphere with a greater respect for traditions, accompanied by antiquated legislative procedures.

The one difference that really stands out among all the others is that in those days many more members seemed to be members who loved, respected, and revered this House and its accoutrements.

In those days, motions and parliamentary procedures were agreed upon by the antagonists in a gentlemanly fashion before the battle, rather than trying to trick someone with a last-minute, devious move.

In those days, when a ruling by the chair was attacked, the first people to go to the chair's defense were the leaders of the loyal opposition, for they respected the tradition of the office if not the man who held it.

Maybe it is nostalgia, but there appeared to be a friendlier rapport among the members, a greater comradeship, a greater understanding, a greater trust of each other's motives, foibles, and concerns.

I see a significant difference that on the last night in those days, the forces of opposition were here till the closing gun. They loved this legislature and they didn't really want to go home as long as there was an excuse to stay with their friends, their comrades, and their adversaries.

Now on the last night, we find the opposition making their speeches, issuing their press releases, and all returning home—all but one, who immediately demands a quorum call!

I know there has been much talk about the Citizens Conference of State Legislatures ranking us thirty-eighth in the nation but many of you do not know of a Michigan University study which rated legislatures on their innovative qualities. They took one hundred bills that had been passed in forty of the fifty states and determined what states passed these measures and in what order. New Hampshire was ranked eighth nationally and was the only small state in the top ten in that study.

There are those who criticize this General Court and hold it in contempt, but I look back at her record of accomplishment over these ten years and I am proud.

As I look at the major accomplishments of the past ten years, one stands out above all the others. Some of you will laugh and perhaps disagree with this, but it is a fact we have made a most important change in our tax structure with the passage of the business profits tax. In this we rejected the long-held theory of taxing an inventory a merchant couldn't sell and of taxing the machines with which he produced his goods. Instead we established a tax on the money he makes from the goods he has sold. I would predict that we will shortly reject the ancient theory of taxing property a man owns and we will replace it with a tax based upon the money he makes. The passage of the business profits tax and the repeal of twelve ancient and inequitable taxes was the single greatest tax reform achievement in our state's history.

In these ten years this legislature has effected long needed reforms in our judicial system with the establishment of a district court system that has modernized the judicial process in this state.

I take personal pride in the fact that this legislature has modernized its own rules and procedures to a point where it is considered a model of efficiency by many of our sister states.

As I travel across this country and hear the problems of our sister states, I think we may take pride in the fact that in this decade we have twice reapportioned this House, free of dispute, free of judicial challenge, and in a manner that is fair and just.

The 1963 General Court granted our cities the power to run their own affairs by the passage of a home rule bill making democracy on the local level more meaningful.

In pioneering the sweepstakes program New Hampshire has maintained a longstanding tradition that this legislature is not afraid to pioneer and meet the challenges of our times with imagination. This program is now being copied by many states across America.

The passage in 1965 of the highest percentage of state support to local communities for water pollution abatement in the nation, plus the passage in 1967 of House Bill 111 safeguarding land development, demonstrates our leadership in the area of ecology. Unfortunately, we have not seen fit since then to adequately fund these programs nor to resist the blandishments of developers. Indeed, in this area we are becoming followers, where we were once and should be leaders.

We have enacted legislation to combat the growing problem of air pollution to ensure that New Hampshire's air will continue to be the cleanest in the entire nation.

One of the major problems facing America today is drug abuse. We take pride in the fact that our drug abuse statutes preceded those of the federal government, that these statutes are considered better than those of most of our sister states, and the undercover narcotics division of our State Police is considered the best in New England. Just recently we have undertaken a new comprehensive attack on this serious problem, coordinating education, rehabilitation, and law enforcement.

We implemented Title 19 of the Federal Medicaid Act providing medical care to thousands of our elderly and poor not on welfare rolls but whose incomes are low and who cannot afford effective medical treatment.

We have developed a highly successful community mental health clinic program throughout our state so that our people may be treated in their home localities rather than in our state institutions. Like many other areas of need, this vital program is far from fully funded.

We have enacted legislation that will permit us to implement the National Highway Safety Act of 1966. This, together with the passage of my Habitual Offenders Act, is a major step in our continuing effort to reduce traffic accidents, thereby getting people off the road who have been causing numerous accidents.

During this period we have constructed eight hundred and eighteen lane miles of new highways at a cost of two hundred forty-five million dollars.

We have, through the Highway Beautification Act, moved to protect the scenic beauty of New Hampshire for all to enjoy. This act, coupled with billboard control, assures our people today and tomorrow that our natural heritage will be protected from despoliation and commercialization.

We changed the holiday law so that we could have more three-day holidays—a boon for both the business and the tourist trades.

We have enacted legislation giving our State Banking Department jurisdiction on loans up to five thousand dollars. At the same time, we have reduced the interest rate on loans up to six hundred dollars from twenty-nine percent to twenty-four percent; we have reduced the interest rate on loans from six hundred dollars to fifteen hundred dollars from twenty-three percent to eighteen percent; and we have given the Banking Department jurisdiction on all second mortgage loans.

Wholly conscious of the need to continue to expand the economy of this State, this legislature has approved a branch banking bill that is fostering economic growth.

We passed an improved Management-Employee Relations Act for our State employees.

We established a new, soundly financed state retirement system through the consolidation of existing policemen's, firemen's, teachers', and state employees' systems.

We have consolidated the university system and brought to reality a dream of our State Teachers Colleges to offer a comprehensive curriculum.

We established the Merrimack Valley Branch of the University of New Hampshire to bring higher-education opportunities closer to the people. We have provided a technical-vocational school system that is one of the best in the nation.

We have approved the right-to-know concept ensuring that public meetings at every level of government will be subject to public scrutiny as they should be.

We have learned during this special session that this legislature can live with the enactment of the right-to-know concept.

We have once again given the voters of New Hampshire an opportunity to decide whether or not the legislature should meet annually.

We have enacted child abuse legislation to protect children by having these cases reported to Child Welfare, where proper authorities can use the protective services of the state.

We have participated in the Title 4 Work Incentive Program of Social Security whereby useful people are working at useful jobs.

Over the past few years we have enacted a broad spectrum of consumer-oriented insurance legislation to protect the interests of New Hampshire citizens. New Hampshire was the first state to provide protection for its citizens against the possibility of financial loss resulting from the insolvency of insurance companies, and as a result, all of the policyholders of the defunct Sutton Mutual Insurance Co. were protected. We have enacted statutes relating to unfair trade practices, which give the insurance department the power to move swiftly against any unfair or deceptive acts or practices in the business of insurance. This legislature has protected New Hampshire citizens who are refused insurance or whose policies are canceled or not renewed through no fault of their own.

We have revised our criminal code by updating all our statutes to become effective in 1973.

We have created a unique work program at our State Prison—a program of rehabilitation rather than incarceration.

Our efforts to improve the Laconia State School have resulted in the first-in-the-nation grandparents project, whereby our elder citizens are compensated for valuable service to children, thus relieving the heavy burden of professional staffing.

These programs are examples of our efforts to recognize, at the state level, the social obligations where those requiring state custodial care are reborn human beings.

Each of us takes pride in the accomplishments of our legislature. After ten years of service, I look back with pride on some of my achievements in the Legislative arena. I see bills I have sponsored resulting in new state facilities that have long been overdue, new schools, and better highways for the citizens of our State.

These are the monuments that will last long after we are gone—the technical-vocational school in my hometown of Nashua, Health Careers College here in Concord, the turnpike liquor stores in Nashua and Portsmouth and soon in Hooksett.

My sponsorship of the turnpike liquor stores has raised substantial revenue for the state to help finance unmet needs I have repeatedly spoken about.

My support of the turnpike extension in Nashua has spawned a sixty-store shopping center and an eight-million-dollar industrial plant. I am proud that I originated the integrated toll road concept that will develop over the next ten-year period.

I also succeeded in sponsoring and you passed many bills to cut costs in state government. Many of you perhaps have forgotten I was the sponsor of legislation permitting cities, towns, and counties to put welfare recipients to work as a condition for receiving welfare funds. I was the sponsor of the surcharge on delinquent fathers who did not maintain their child support payments, which resulted in decreasing our welfare costs. The General Court, this session, passed my bill requiring Social Security numbers of divorced people to be furnished by the Probation Department to help us cut down on our aid for the families with dependent children program.

We have also succeeded in passing my legislation providing welfare abuse penalties and I have sponsored increases in unemployment benefits.

I fought to retain New Hampshire holding the first in the nation presidential primary, which does so much for this state's public relations and promotion program. The primary in itself is worth an estimated $10 million to our economy.

Together you and I have enacted many other bills and programs which I have sponsored and supported:

A. Requiring ramps on all public building for the physically handicapped.
B. Appropriations for alcohol and drug abuse.
C. Higher allowable earning under the retirement program for teachers and state employees.
D. Strong flammable fabric legislation for consumer protection.
E. Specialized vocational-technical programs for boys and girls at the Concord Technical Institute.
F. An interstate compact for the cleanup of the Nashua River.
G. Providing for a property tax survey committee.
H. Providing for a study on the feasibility of an east-west toll road.
I. Making the right-to-know law apply to all actions of this legislature and its committees.
J. Abolishing the Legislative Council and making all house committees standing committees.
K. Improving our parole procedures.
L. Memorializing Congress to pass federal-state tax sharing measure.
M. Reduced residence requirements to thirty days for Presidential elections.
N. Limiting administrative costs of charitable fund drives to fifteen percent.
O. Twenty-five-year retirement program for police officers.
P. Constitutional amendment providing for freedom of speech in the New Hampshire Bill of Rights.
Q. Included in the budget additional funding for psychologists and psychiatrists at the State Industrial School.
R. Construction of an infirmary at the State Industrial School to provide for both medical and rehabilitation care in drug abuse.
S. Setting up a concentrated attack on drug abuse and including funding for our best-in-New-England undercover narcotics squad, as well as funding for drug education and rehabilitation. Also regulating the sale of hypodermic needles.
T. Eliminating the waiting list at the Laconia State School.
U. A new facility at the Soldiers Home in Tilton.
V. Allowing the New Hampshire College and University Council to buy through the Director of Purchase and Property.

In this special session I sponsored and you passed:
A. Establishing the rights of policemen.

B. Providing free tuition for children of prisoners of the war in Asia.
C. Allowing families of prisoners of war in Asia to take legal actions.
D. Increasing the salaries of state employees and establishing a personnel study commission.
E. Requiring the filing of social security numbers with the Department of Probation.
F. Providing for the construction of liquor stores at the Hooksett Toll plaza.
G. Increasing the limit of earnings of retired teachers and state employees.
H. Controlling the sale of unsafe flammable fabrics with special emphasis on children's nightwear.

These are some of the tangible results of my ten years of service in these legislative chambers. Many of you helped me get these measures enacted into law.

Yes, these things I have listed are among the two thousand seven hundred and eighty-eight laws passed by this House in my tenure.

Yes, my sense of accomplishment in the bills I have seen passed concerning better roads, new buildings and schools, which have come into being as a result of my legislative efforts, is important, but the thing that means the most to me is the recognition of one's peers in this great legislative body.

I am grateful that despite controversy you have honored me by twice electing me as Speaker of this House and once as Majority Leader for one term.

I take pride in the fact that my fellow legislators across America elected me chairman of the Republican Legislative Conference and have chosen me one of ten legislators in America for the Executive Committee of the National Legislative Conference, a division of the Council of State Governments.

I take even greater pride in the fact that despite differences of opinion, many of my political enemies pay respect to a man able to get the job done.

While I take pride in these accomplishments, there have been some regrets as well.

Former Governor John King perhaps said it best in his 1967 prorogation speech—I quote:

"Of course all of us have been subjected to criticism from those who have not yet recognized the twentieth-century criticism that there was no

186

need for new revenues. These tired old voices of yesterday would have us turn our back on the medically needy, the aged, the patients at our state hospital, and the thousands who receive care at our community mental health clinics. These critics would deny our state employees a decent week's pay, and they would allow the pollution in our streams and rivers to continue unabated."

I regret the erosion of public and legislative confidence in our state university, which has caused reduction in the state's share of the university's budget from fifty-two percent in 1963 to thirty-two percent in this biennium.

I regret our foundation aid program for education in 1963 was 7.4 percent of the state's net budget helping ninety-seven school districts and today we allocated 3.3 percent of the net budget, which helps only sixty-eight school districts.

I regret that we have failed to meet our responsibility in helping the disadvantaged child, the handicapped, the emotionally disturbed, and the retarded.

As Thomas Jefferson said: "The care of human life and happiness, and not their destruction, is the first and only legitimate object of good government."

I regret that we are ranked fiftieth in the nation in state aid for rehabilitation, thus losing federal funds in a vitally needed program. I regret the loss of extremely competent state personnel, among them the directors of mental health and vocational-rehabilitation. When such men move to other states, we lose skills and administrative capabilities we cannot afford to lose.

I regret that there are some members of our legislature who worship at the altar of public opinion and are more concerned about getting re-elected than about being able to do what they know ought to be done in the best interest of the people.

I believe, as John Quincy Adams said, "Always vote for a principle, though you vote alone, and you may cherish the sweet realization that your vote is never lost." And as Andrew Jackson said, "One man with courage makes a majority."

In a world where we can put a man on the moon we should be able to educate every child in New Hampshire.

As John F. Kennedy said:

"Of those to whom much is given, much is required. And when at some future date the high court of history sits in judgment on each one of us recording whether in our brief span of service we fulfilled our responsibilities to the state, our success or failure, in whatever office we now hold, will be measured by the answers to four questions—were we truly men of courage . . . were we truly men of judgment . . . were we truly men of integrity . . . were we truly men of dedication?"

We must recognize the great challenge faced by our state—the avalanche of change.

New Hampshire is caught up in mushrooming growth, making us the fastest growing state in New England and one of the fastest-growing in the nation.

New Hampshire is a growth state. Growth has its positive side, which is measured in greater job opportunities for our citizens, but it poses new challenges as well. The purity of our air and water is under increased attack, and our school and transportation systems have been severely tested and found wanting. Put simply—we must master the forces of growth and change or be overwhelmed by them.

Unfortunately, in facing the challenge of change, the emotions of the times . . . the polarization of our people . . . has resulted in the erosion of respect for the General Court.

I regret the emotional climate in which we have been forced to operate and make our decisions.

Ralph Waldo Emerson said, "He who corrupts the public mind is more contemptible than he who steals from the public pocketbook." It is corruptions of the public mind and its ally of misinformation that challenges us as legislators to serve the people of New Hampshire courageously despite outside pressure upon this great institution.

I believe deeply and I am convinced most of you agree that it is the duty of the Speaker to provide leadership, to take unpopular stands, to fight for those programs that are in the best interest of the people of the State of New Hampshire. This I have always tried to do.

My fondest desire would be to come back here as a spectator in some future year and find all members acting as ladies and gentlemen, never booing, never hissing, never falling prey to the emotional attacks that have so polarized us in these unstable times. I urge you to respect this institution, respect each member's individual rights to be heard on an issue no matter how unpopular his or her viewpoint might be, and bring back to these chambers the spirit of '63—a time when we could disagree without being disagreeable.

My one strong, prevailing hope for the future is that after I am gone from this chamber, some of you here today will pick up and carry the torch forward, restore this institution, this House, to the rightful place of respect it deserves.

I would urge this legislature in the future to restructure its staffing situation so that the legislative budget assistant's office comes under the Speaker's office. There can be no effective chain of command unless the employees report directly to the man who must be responsible for the institution's ultimate decisions.

I would urge this legislature in the future to give both the legislative and the executive branch the tools—the necessary tools, such as research and staff potential—to enable them to perform efficiently and adequately. I believe this is one of the many challenges that lie ahead for this body.

I would urge this legislature to face up to the necessity of reducing the size of this House to two hundred and fifty members and increasing the Senate to forty members plus increasing the compensation of its members so all age groups can afford to serve in this important body.

I would urge substantial additional compensation for future Speakers and Presidents of the Senate because, as Prime Minister Pierre Trudeau has said, "It takes a hell of a lot of time to be Prime Minister."

As I look around this chamber, I see so many friends. In my mind's eye, I see, too, many of those no longer with us. And I see their empty seats. It has been beyond question the greatest experience of my life to have spent ten years among you, my friends.

There have been joys, there have been accomplishments, there have been sorrows and defeats. All of these have been shared with you, with my friends, both past and present.

The very first day I was elected Speaker I said in my acceptance speech, "I hope at the conclusion of this legislative session each and every one of us can say 'I am proud I served in the legislature.'" I think when we reflect on the record of the past ten years I have just recited, we can truly say I am proud I served in the New Hampshire Legislature in these trying times.

I think we have written a record of which we can be proud. We have had our troubles and our tribulations. We have done a good job, but there is much left to be done.

I have enjoyed serving with each of you. I have been honored to serve as your Speaker. As you know, I believe what Abraham Lincoln said: "I do the very best I know how—the very best I can; and I mean to keep doing so until the end. If the end brings me out all right, what is said against me won't amount to anything. If the end brings me out wrong, ten angels swearing I was right would make no difference."

I have tried to do this and will continue to do it in whatever role the future holds for me. My credo has always been:

> I am only one
> but I am one
> I cannot do everything
> but I can do something
> and what I can do
> by the grace of God
> I will do.

I wish each and every one of you Godspeed and good luck and thanks on behalf of the people of New Hampshire for a job well done.

I walked off of the Speaker's podium for the last time to a standing ovation. I went up to my office on the third floor, where my family and friends had gathered to support me. My eight-year-old daughter, Laura, and her cousin, Lisa, came running into the room screaming, "Daddy, Daddy, we counted to 100 three times and you were still talking!" That brought me back down to earth.

CHAPTER 50

Governor Peterson's Prorogation Speech

Governor Peterson also addressed the joint session of the legislature and delivered his prorogation speech, which highlights many of our joint accomplishments.

Mr. President, Mr. Speaker, and Members of the General Court:

The 1970 Special Session is about to come to an end. It has been, in my judgment, a most productive and progressive session, and I hope you are as proud of the accomplishments of the last five weeks as I am.

There has never been a Special Session in our history to match this one. I am told that in the thirteen previous special sessions in New Hampshire history, going back 187 years, a grand total of 105 bills was passed, with twenty-five being the highest total of any one session. In this session alone you have considered and passed some seventy-five measures.

This record of accomplishments is a high tribute not only to your determination to face the issues before you, but also to the dedication and considerable organizational skill of your leadership. No session of the legislature within my memory has been as well organized as this, nor —considering the severe limitation of time—as productive. I hope—and I believe—that the citizens of New Hampshire appreciate your hard work and the good works of this session.

It requires no special insight for me to tell you that here in New Hampshire, as well as in most other parts of the country, we live in an era of rapid growth and change. This puts new stresses and strains on government—in fact, on all the branches of government: the executive, the legislative, and the judicial—and we have all come in for our share of criticism, some of it fair, and some of it unfair. We never will succeed in carrying out the particular wishes of every citizen, nor redress every personal grievance, but we can try to do as well as we can within the limits of reason and budget to keep pace with the legitimate needs of our growing state.

If there is a cynicism these days about the responsiveness of government, by your action here you have dispelled a good deal of it. It has been said that the great problem facing us in the decade of the 1970s is to make government work. I think we have made a good start here in 1970.

I know that in the public's mind the business profits tax is probably considered, for good or ill, the most memorable piece of legislation you passed at this session. And it was, together with other measures, the key that opened the door to much else.

But I can't let you go home without a word about this major reform of our revenue structure, the greatest single tax reform achieved in our history. House Bill 1, I remind you, repealed twelve ancient taxes, all of them inequitable, anachronistic, and justifiably unpopular. Their only virtue was that they were predictable—and one of the things you could predict about them was that they were leading New Hampshire down the road toward serious social consequences. In many communities the stock-in-trade, machinery, and other business property taxes had reached, if not exceeded, the limits of their productivity without adversely influencing the business climate in New Hampshire. I think if this legislature had been called together to enact, instead of to repeal, these taxes, you would have rejected them out of hand.

Let me mention, for the record, the other results of your action:

It made possible the repeal of the inheritance tax on lineal descendants.

It made possible additional state aid to local schools, as well as a new program of aid to communities with financially troubled parochial schools.

It made possible a vastly increased effort in the field of pollution control, in a time when the public clamor for preserving our environment has grown much louder.

It made possible a redoubling of our effort to combat drug abuse.

Your action made possible much needed transfusions for our state hospital and for our community mental health centers. It brought a vital cost-of-living increase for recipients of state aid programs.

And it made possible a pay raise for state employees, with a special boost for those in lower grades.

At the same time, this legislature took steps toward reorganization of state government. It will be awhile before you see the good results of having a state budget director, or of making the state's planning office into a true state planning office, but you have given a governor and future governors better tools to plan and coordinate state activities, and this cannot help but improve the management of the taxpayer's business.

You have given the voters of New Hampshire an opportunity for annual sessions of the legislature and for a four-year term for governor. I believe you have done the right and necessary thing, and I hope you will join in urging our citizens to approve these constitutional amendments.

The list of all the measures you have passed is too long to recite. Let me just say that although little may have been said about many of them, taken altogether they move us in the right direction.

I have long believed, as a legislator and now as governor, that this General Court, given adequate and honest information, will always act in the best interest of our state. Last year you authorized and appropriated $190,000 for a Citizens Task Force. Your judgment, I think we can now say, proved correct. The Citizens Task Force laid the groundwork for this special session. It did the research necessary for us to understand where we are in 1970, and it gave rise to fruitful public debate on the important issues facing us now and in the foreseeable future.

The three hundred unpaid volunteers who made up the Citizens Task Force deserve our deepest thanks for the efforts they made toward the success of this Special Session.

This session is now at an end, but it is really just the end of the beginning. What you have done here is to start New Hampshire on a new road, and it is anything but a dead end. We can expect, as the task force pointed out in what it called "Blueprint for the Future," that our problems will become larger and more complex, and I believe that you will rise to the occasion next year and in succeeding years to deal with them.

We made progress toward preserving our environment at this session;

We made progress toward an equitable and productive revenue structure;

We made progress in meeting the needs of citizens and institutions;

We made progress toward a modern governmental structure.

But the task of shaping government to make it efficient and economical, responsible and responsive, is never-ending.

We made a great deal of progress in this special session and I know the people of our state will be grateful as they look back on your achievements. But this historic session is a harbinger of things to come.

The courage and common sense you showed in the last few weeks fill me with confidence about the future of New Hampshire.

Thank you . . .

CHAPTER 51

"No, Brutus"

When I first made a run for the Senate, my campaign advisers and I had a big discussion about whether it was all right for me to date now that I was legally divorced. Perhaps I should try to hide the fact that I was a normal human being who liked women. My advisers said New Hampshire is too small a state to hide those kinds of things, so I might as well do my dating publicly. I'd never get away with a clandestine relationship in New Hampshire.

I plunged into the dating scene. One of the first women I met—she actually picked me up—was a singer at the Colonial in Lynnfield, Massachusetts, who had dated Bobby Orr, "Ace" Bailey, and several other hockey players. She was very attractive, and very talented, and very personable. She and I started a relationship. It became kind of the talk of the town.

Later, I was dating another woman, and she had a big great Dane whose name was Brutus. Usually, when the bars closed, we would go to my house because she had teenage children. One particular evening she said to me, "Why don't you come to my house tonight? The kids are gone to visit their father and I need to feed the dog in the morning." I said, "Fine, there's no problem with that."

The next day, everything was going great. At an inopportune moment in bed my friend seemed to freeze. Then she screamed, "No, Brutus." I looked over my shoulder. A quarter of an inch from my rear was Brutus, with his mouth wide open ready to do major damage. I was petrified.

My friend finally got the dog away from me. She pledged me not to tell that story to anybody. We went to a holiday party the next day, and after she had a number of drinks, she told everybody the story. Soon it was all over Nashua. I kept hearing about "No, Brutus" for some time thereafter.

CHAPTER 52

Live Free or Die

One of the accomplishments during my tenure as Speaker is that we passed legislation putting the immortal words of General John Stark, which were already serving as the state's motto, on our state automobile tags. The legislation was sponsored by leading conservative spokesman Bob Lawton.

The liberal *Concord Monitor* editorialized against putting "Live free or die" on our license plates, saying, "It is a ringing motto, high in principle and determination. But it doesn't belong on a New Hampshire license plate." The reason? It had sixteen letters and the then current motto, "Scenic," has only six spaces. The *Monitor* suggested options such as "Cheap Booze" and "Gamble Good," which it said would promote our horse racing and lottery. Other suggestions were "Play the Ponies" and "No Fair Taxes."

The *Monitor* concluded that the best motto for tourists to see on our state license plates was "Bring Money." We ignored the *Monitor*'s advice (as usual) and passed the legislation with an overwhelming vote.

I have always wondered why liberals get mad at the words "Live free or die" yet praise Patrick Henry's very similar "Give me liberty or give me death."

CHAPTER 53

How to Run the State on the Profits from Booze

I became a major player in the sale of booze for two reasons. First of all, I had been convinced by Liquor Commissioner Chick Tentas to sponsor legislation to put the new liquor stores on the turnpike. For years, New Hampshire had a liquor system that was based on the appropriations process. No one paid attention to the net profit that came from liquor.

The budget contained the appropriation's costs for the clerks who were hired to run the stores and for the rent of the buildings. The revenue went into a separate budget category. This had led, over the years, to the budget being cut in a shortsighted way.

The money available to pay rent was one of the casualties, so the state's liquor stores were located in back alleys and on back streets, in small buildings with grungy facilities.

All of the stores had a green sign on the front saying NEW HAMP-SHIRE LIQUOR STORE. The stores were affectionately known as "Dr. Green's" because of these signs. The Liquor Commission recognized that it needed to sell, merchandise, and market the sale of alcohol better.

The commissioners wanted to put some stores on the turnpike and they came to me with the idea. I thought that made all kinds of sense. I said famously: "If we're going to be in the business of selling liquor, we ought to locate our stores the same way Jordan Marsh does," referring to a prosperous New England store. Thus, I sponsored, on the Liquor Commission's behalf, legislation to locate two new liquor stores on the Everett turnpike.

There was a major debate. At that time, I was still a moderate. To say the least, the conservatives didn't like me very much. The day the vote came, every conservative worth his salt got up and took the floor, declaring, "I haven't voted with Speaker Cobleigh since I've been here but I'm going to vote with him today to put those liquor stores on the turnpike!"

The measure passed overwhelmingly. New Hampshire had an expanded source of revenue.

The subject came up again when there was a highway strip leading up to the bridge across the Piscataqua River into Maine. There was a series of gas stations that sold gasoline and cigarettes. In the middle of them was the state liquor store of the traditional Dr. Green prototype.

When they decided to build a new bridge over the river, it was going to bypass this golden mile of gas stations and the liquor store. This was going to cost the state some twenty-seven million dollars in revenue. In cahoots with the Liquor Commission, we decided we should build a major liquor store at the rotary leading up to the new bridge.

The merchants that were being bypassed fought fiercely to have the road go by their places of business. This wasn't very realistic, frankly, considering the type of traffic that we could expect in the future.

I had put in legislation to build a liquor store at the rotary and to have it sell cigarettes, tobacco, and sweepstakes tickets. The stores and the gas stations were against the sale of gas and tobacco at the new rotary liquor store. It ended up only selling liquor and sweeps tickets.

I determined that the legislation would probably best come up near the end of the session, when the leadership would get through its pet projects.

There was a rule that all legislation had to be filed by title by a given day. I had filed the bill by title. In a flip moment I'd called it "Cobleigh's Sin Center." I figured they'd straighten out the title later on, but knew what the title was for. The members were upset at me for my aggressive leadership and for passing too many of my bills near the end of the session.

They voted to require the printing in the House *Journal* of all the titles of legislation that would be coming up before them at the end of the session. I lost that full disclosure battle. The members voted to require all the titles to be printed.

I was at the Highway Hotel bar that night working on the next day's agenda. I got a harried call from a dedicated legislative services staffer, Dwight Dobbin, at about midnight. He said, "Mr. Speaker, you don't really want to call that big liquor store complex at the Portsmouth traffic circle Cobleigh's Sin Center, do you?"

Fortunately, the clerk had caught the fact that I had filed the bill under that title. He helped me escape from a lot of bad publicity by being alert enough to call me. We changed the title to "A New Revenue Source for New Hampshire." The bill to create the new Portsmouth traffic circle liquor store passed.

I always bragged that the top five grossing liquor stores in the state are the ones for which I sponsored legislation. We put them at the major traffic crossroads in the state or, in effect, located the stores the way Jordan

Marsh located its stores. These stores are still the leading liquor grossing sales in the state (though the Jordan Marsh company sold out to Macy's a couple of years ago). Those turnpike liquor stores are a daily reminder of my service to the state of New Hampshire.

I also determined that we ought to know what the optimum price was for liquor. We passed legislation requiring the Liquor Commission to bring in Arthur D. Little to do a survey to find out the price at which New Hampshire could sell liquor to obtain the highest gross revenue.

Members thought I had gone daffy because I wanted to bring in some management experts to tell us what the prices should be. It was the first time we had used business consultants in the state of New Hampshire to determine the price of liquor and what the tax should be on tobacco.

The Arthur D. Little study showed that 37 percent of our tobacco sales and 55 percent of our liquor sales were to out-of-state customers. They set up a process to market them at a price and a tax load for cigarettes. (There is no tax on liquor. We just make a profit on the margin.) I like to say that Korvette was not the first discount house in America to preach low-markup, high-volume sales. It was the state of New Hampshire.

By keeping the price lower, you increase the amount of sales and the gross income to the state.

In a nutshell, we were trying to maximize our income by increasing sales and setting the price of tobacco and liquor at a level that would attract out-of-state buyers to purchase our products.

It has been a major reason why New Hampshire has had no general sales tax or income tax—because of their effective pricing of the sale of both liquor and tobacco to out-of-state people. I still believe one of the problems that the state has in its current revenue crisis is they have, because of the so-called evil of tobacco, priced it so high that they've destroyed their competitive advantage and decreased their gross revenue as a result.

By the way, the New Hampshire Liquor Commission informed me in late November 2004 that the three stores I sponsored legislation for (the two Hooksett stores on the turnpike and the one at the Portsmouth rotary) have generated $886,155,564 in gross sales. At the normal 28 percent profit margin that the state takes in from these stores, the state has received $248,080,000—almost a quarter of a billion dollars—since my legislation passed. The sweepstakes commission estimates that these three stores have generated an additional $18,000,000 in revenue earmarked for state education. No wonder the conservatives all wanted to be recorded as voting for the Speaker's turnpike liquor stores.

When Governor Mel Thomson was defeated, his executive council was dominated by liberals: Lou D'Allesandro, Malcolm MacLean, Ray Burton, and Dudley Dudley. They were turning down every nomination the governor made. Traditionally, outgoing governors nominate key friends and supporters before leaving office. The liberal axis of MacLean, D'Allesandro, Burton, and Dudley was determined to stop Thomson from appointing anybody.

At one stage, Thomson had decided to appoint me as a member of the Public Utilities Commission. The council said, "No, we won't do that." Thomson said, "Why not? Cobleigh is eminently well qualified. He has been the energy chief of the state. He's a good administrator. He's liked by the legislature. It's an appointment that makes sense." The liberal councilors said, "No, Cobleigh drinks too much, he doesn't wear neckties, he stays out too late, and he's a womanizer."

Thomson told them, "Look, I know he doesn't dress pretty. He doesn't always wear neckties. I know he stays out at night. I've heard rumors that he drinks and chases women. The only thing I can tell you is that he's the first guy at work in the morning. He comes with a clear head. As his boss, that's all I can really ask. I'm sure if you confirm him and make it a requirement that he wear a suit and necktie, he'll do so. I don't think you should stop him on those grounds."

The council was not persuaded and the liberals voted to reject me, just as they voted to reject a number of other appointments of Thomson at that time. The next morning, I got a call from U.S. Senator Norris Cotton. "Marshall," he said, "I want to tell you one thing. There's only two men in the history of the state of New Hampshire who've been turned down by the governor and executive council for drinking and screwing. I was the first and you are the second. Congratulations on joining my club!"

A sampling of Bob Murphy's cartoons that the Union Leader *used to discredit Marshall. All given to MC by Bob Murphy.*

The day after our 1980 election losses.

3 col. x 7½
THURSDAY EDIT. U-L

FRIDAY EDITORIAL
3 col. x 7½" – U-L

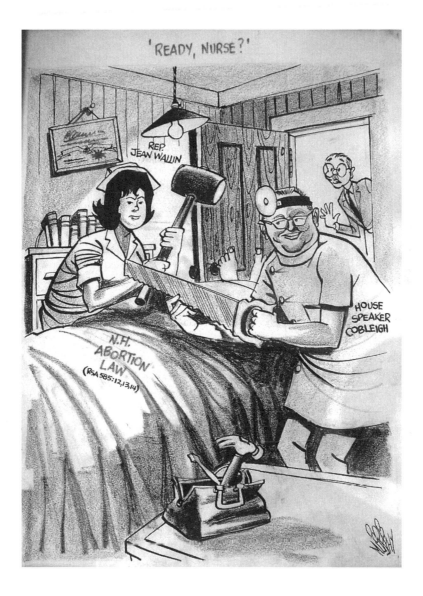

More Vignettes

When John Connally came to New Hampshire to set up his presidential campaign, he asked me to arrange meetings for him and I did. The schedule was a hectic one that started out with Mike Dingman, of Wheelabrator Frye; then Bill Loeb, publisher of the *Manchester Union Leader;* and Tom Gerber, editor of the *Concord Monitor*. It included, among others, the executive committee of Sheehan, Phinney & Bass, the biggest law firm in the state at the time.

After Connally finished his speech and fielded questions from key members of the firm's executive committee, we left the building. As we were going down the elevator, Connally turned to me and said, "That young lawyer, Rudman, he thinks he should be president, not me." It showed me how perceptive Connally was. For many reasons, I have always believed that John Connally was the most able of all of the presidential candidates I ever met. And for the record, I have met every U.S. president since Harry Truman as well as hundreds of wanna-bes.

Here is an illustration of Governor Mel Thomson's compassion. Mel had, early in his gubernatorial career, put out an edict banning alcohol in the statehouse. This caused a great deal of consternation because for years there had been parties on numerous occasions in leadership and gubernatorial suites.

The day before Christmas, I received word that my closest childhood friend, Bob "Pinky" Johnson, had succumbed to leukemia. This upset me deeply. I was a relatively young man and I was not used to my friends dying.

Mel and Gale were on their annual Christmas tour of the county nursing homes, delivering candy treats to the residents. One of the great stories Gale liked to tell was about an old lady who was informed by the head nurse that the woman coming down the hall giving out the candy was the governor's wife.

The lady, whose memory wasn't what it used to be, greeted Mrs. Thomson by saying, "Oh, Mrs. Dale, it's really nice to meet you." Dale had been governor about thirty years before Mel. This lady was obviously living in the past.

Anyway, because of the candy delivery, the governor's office was empty. Peter Thomson, sensing my emotional turmoil, got a hold of a bottle of booze and some ice cubes and made a drink for me. Peter told me to sit in the governor's office as long as I wanted to and get my thoughts together. He left me with a drink in my hand. About forty minutes later, the governor and Gale returned to the office unexpectedly. Peter had warned Mel that I was in the office and that I was distraught over the loss of a close friend.

The governor came into the office and put his arm around me. He consoled me and never mentioned the fact that I was drinking booze in his office. He was compassionate and understanding. Then he turned around and said, "Stay here as long as you want. I'll go down to the library and work on a project that I'm doing." With that, he left me alone in his office.

After about a year of negotiations, my divorce was going to be final. I was ready to go to court. I had not dated anybody during that period of time, but just before the divorce became final, I was sort of picked up by Mary Ellison and we had started dating. She was an extremely attractive woman, with a great deal of personality and a lot of accomplishments in all kinds of diverse areas—like being an outstanding golfer and a pilot, as well as a good enough carpenter to shingle her own roof.

I had been away from a woman's companionship for about a year. I became mesmerized by her charms. The day before the divorce was to go to trial, I talked to my attorney, Bill Phinney. He asked me if I had been involved with any women. I said, "No, up until a couple of weeks ago, then I started dating Mary Ellison." He knew of her and knew that she had been a supporter of Wesley Powell.

Phinney, being a lawyer, was convinced that Powell had sicced her on me to take advantage of me. He told me, "I don't want you to see her at all before the trial. I don't think you should have any conversation with her about the divorce proceedings."

I had already made arrangements to meet her at the Cracker Barrel Bar, which was right across the street from Phinney's office, just before I was going to get my last-minute briefing from him on the court procedure.

Jack Bradshaw, the Senate president and my close friend and roommate, accompanied me to Manchester. Knowing how upset I was, having been through a divorce himself, Jack was being, as usual, a compassionate good friend. We were sitting in the bar with . . . Mary.

We decided that Jack should sit beside Mary. I would sit by myself to at least give lip service to Phinney's edict. That worked until a well-known couple from Keene, where Bradshaw's business was, came into the bar. They knew Jack. They knew his wife. They knew that Mary wasn't his wife. Jack went to the men's room. When he came back, he said, "You've got to sit with her now, Marshall, I can't sit with her."

When the people from Keene left, Bradshaw went back and sat with Mary. In the meantime, when they were in the bar, I had to sit with Mary. We felt like idiots playing musical chairs. The next day, we went into the trial for the actual divorce proceedings. It was a quasi-holiday—Columbus Day. The courthouse was basically closed, but they had agreed to hold our divorce hearing that day. Of course, the *Manchester Union Leader* sent its notorious scandal-mongering reporter, Arthur Egan, to cover the divorce. Phinney told me to sit in the waiting room while the lawyers were in conference.

The lawyers were in conference off and on most of the day. I was sitting there with my soon to be ex-wife, wondering what the hell was going on. Most of the time the only other person waiting was Arthur Egan, the reporter for the *Manchester Union Leader*. I knew enough not to talk to him for the first couple of hours. Eventually, we both got bored and tired of the charade, and we started a conversation that went on at great length. I tried to skirt the issue of the divorce trial.

Eventually, Phinney came back out of the conferences and said, "It's all agreed," and gave me the specifics. He and I went into another conference room, leaving the *Union Leader* reporter outside. Phinney told me, "Now Judge King knows the *Union Leader* reporter is here, but under the law he's required to ask you a number of questions. He wants you to answer the questions in as soft a voice as possible, so that the *Union Leader* guy can't hear anything you say. King doesn't care what your answers are. We've agreed on a settlement, but he wants you to answer the required questions, but do it so softly that nobody can hear you."

So I mumbled replies to questions that neither the Judge nor the reporter could hear. Then the divorce was granted. It was an interesting day, to say the least.

About the time of the divorce, I went to a high school reunion. There was, as there is in every class, one girl who had tremendous sex appeal. She was extremely well endowed. In fact, we called her Jane Russell, after the reigning sex symbol of Hollywood during that period. They had similar endowments.

She showed up at the reunion with a fancy fur coat and an extremely low-cut blouse. Soon, every married guy at the class reunion was going up to the bar where she was sitting and ordering drinks—having, of course, a conversation with a woman they'd always been in heat over, but had never been able to get near when they were young and shy.

The word spread like wildfire that she was now a hooker in Boston. You could get her phone number if you went up to the bar and bought a drink. Many of the guys who'd been faithful ever since they'd left high school were heading for the bar to get her phone number. We were all fired up for the chance to finally connect with our former high school sex symbol—or whatever you do with hookers, if it isn't love.

Unfortunately, a week after the class reunion, there was a front-page headline in the *Nashua Telegraph*: "Local Woman Dies in Boston Hotel Fire." Sure enough, she was in a room with a guy, the hotel caught fire, and she burned to death. All of these guys who thought their dreams would come through found out that their dreams had gone up in smoke.

President Nixon sent an invitation to the legislative leaders of the various states to meet with him in Washington.

At the last minute, one of our Democratic leaders, Ernie Courtemarche, couldn't get off from work to go. The minority leader, Bob Raiche, came to meet with me. He asked if we could bring his father down to Washington with us. His father had never been to Washington, he had never seen a president, he had never been in the White House.

I agreed that Raiche should take his father, using Courtemarche's credentials. The morning before the White House meeting, we went to a topless breakfast restaurant. It surprised the daylights out of the elder Mr. Raiche.

The next day, we got up to the White House gates. The Secret Service was checking our credentials. They got to Mr. Raiche and asked him his name. We had him briefed to say his name was Ernie Courtemarche. Mr. Raiche told the guy his name was Ernie Courtemarche. The Secret Service guy said, "How do spell that?" Mr. Raiche had no idea in the world how to spell Courtemarche! Fortunately, I overheard the exchange. I called the Secret Service guy aside, showed him my credentials, told him I was Speaker of the New Hampshire House, and said, "He's a French Canadian who doesn't understand much English, but it is Ernie Courtemarche. I can vouch for him."

And so Mr. Raiche got into the White House with us. They served coffee and Danish. All of a sudden, I heard Bob whisper to his father, "Don't you even think of it." I couldn't figure out what was going on. Bob Raiche said he knew that his father was going to try and take the White

House spoon. He didn't want any more incidents, so he forbade his father to even think about taking the White House spoon to add to his wife's spoon collection!

My friend Zandy Taft used to tell one of the great stories about the legislature. It was about Arthur L. Bouchard, a diminutive French-speaking representative from Berlin who used to claim that he was on welfare and thus understood poor people's problems. He also claimed he was a bank director and thus understood the problems of the working people. We called him "Bush."

One day the Public Health and State Institutions Committee was going to make an inspection of the state mental hospital to see what its needs were legislatively for the coming year. In the first ward they visited, which happened to be the forensic unit, Bush met an old friend from Berlin and started to talk with him. The forensic unit is where they keep people who are convicted of murders and attacks and rapes and who are mentally ill and so not in jail. Many of them are diabolically clever in ducking their way out of things. That is how they ended up in a mental hospital, not jail, in the first place!

When the committee was ready to move on to other parts of the hospital, Bouchard stayed behind to talk further with his friend. After a long conversation, he decided it was time for him to join the rest of the inspection team, so he walked over to the door to leave. To his consternation, the door was locked.

He said to a nurse, "Will you please unlock this door? I need to join the rest of my inspection team." She said, "Oh no, we can't unlock the door."

He said, "I'm Arthur L. Bouchard, representative of Ward 3, Berlin, New Hampshire. I'm in the legislature. I put the inspect on this place. I saw my friend Pierre. I stopped and shot the shit with Pierre. Now I want to join the rest of the team and inspect the rest of your g-damn place."

"Gee, that's a nice story, but I can't do that, sir. You'll have to stay."

He demanded to see the head person, and the head nurse was brought in. She said, "What seems to be the problem over here?"

Puffing himself up, Bush said, "I'm Arthur L. Bouchard, representative of Ward 3, Berlin. I've come to put the inspect on this place. I met my friend, Pierre. I shot the shit with Pierre. Now it's time for me to join the team and inspect the rest of your g-damn place. Please let me out of here."

She said, "That's a very nice story, but I can't let you out of here."

Bush then demanded to see the supervisor of the hospital. After much screaming and hollering and delay, the supervisor arrived and said, "What seems to be the trouble?" Bush said, "I'm Arthur L. Bouchard, representative of Ward 3, Berlin. I came to make the inspect on this g-damn place. I saw my friend Pierre from Berlin and I shot the shit with him. Now it's time for me to join the team and go put the inspect on the rest of your g-damn place."

He said, "That's a likely story, Mr. Bouchard, but we know you're a patient and you can't leave here."

Bush said, "Listen, I'll tole you what you do ... you count up all your g-damn nuts, you got one left over, that's me, Arthur L. Bouchard, representative of Ward 3, now let me out of here."

One time in the legislature there was a very hard-fought battle between the School Board Association and the Teachers Association. I did not have a dog in that fight. I was presiding but utilizing the time to read and sign my mail and perform other chores that weren't really related to the fight.

Eventually, it came time for a vote. I called, All those in favor, say aye. All those opposed, say nay. They ended up having a roll-call vote. When the roll call was over, the clerk was standing in front of the Speaker adding up the totals. When he finished he said, "Jesus Christ."

With that, as they tell the story, I popped right up and said, "What's the matter?

He said, "It's a tie."

I said, "Are you sure? Have you checked your numbers?"

He said, "I've checked them three times and it's a tie."

So I promptly said, "House attend to the state of the vote, 191 voting yes, 191 voting no, the Speaker votes no, the motion fails." I then declared the session adjourned. With that, several of my lieutenants who were school board advocates—Jim O'Neil, George Roberts, Rai Bowles, and others—rushed to the Speaker's podium, saying, "You can't do that. What are you doing? Why did you do that?"

I said, "Well, it was a tie. I had to break the tie. I voted in favor of the teachers. I know you guys were for the school boards. I'm going to be running for the U.S. Senate. Let me tell you one thing, there's a hell of a lot more teachers than there are school board members."

To say the least, the Speaker's troops were upset with him for the next ten days or so.

Now part of New Hampshire history is how presidential frontrunner and senator from Maine Ed Muskie allegedly either cried in front of the *Union Leader* office or had snow in his eyes, depending upon whose version you believe.

One of the great trivia questions that nobody can answer unless he reads this book is, "Whose flatbed truck was Muskie standing on and who was driving it?"

Here's the scoop: Hugh Gallen, who later became governor, had been one of Muskie's leading supporters. He went to Fred Sicotte, the head of Auclair Trucking, and asked to borrow a truck. Sicotte said to Gallen, "You can borrow a truck, but I don't want any kid driving it. If you're going to borrow the truck, I want you to personally drive it so I know that it's going to be in good hands." So the answer to the question is that it was Fred Sicotte's truck and Hugh Gallen was driving it when Muskie allegedly cried on the back of a flatbed truck in front of the *Union Leader*.

Another Muskie story occurred the first time he came to speak to the legislature. I was presiding. As the presidential frontrunner, he was accompanied by a huge press corps. When Muskie came up to the podium to greet me, the press horde gathered around with all kinds of cameras and other equipment. The press were blocking the view of the members of the legislature. The elected legislators proceeded to signal to me at the podium that the reporters were blocking their view.

Being very high-strung and nervous with this large national press corps in attendance, I committed a major faux pas. I declared to the national media: "I am not going to start this show until all of the national press kneel down in front of me."

I got a lot more national publicity on that statement than I needed.

Here's a story from the half-dead club, friends of mine. I was giving a speech in California to the Chief Justices of the State Supreme Courts. The Chief Justice of the New York Supreme Court was named Milonas. I told him that I had a friend with the same last name. He asked, "Well, what does your friend do?"

I said, "He distributes jukeboxes and poker machines and sells cigarettes through vending machines in various lounges in the state."

The New York Supreme Court Justice, knowing the background of those trades, said to me, "Your friend is in the same business as I am, but on the opposite side."

CHAPTER 55

No Longer a Viable Candidate

My elective career came to a screeching halt in a most unusual manner. After I lost for Congress in 1980, Senate President Bob Monier hired me short term to help in his office. Monier also helped me get a job with Jerry Carmen at the General Services Administration in Washington. I was named director of Program Control. I eventually served as de facto administrative assistant to Carmen. He never would give me the title.

One time, in a moment of weakness, Carmen told me, "Sometimes I do really weird things. I want you, if you see me doing them, to stop me from doing them because you will actually be helping me if I try to do something crazy that is beyond the bounds of what I should be doing."

I accepted that challenge, along with many others, from Carmen, who was a most demanding boss.

When I learned that Arthur Drake, who had been a close friend, ally, and my Appropriations chairman, died, I told Carmen I was going back home to New Hampshire for the funeral.

I had a lot to drink at the wake with a lot of my friends and contemporaries, who joined me in lamenting Drake's passing. After the wake, I returned to the Vault, in Manchester, for something to eat. I was told by the owners that an old girlfriend was in the bar asking for me. I told them not to tell her where I was. I left by the other door. I went over to the North American Club to visit my friend and former roommate Alan Peduzzi, who was tending bar. I wasn't there very long when the same girl showed up and insisted on dancing with me.

She came on like gangbusters. I succumbed to her charms. I arranged to get some beer to go, which was illegal. We went to her house. We had some beers. We started to make love on her living room rug. In the middle, she got up and left for a minute. I assumed she was going to the bathroom. She didn't return. I wondered where the hell she had gone. I started looking around the house for her, calling her name. Eventually, as I got near her bedroom, I heard sobbing. I went into the bedroom area. The sobbing was coming from behind a door. I opened the door.

It was a large walk-in closet. The woman was lying naked on the floor. I tried to console her and find out what was wrong. She said, "This is what your cell is going to look like." I didn't know what the hell she was talking about. That's all she would say. I decided that if she wasn't making sense, I should get out of there, so I left and went home.

I was awakened the next morning by a call from the Manchester Police Department. They told me that I was being charged with rape. They told me I should come to the police station by noon, that it would be wise for me to have a lawyer with me because these were serious charges. I started wondering how the hell she could say I had raped her, because she had clearly been the aggressor up until the time she disappeared. I had done nothing in the closet other than console her and caress her. I thought back over our relationship. She had been a strange one from the beginning. Her favorite song was a Buffy Sainte-Marie number entitled, "It's Time for Me to Go." Whenever it played on the jukebox in a bar when I was with her, she would leave—she would just disappear.

I knew she wasn't the most stable ship in the sea, but she was sexually active. I enjoyed being with her. I had seen her from time to time. She was always the aggressor in that very sexual relationship.

I called my friend Attorney Bill Craig, who had been the Democratic minority leader, to represent me.

Craig said we would be better off to have his partner, Vin Wenners, represent me because he was more adept at criminal cases and he was friendly with the people who run the Manchester Police Department. Wenners and I showed up at the police station at noon. We were told that the woman was charging me with rape, claiming I had broken a window to get into her house and attack her. They asked if this was true. I vehemently denied it. I offered to take a lie detector test.

Wenners kept discouraging me from taking a lie detector test, saying that they were erratic. He told me, "We'll just get all the facts out here. We will talk about lie detectors later."

A detective asked me about breaking the window. I told him I did not break the window. The woman had let me in. She had met me at the North American Club. I told the police that I had witnesses to the fact that she had been there. And that I left with her to go to her house.

I had witnesses to the fact that she had been at Alan's club. That I left with her to go to her house. I told them exactly what had happened, and that I'd found her in the closet, and that she said, "This is what your cell is going to look like," and that I had left.

But the whole situation was touch-and-go for a couple of days. I had to return to Washington and I notified Carmen of my problem because in politics you have to do those things. My law firm had been trying hard to keep the story out of the newspapers and the media and so far had succeeded.

My friend Alan Peduzzi knew some of the cops who were investigating the case. Alan had talked to them. He told them about her coming to the club. Alan had helped get the story out to the investigator that I was a decent guy. I wouldn't do something like that. Eventually I became aware of the fact that she had not one but two children who died of SIDS (sudden infant death syndrome). She was mentally unstable since their deaths.

I came home the next weekend. Again, I visited with the Manchester police at their request. I went over my story and they questioned me at some length. I demanded to take a lie detector test but my attorney didn't think that was wise. The request was withdrawn. Later, the Manchester police told my attorney that they were going to let me go—they did not believe the woman's story and had proved one aspect of her story false.

I swore I never broke a window, but when the police got to the house, there was a broken window. However, an investigation by the police determined the window had been broken from the inside, not the outside. Therefore, it was likely that the woman had done it herself. The charges were formally dropped.

But not before the *Manchester Union Leader* printed an article stating in effect that Cobleigh was a suspect in a case with unspecified charges. Craig and the paper had negotiated the wording, but while it didn't clearly say anything about rape, it certainly made it look like something serious was happening. Eventually it was publicized that the charges had been dropped.

The toughest part of the whole situation for me was that I had to call up my young daughters and tell them what had happened and try and explain it to them. It was one of the toughest things I ever did. Recently, my daughter Laura told me she had a strong memory of how direct and honest I was in telling her the facts of the case.

I returned to Washington to work. Of course I was under a great deal of emotional strain. There was a bureaucratic turf battle going on in the GSA Agency at the time over legislative policy. All departments were instructed that nobody testified up on the Hill without getting my approval of their testimony.

When two of the department heads of the agency got into a battle about the budget and who was going to testify, Carmen decided to have a woman, Pat Shoney, who was playing up to him, do the approval of the testimony instead of me. This really irritated me. That day, when Carmen came in the office, I continued to read a newspaper rather than pay attention to him. Carmen became very annoyed over the disrespect.

I told him, in essence, Look, if you're not going to use me, if you don't want me to do my job, I might as well do something important and read the papers and find out what's going on down here rather than just pretend things are like they were.

The next day, the senior ethics lawyer of the GSA, a close friend of Carmen's, called me and told me that I was being fired because the episode in Manchester was all over the street. He claimed that the charges were widely known in Manchester.

Carmen couldn't have somebody as a key employee who was involved in such things. I was to take a leave of absence. The paper, of course, printed the fact that I was on a leave of absence and repeated the story about the mysterious charges that I was under investigation for. I was now out of work.

Carmen later said that if I had called and apologized, I would have gotten my job back, but there was never any indication of that at the time. So there I was, cleared of the charges, yet I had been fired because of them. I had to return from Washington in disgrace with no job and no income.

An ironic twist to the story is that about a year later, a state representative who was related to the chief investigating officer of the Manchester police force told her that if he ever thought I was guilty at the time, he was positive now that I was innocent.

It seems that the same woman had made almost identical rape charges about two other men. She invited them to the house together and ended up, nude, in the same closet. She told them the same thing: "This is what your cell is going to look like."

The detective said it was eerie: "It was almost like I was hearing Cobleigh tell his story again because I was getting word for word the same story from these two poor fellas who had been charged with the same rape offence by the same lady. If I didn't believe Cobleigh in the beginning, I sure as hell know he was telling the truth now!"

But the fact remained that my elective political career was ended. With these charges widely known, if I tried to run for office in the future, the charges would be dragged out by an opponent. They would be printed and disseminated even more widely than they had been. There was no chance that I could be elected to anything after this unfortunate episode, despite my innocence.

About that time, some right-wing nut in Washington proposed the death penalty for adultery. Senator Denton, of Alabama, took the floor: "If we pass a law making death the penalty for adultery," he said, "we'd lose Strom Thurmond. We'd lose half my constituents and two thirds of my colleagues."

CHAPTER 56

Young Men Can Change the World

Episode Two

During my Jaycee career, I became acquainted with, and later a friend and great admirer of, Dick Chaput. Chaput had been stricken with polio when he was eight years old and lived, as was the custom in those days, in an iron lung. Eventually, Dick could be out of the iron lung during the day, but he still had to sleep in it at night.

Dick had tremendous speech problems, as he had to gasp for air as he spoke. Every sentence was broken up by several breaths, which was disconcerting to him and to others. But at least he could talk and make his wishes known.

I had become an instructor in a program called Speak Up a Jaycee, which was in essence a speech training class for young men to help them improve their public-speaking skills. Dick signed up for my speech class. The first time I called on him to make a speech, there was a great deal of trepidation felt by the rest of the class. I was known for being a tough critic: I would give a neophyte speaker suggestions and clues as to how he could improve his effort.

Dick took his assigned subject and, frankly, his speech was terrible. He was so concerned about the fact that he was gasping for air after about every third word that the content wasn't very good either. When it came time for my criticism of Chaput's meager effort, the whole class was full of anxiety. I said, "First of all, Dick, you lay there in your stretcher with your eyes staring at the ceiling all the time. Your posture stank."

After I got Chaput laughing, I said, "Why don't you try it again, Dick. You can do better than that. Just ignore the fact that you have the speech impediment and do the best you can." Chaput tried it again and he did do better. He eventually went into the world of public speaking. He wrote a book, which was a remarkable accomplishment because he was paralyzed from the neck down. A typewriter keyboard was positioned over his head and he held a stick in his mouth. He pushed the typewriter keys with the stick, one letter at a time, as he wrote *Not to Doubt*.

Cardinal Cushing wrote the foreword, which made it an instant success. The book basically said that if you think you have troubles, look at me with polio, paralyzed from the neck down, typing a book by holding a stick in my mouth and hitting a typewriter keyboard hung above my head, one letter at a time. "God put me on this earth to show you that when you think things are bad in your life, think about me. Then you'll realize that your life isn't as bad for you as you think it is." It was a tremendously inspirational story.

Dick Chaput eventually was named one of the ten outstanding young men in America by the same Jaycees who inspired me many years before. After receiving the award, Chaput traveled in his iron lung in a van. He would give speeches to other organizations about his book and about his philosophy.

One day, at the height of the Seabrook nuclear power crisis, I was having a couple of beers in a bar when I was joined by Donny Caouette, who was the president of the Iron Workers of the AFL-CIO. We were lamenting that the Clamshell Alliance and the anti-nuclear protesters were getting all the publicity. There was no publicity for the people who believed that Seabrook was necessary and a valid use of government funding.

We talked about the idea of sponsoring a hard-hat demonstration saying that Seabrook is good! After a couple of drinks, it seemed like a great idea. I called Governor Thomson at home and told him that I was sitting with Donny Caouette and his union would like to sponsor a hard-hat demonstration in support of Seabrook. Thomson thought it was a wonderful idea. He gave us the go-ahead.

Later, in an incidental conversation with Dick Chaput, I found out that he was a great believer in the Seabrook Nuclear Plant too, because electricity was required to keep his iron lung going. I asked him if he'd like to speak at the demonstration in support of Seabrook. Chaput, who had a strong ego drive, thought it was a wonderful idea and signed up to speak. Caouette arranged for a large turnout of union folks. Thomson, of course, was there in his glory. There was a very successful demonstration of hard hats in support of Seabrook at the statehouse.

The feature event was Dick Chaput in his iron lung. He said, "You guys are for Seabrook because you want electricity. You want television. You want things like that. I'm in support of Seabrook because I need electricity to keep alive, and if there's no electricity for me, I die." It was a very moving speech, especially with the intermittent hesitations after his words all through the speech. It really got everyone's attention.

The liberals, of course, were wild at me for parading a disabled man in support of Seabrook: "You'll stop at nothing to get your way, including that maudlin approach of the guy in the iron lung gasping for breath as he proclaimed his support for Seabrook nuclear station so he wouldn't die."

As his friend and speech teacher, I was honored to be chosen as one of Dick Chaput's pallbearers when he died—at the young age of twenty-nine.

CHAPTER 57

Charlemagne

I continued my women's basketball coaching career at the Nashua YWCA after leading the national champion girls basketball team at Patuxen River, Maryland, Naval Base. My Nashua Y team won the state championship. We went on to play in the New England championship in Swanton, Vermont.

I looked at a map and figured that it would take a couple of hours to drive there. It turned out that with the bad Vermont roads, it took about four hours. The team arrived at the tournament game five minutes before play was to begin. My girls had road legs after four hours in the car, and we got off to a horrible start. We lost a game that we should've won. That night I was disgusted with my lack of judgment in not knowing the correct driving time.

I went into Montreal to drown my sorrows and found myself in a nightclub with a strip show. The feature entertainer was a woman named Charlemagne, a good singer, very beautiful and very well built. The more songs she sang, the darker it became and the bluer the lights and the more clothes she took off.

At the end of her final song, the master of ceremonies said, "Okay, now let's have a big hand for Charlie Maine." With that, Charlemagne whipped off her wig and whipped off her bra—and the audience was surprised to find Charlie was a guy in drag.

A week or two later, I was at the Coffey Post American Legion watching the National Football League championship game between the

Detriot Lions and the Cleveland Browns with a friend, retired all-pro Cleveland Browns football player John Kissell.

Kissell had been cut from the Browns that year after a distinguished career. He had played in the Canadian League. Paul Brown thought he was now a bad influence on the young players. All during the game, Kissell would pound the table and say, "When you get inside the ten-yard line, it's the beer drinkers, not the Goddamn choirboys, who win the game."

With that he would pound the table and the beers would rise about six inches into the air and then plop back onto the table. The drunker Kissell got, the more he said, "It's the beer drinkers who win the games inside the ten-yard line—not the choirboys." The Browns choirboys were badly defeated by the Lions that day.

After the game, Kissell and I went across the state line into Massachusetts to Duke's Club in Tyngsboro. In those days, the bars in New Hampshire closed at nine o'clock on Sunday nights. We were going to watch the strip show there. Lo and behold, the feature act was a stripper named Charlemagne. Having had a number of beverages, I kept saying, "You're not going to fool me again: I know you're a guy, Charlemagne."

The woman got so mad that she refused to continue her dance. The manager came over—nervously—to the six-foot seven-inch, 295-pound Kissell and said, "You fellas have got to quiet down. You can't keep saying she's a guy, cuz she's not a guy, she's a woman." Kissell told the manager, "If Marshall says it's a guy, it's a guy!"

Eventually, the manager brought the lady over to the table and had her show us her breasts. She proceeded with her act. But Kissell kept proclaiming, "If Marshall says it's a guy, it's a guy!

I had formed a fast friendship with the Massachusetts Senate president, Maurice "Mossie" Donahue. Donahue was an Irish bachelor whose idea of a good time was to put together a bunch of legislators and find a lobbyist to pay for a cocktail party and scrumptious dinner. After dinner, everybody had to entertain.

Some would sing songs, others would recite poems. I was always called on to tell jokes. Over a number of these occasions, Donahue and I became bosom buddies. One time, Donahue asked me to give a talk at a convention in Boston. I was on a speaking tour then and arrived in Boston just in time to make the speech, which was at noon a major hotel.

I checked in to the hotel to put my luggage away and clean up before I went down to give the speech. I followed the bellboy to the room. The bellboy opened the door with a flourish, only to find a naked woman just coming out of the shower. She was a guest and tried to cover up. The bellboy was trying to shut the door and apologize to the woman. It turned out they had assigned me to a room that was already taken. Getting assigned to another room made me just a little bit later to get down to give my speech.

When I arrived, they were just about ready to introduce me. I told the story about how I had arrived at the hotel. I was taken up to my room. With a flourish I had opened the door. There before me stood a naked lady. I turned to the audience and said, "That Mossie Donahue thinks of everything!"

Once Donahue was entertaining a bunch of the troops at an insurance commissioners meeting in Hawaii. We spent the day on the beach ordering drinks and ogling the beauties who were walking in the sand. At about six o'clock, it was time for us to go up to our rooms, clean up, then head for a major cocktail party. A lobbyist walked through the hotel at about the time we were ready to leave. Donahue summoned the lobbyist and said, "Here, sign this check." The guy hadn't been with us at all. The check was for three figures, yet Donahue thought nothing of telling him, "Sign the bill for my friends."

In fact, he regularly brought lobbyists with him on trips like that just to take care of this kind of contingency.

At one of Mossie's gatherings I told Fritz Wetherbee's classic story about the "Sex Act."

It went like this: To stave of the dreaded broad-based tax, New Hampshire should enact the Sex Act. The legislation would call for each citizen to pay one dollar for each orgasm she or he had during the year. It would be self-policing. You would tell the state how many orgasms you had and pay a tax amounting to one dollar for each orgasm you had or claimed to have had. The results would be printed in every local newspaper and in all town reports. Human nature being what it is, everybody would claim inflated numbers, so the tax take would be huge.

A young business-type legislator went home and filed the legislation to pass the Sex Act in his state. The publicity he received was so bad that he left the legislative arena.

Thomson was trying to put in Fred Goode, a member of his staff, as a judge. The bar association wanted Carl Randall, a respected veteran clerk of the Hillsborough County Court, to be a judge. Thomson and the bar association couldn't agree on one or the other.

Finally, a second judge conveniently died. Thomson and the bar association made a deal. They'd give him Goode, whom they hated, if he would appoint Randall, whom they loved. Thomson reluctantly made the deal. He came back to the office on Friday afternoon and said, "Well, I gave in on the judgeship. Fred's going to get a judgeship, but we've have to take this liberal guy, Randall, too. We need them both in here at ten o'clock Monday morning. We'll get the council in and get this done and confirm them."

Thomson asked, "Who knows Randall?"

I said, "I do. He's a friend of my father."

Thomson said, "Well, call him and get him in here for ten o'clock Monday morning. Tell him we made the deal."

So I started calling Randall that night. I couldn't find him Friday night. I spent most of Saturday trying to locate him. Finally, at about ten o'clock on Saturday night, I tried one more time. Randall answered the phone—obviously not on his first beverage. I said, "Carl, this is Marshall Cobleigh."

He said, "How are you, Marshall? What can I do for you?"

"The governor is going to make you a judge Monday morning at ten o'clock."

He replied, "Fuck you, Cobleigh," and hung up the phone.

This went on four times until I finally convinced him that it was true and that I was not pulling his leg. They always said that a judge was a lawyer who knew a governor.

CHAPTER 58

Working for Mel

After I lost the election for the Senate, I found it necessary, of course, to get a job. I had left the Trade Association, which had been so good to me over the years, when I ran for the Senate. I didn't get much help from my liberal friends, but the one place I received some support from was conservative governor Mel Thomson.

Thomson remembered when he had beaten my effort to pass a tax in New Hampshire. When everybody else was attacking Thomson after his victory, I was gracious enough to show up at his victory party and congratulate him. This always impressed the gentlemanly Thomson. He had high personal regard for me even though he didn't agree with me philosophically. He arranged a job for me working for Aristotle Onassis in his fight to put an oil refinery in New Hampshire.

Thomson's people argued about whether to hire me, because I was considered the enemy. But they realized they needed somebody who could talk to the non-conservative members of the House. I was as good at that as anybody else they knew. They proceeded to have a meeting at the Bridges House to discuss the matter. They decided to hire me to lobby the liberals for Onassis.

Ironically, everybody at the meeting told me everybody else was against me except them. Each said he personally spoke up for me. That's why I was hired. It's called revisionist history, I guess.

At one of the first meetings of Governor Thomson's key advisers, they were going over a list of legislators to see who was leaning which way. They kept calling on me. I'd say, Well, this fellow sells sand and gravel to the state. The highway commissioner can get him. This guy wants to be on the Parks Department Advisory Board. This guy's looking for a job for his son to be a lifeguard on Hampton Beach this summer. I knew the background and intimate details of all members of the House, along with their goals, aspirations, and wants.

After going through twenty members of the House, Thomson looked at me and said with admiration, "No wonder you always beat me."

After the Onassis refinery went down in flames, I didn't have a job. The liberals were even more upset with me now because I worked for their mortal enemy, Mel Thomson. About this time, Carolyn and Bill were trying to sue me because they claimed I was behind on child support, which wasn't true but it was part of the deal to muddy me up in the courts and destroy my reputation.

Governor Thomson saw it in the paper and said, "We must get a job for Marshall." He tried to get me placed on the New England Regional Commission staff. This outfit was often used as a holding pattern for political hacks from each of the six New England states. Thomson couldn't understand why they wouldn't give him a job for me while all the rest of them had people there. This was primarily because when the rest of them were putting their hacks on staff, Thomson opposed them; thus, they weren't about to hire one of his hacks.

Thomson got teed off and decided that if they wouldn't hire me, he would hire me to help run his Energy Office, utilizing their funding. So I went to work for Governor Thomson. When the legislature got back in session, it made sense for me to lobby members on behalf of Thomson.

There was one major problem, however, in that Thomson and I had very divergent views on a number of subjects. We finally reached an agreement that I would not testify on matters like abortion and taxes on which we disagreed, but I would testify on non-emotional issues where I could represent the governor's position. They said it was like a law firm, where I specialized in those matters that were not against my principles. Thomson's other aides testified on such issues as taxes and abortion that mattered so deeply to Thomson. Mel and I became a team. We formed a partnership and actually built a very strong personal relationship.

One of the ironies of my working for Governor Thomson occurred on a summer day when Lucille Lapinskis, a notorious right-wing woman whom many people consider a little on the wacky side, showed up at the governor's office demanding to see Thomson. Thomson was out of state that day. His receptionist, Betty Hancock, said, "The governor is out today, but I'll let you speak with his administrative assistant, Marshall Cobleigh. He will take down the message and get it to Governor Thomson."

Lapinskis haughtily refused, saying, "We elected Mel Thomson to get rid of Marshall Cobleigh! There's no way I'm going to speak to him." So we found out that the woman wasn't as crazy as we thought she was.

Cathy Dube, who was the governor's very competent but highly emotional secretary, had convinced the governor to have her state trooper husband replace the governor's longtime state police aide, Hank Byrd. No sooner had Cliff taken charge of the security detail in the governor's office when we got a letter from the FBI saying there was some nut loose who was promising to kill both the president and Governor Thomson.

Cliff, of course, had to increase security around the statehouse. He was unsure about just how to do it and his wife was trying to tell him what to do. It became very tense. I realized that there was a good deal of apprehension and fear in the office. I sensed that they needed to lighten the mood a bit. I went into the men's room with a piece of cardboard. I made up a sign that said, "I am not the governor, he's in there," pointing to the governor's office. I sat right in front of the office door with that sign on my neck, which got everybody laughing. It relieved the tension some and Cliff was able to do his work. The governor would be protected.

CHAPTER 59

Mel Thomson and the Taiwanese Flag

Governor Mel Thomson was famous for lowering flags to half-mast and for putting up flags along with the American and state flags atop the statehouse building. At time of the 1976 Olympics, the Taiwanese team had come to Boston en route to the Games in Montreal.

When they got to Montreal, they were informed that they were barred from the Olympics because China was to be represented only by Communist China. Taiwan was not recognized as a separate nation but simply as a subsidiary of Communist China, which, of course, the Taiwanese could not accept. When Thomson heard this, he invited them to come to Concord and enjoy a reception at the Bridges House.

I was informed that my main job that weekend was to get a Taiwanese flag. Did you ever try to buy a Taiwanese flag in New Hampshire on a Sunday? It was an almost impossible task. I finally reached a telephone company executive who gave me the phone numbers of the Taiwanese embassies in both Boston and Washington. I placed calls to them—and got a Taiwanese flag. When the Taiwanese Olympic team was hosted at a reception at the statehouse and later at the Bridges House, there was their flag flying next to the American flag on the statehouse of New Hampshire to demonstrate our empathy with them for being a separate nation. They should not have been barred from the Olympics.

There's more to the Taiwanese story. When Thomson hosted the reception for the Taiwanese Olympians, we didn't really know what they liked

219

to eat or drink. We had milk, lemonade, and Coca-Cola. The women from the office passed out trays with these three choices of beverage. The Taiwanese, being superbly polite, took their drinks in order. If the first guy took lemonade, the next guy took milk and the next guy took Coca-Cola, and then back to lemonade, milk, and Coca-Cola. Nobody took what he wanted; each took what came up next in the rotation, which really amazed us.

Another notorious Mel Thomson episode was during the Clamshell Alliance demonstration, which was protesting the Seabrook Nuclear Power Plant. Thomson had made plans with security to keep them off the grounds. When they tried to climb the fences, he had 1,414 of them arrested. There was obviously not space enough in our jails to hold 1,414 additional prisoners. They were bivouacking into the State National Guard Armories, where they were held prisoners by the National Guard until their court cases could be disposed.

Unfortunately, an epidemic of crabs started among the demonstrators. We had a severe medical problem that we did not want to get into the press. I was dispatched to buy the liquid medicine 712, which is allegedly a cure for this unpleasant case of scabies. (We didn't want the press to know about it.) This was before the days of big chain drugstores, so I had to put together a team of folks to go to just about every mom-and-pop drugstore in the state to buy two bottles of the stuff each. We didn't want to tip off people that we had this epidemic of scabies running through the armory.

Another traumatic vignette in the Thomson years was when the governor received a telephone call from his counterpart in Tennessee, who said we had arrested one of his truck drivers who was bringing back from Canada an important cargo of liquid gas. This gas was needed at the height of the energy crisis.

People were freezing in Tennessee as a result of our holding hostage this driver's truck because the truck was carrying an overweight load. This was allegedly happening in Lebanon, New Hampshire. Thomson assigned me to look into it. I called the sheriff of Grafton County, the state police, and the Lebanon Police Department. Nobody knew anything about an overweight truck loaded with natural gas.

We swore it was true. We told the area police the truck company name and the driver's name. We asked the police to find out about it and released the truck and driver because people were freezing to death.

After our substantial police investigation, it was determined that there was no truck being held up for carrying an overweight load of natural gas. The truck driver had fallen in love with a local maiden. He had spent the weekend in a local motel with this fair damsel. He had called his superiors to say his truck was being held up for being overweight so that he could spend the weekend with his new love. We notified the governor of Tennessee. The owner of the company called the motel. He told his guy to leave the girlfriend and get down to Tennessee with the gas. Thus, our good police work found out that there was no case of a truck being held hostage by New Hampshire. There was a young maiden who had convinced the driver of her charms. He had made a voluntary choice to tell this tall tale in order to avoid leaving New Hampshire until Monday.

The situation was rectified. The driver was on his way. I had done my duty.

CHAPTER 60

My Favorite Governor

I have written a book about my favorite governor, called Memorable Words *and* Memorable Actions *of Mel Thomson. It is now out of print, but you may obtain it from any library in the state of New Hampshire. This is my intro from that book:*

Mel Thomson's memorable words and memorable actions are just that. Memorable! Mel was a rare breed in the political arena. He said what he believed. He did what he thought was right all of the time.

If Mel thought it was right and the whole world thought it was wrong, Mel went ahead and did it or said it. If the whole world thought it was wrong, Mel went ahead and did it or said it. If the whole world thought it was right, but Mel thought it was wrong—heaven and earth could not get Mel to do it or say it.

His friend, the late U.S. Senator Norris Cotton, describes Mel well in his review of Mel Thomson's book *Live Free or Die*. Cotton says:

"Mel Thomson is a complex personality. For many years I knew him as a quiet, gentle man. It was not until he emerged as a public figure, first as a candidate and then three times governor of New Hampshire, that I became acquainted with the second Mel Thomson, who when his principles were involved would fight anyone at the drop of a hat.

"The more powerful the opposition, the more he loved the battle. Whether it be the federal government encroaching upon the sovereignty of his state or the disciples of tax and spend among our own citizenry, he can be utterly relentless, almost to the point of ruthlessness. What a paradox! Loving and tender in his family circle, warm and sympathetic in his friendships, he can turn into a veritable tiger in his public relationships."

"There is not one millimeter of compromise in Mel Thomson. When his convictions are involved, he is utterly inflexible.

"I always knew him as a master of the English language, but it was not until he went the whole way in expounding his philosophy of government that I came to fully appreciate his gift for pungent phraseology.

"Whether he is dealing with the loss of state sovereignty; the nation's tragic energy debacle; human rights; gun control; or taxes; he can be spicy, sarcastic, and whimsical in the same paragraph and sometimes in the same sentence."

I cannot help comparing him to William Lloyd Garrison, who expended himself for the cause of abolition. When I read the words of Garrison, I can hear Governor Thomson speaking:

"I am aware that many object to the severity of my language; but is there not cause for severity? I will be as harsh as truth, and as uncompromising as justice. On this subject I do not wish to think, or speak, or write, with moderation. No! No! Tell a man whose house is on fire to give a moderate alarm; tell him to moderately rescue his wife from the hands of the ravisher; tell the mother to gradually extricate the baby from the fire into which it has fallen; but urge me not to moderation in any cause like the present. I am in earnest—I will not equivocate—I will not excuse—I will not retreat a single inch—and I will be heard."

Mel was unique among political leaders in that before reaching a final decision, he sought out dissenting opinions from key staff and others whose judgment he trusted. I often argued with him when I thought he was right just to make certain that he had examined all sides of the issue in question.

Early on in his political career, Mel, like so many other political leaders, acquired several sycophants who told him what they thought he wanted to hear, rather than telling him all the relevant facts that he ought to be aware of before reaching a final decision. This led to several missteps that colored people's opinion of the good governor.

One of my key roles on his team was to change the decision making procedures so that he got all the facts. His son Peter and I had a tactic of last resort when we could not persuade Mel that he should rethink a contemplated position. It happened rarely; but when it did we left a handwritten note on his pillow at the Bridges House asking him to take one more look at the issue and he always did. But we didn't usually prevail.

I bring this up to let the reader know that the memorable words and memorable actions contained in this booklet were not the typical rhetoric of politicians seeking favor by supporting issues that resonated with the views of the public in the eyes of pollsters. Mel did not pay attention to pollsters.

What Mel Thomson says and does are deeply rooted views from the most sincere man I ever met in the political arena.

Where else would you find a politician who says and honestly means "I believe that a leader, in pursuit of service to the people and in the development of a worthy heritage for our posterity, must be willing to risk defeat at the polls."

In this age of slick 30-second campaign commercials it is particularly necessary for aspiring political office seekers to take a hard look at this unique leader's philosophy.

Citizens of New Hampshire and America should study Mel Thomson's words and actions to re-examine their role and responsibility in making our democracy work.

We must ask ourselves without Mel at the helm "Is New Hampshire still what America was?"

We remember Mel's immortal words:

"People Above Politics."

"My Tax Pledge To You: As your Governor, I promise no sales or income tax, no new taxes and no increase in present taxes. I will work diligently to keep the greedy hand of Government out of your pocketbook!"

"Like you and everyone else, government will have to tighten its fiscal belt if we are to return to prosperous times."

"Protecting your pocketbook will be my first and foremost concern."

"Wherever you find taxpayers struggling to keep the taxes on their homes paid, striving to provide an education for their children, wrestling with hospital bills or the problems of old age—there you will find men and women determined to see that public officials give them full and honest value for every tax dollar spent. These are the people whom I strive to serve."

When I was working as Administrative Assistant for Mel Thomson, the Governor would always take all kinds of papers and staff reports to the Bridges House to read and study. He always got way behind and there were stacks and stacks of unread reports and grants. Every once in a while there would be a time when something would come up that had to get to the Federal Government by a given day.

I knew the missing document had been sent to the Bridges House, but couldn't get access to it. I made the departments redo the reports. This caused a good deal of consternation. I kept begging Governor Thompson, "Let me, when you're on this next trip out of the country with your wife, let me go over to the Bridges House [the Governor's mansion] and go through all those old reports. I'll see what is important in there and what isn't."

Thomson resisted and resisted. After a couple of months of badgering, he finally said, "Look, I'm going on a trip. You can go clean up all those things, but don't you destroy anything important that I need to see."

I went through these papers. I found all kinds of reports that were due . . . all kinds of things that needed to be submitted to the Federal Government. Most important and most amazing, I found $37,000 in campaign contributions which had been sent directly to the Bridges House and had not been opened.

From then on, whenever the Governor was going out of state, I had no problem convincing him that I should go back to the Bridges House and clean up. The governor would say, "I hope you're going to find me some more money!"

On the night that Mel lost the election to Hugh Gallen over the CWIP issue, Mel went to bed without knowing the election results. He asked us to come over to the Bridges House when it was official and give him the results. At about 5:00 A.M. Peter and I awakened him and told him that he had lost the election. He said, "I could see it coming the last few days."

He asked me what I was going to do. I told him I was going home and get some sleep. I will never forget what he told me that morning. He said, "Marshall, we have a great staff. They would be an asset to any business in our state. We have lost the election. Between now and January we will be a caretaker administration. So you will have time. When you get rested, I would like you to find jobs for every member of our staff. Will you undertake that one more task for me? I will be forever grateful."

Mel Thomson, after his greatest loss, thought not of himself. He was not melancholy. To him it was God's will. He asked me to take care of and find jobs for his staff. That to me was the measure of the man. This is one of the many reasons why I loved Mel.

By his actions and leadership Mel Thomson removed the hue and cry for broad-based taxes and completely changed New Hampshire's political agenda. Mel left the state with its largest budget surplus, $38.8 million. Under Mel, New Hampshire had the lowest per capita tax in the nation. There was a growing body of evidence to prove that New Hampshire's low tax structure resulted in one of the best economic climates in the nation. In Mel's six years, we attracted 260 new business that brought 20,000 new jobs to the state. Mel's frugality helped produce the best and most prosperous economy in the Northeast.

CHAPTER 61

John H. Sununu

John Sununu invited me to work on his campaign for governor in a show of compassion. He had worked for me in the Energy Office and was a friend. He kept me in the back room because of the controversy surrounding my leaving Washington. When pressed by the media for a title and description of what I was doing, he called me director of Issue Development.

I got in trouble right away. Sununu was unknown except in his hometown of Salem. I decided that he needed visibility. The opportunity came while driving to work, when I heard on the local radio news that a child molester, who had killed a child, escaped from New Hampshire State Prison. The news story said that the prison guard tower wasn't being used due to manpower shortages.

I immediately drafted a press release for Sununu's approval, declaring: "A killer is loose in our midst because Governor Hugh Gallen [our opponent] doesn't know how to set budget priorities," Republican gubernatorial candidate John Sununu charges.

Our press release got a lot of play on both radio and TV. I was proud of that effort, but it raised the ire of Sununu's fancy new Washington consultants, Smith and Harroff. They felt it was undignified for a soon-to-be governor.

I pointed out that Sununu had about zero visibility. My goal was to get his name out to the public and at the same time embarrass Governor Gallen. Smith and Harroff were appalled.

We continued to battle. Everything I wrote that received good coverage raised their hackles because of my flamboyant writing style. I told them we would not get free press in New Hampshire unless we made news. Sophisticated issue papers would not be used, or if they were printed, they would be buried where nobody would read them.

The issue between us finally got resolved when they sent an employee to New Hampshire to muzzle my stuff before it went out. We agreed I could continue to create flamboyant attacks, but not in Sununu's name.

I had been working for the state Senate before I went to Washington. I had a good relationship with the majority bloc of conservative senators, for whom I had been writing stuff during their session. I did daily attacks on Governor Gallen and praised Sununu in the name of a different state senator each day. I would taunt the Washington consultant by telling her, "I'm going over to the *Union Leader* to file my copy."

The sequel to this story is that on the day before the election, when the press will not print or air charges of any kind, I read a small article in the *Boston Herald*. It said that an African doctor had discovered a potential cure for herpes. I immediately faxed this proposed press release to Smith and Harroff's Washington office.

"Republican Gubernatorial candidate Dr. John Sununu hailed the discovery of a cure for genital herpes as a breakthrough that will warm the cockles of many a New Hampshire citizen's heart. As I crisscrossed New Hampshire from Coos to the sea, many people I have come in 'contact with' have expressed their deep concern about this dreaded plague.

"Discovery of a marital partner afflicted with this scourged disease is the number one cause of the breakdown of the family unit in the Granite State. I join the moral majority in saluting those dedicated fellow scientists whose timeless research has resulted in an easing of the emotional strain on countless campaign consultants who by the nature of their work traversing America interact with afflicted members of the great unwashed public.

"Many mothers will breathe a sign of relief that pre- and post-marital interdigitation may now be enjoyed without the awful consequences of herpes.

"Hugh Gallen's poor appointees are the reason that the children of New Hampshire have lain awake countless nights checking their youthful bodies for signs and symptoms of America's leading social stigma. With Dr. John Sununu as Governor, the change for the better starts with the elimination of herpes!"

It blew their minds.

Smith and Harroff swung into action. They called us in the New Hampshire campaign office and ordered us to destroy all copies at once. I laughed for years over that one. It's also clear that I violated their instructions and kept a copy till this day.

Another contribution to Sununu's campaign was the creation of hundreds of different targeted letters to every conceivable occupation list in New Hampshire. This was before the advent of computers. We had an IBM Selectric typewriter and an extremely dedicated, hardworking high school typist named Sue Beaudoin (now Forcier) who worked half the night, every night, getting out those stealth letters, which I believe played a key role in Sununu's election. Years later she is still my right arm as she types this manuscript.

Another sidelight of that campaign is that Dave Carney, now a nationally known political consultant, started his political career wearing a cowboy hat and putting up Sununu signs.

Most people do not know that roly-poly John Sununu is an outstanding softball player. He is one of the best hitters I have ever seen. I once coached a national championship team and am thus qualified to make that statement. John is also proud of his skiing ability, which I am not qualified to judge.

Sununu was an almost complete unknown. No one knew what Sununu looked like or his ethnic background. The Democrats came up with a vicious whispering campaign telling people that Sununu's father bombed Pearl Harbor for the Japanese. The Sununu camp came up with a clever TV commercial to counter that lie. The commercial asked, What is a Sununu? Is it the Sun? Is it the Rising Sun? (People knew the Japanese emblem in those days.) Then a picture of a little bird came on the screen and the announcer said, "Actually, *sununu* is a Lebanese word that means 'little bird,'" then a picture of portly Sununu with the voiceover saying, "This is John Sununu. He's not very little, but he is a professor at Tufts University. He is also a widely respected management consultant who will solve New Hampshire's problems."

We had a competent but bossy office manager named Judy Galluzzo. We lived in fear of the decisions about the campaign she concocted with the Salem wives.

Hugh Gallen and his campaign had been convinced that conservative Senate President Bob Monier would be the Republican nominee to run against them. They had a television commercial in the can, ready to use as soon as the general election started. The theme was that

Bob Monier was the philosophical son of Governor Mel Thomson. When Sununu upset Monier, they redubbed the commercial they had already paid for to say that John Sununu was the philosophical son of Mel Thomson because Marshall Cobleigh would be in Sununu's back room just like he was with Mel Thomson. They ran the commercial for a week and then dropped it.

In the televised debate two days before the election, Gallen brought up this charge again. Always clever, Sununu parried Gallen's charge by saying that I would not be in the statehouse in his administration. I was crestfallen. Sununu told me not to worry; he'd find a way around it. He had led me to believe that I would manage his office. He knew I badly needed a job. I had proved that I was capable of being his chief of staff. We had a good personal relationship.

He went to the national governors orientation session at my urging. He told some senior governors of his dilemma. They told him that if he wanted to maintain credibility with the people, there was no way he could put me on his staff. He told me he would find something for me outside the statehouse.

Congress had just repealed the scandal-ridden CETA program. They replaced it with JTPA, the Job Training Partnership Act. During the transition I had written Sununu a memo outlining this as an opportunity to put business in charge and to take job training away from the Democrat-orientated community action agencies. He called me in. He told me he wanted me to take it over and put it in the hands of business.

That proved to be a tremendous opportunity for me. Under Sununu's leadership, I spearheaded the fight for state control of the program. I eventually was elected national chairman of the JTPA Liaisons Group. In that role I led the battle for more state input into this federally funded program. Sununu kept his promise that I would not be in his statehouse. I received a nationally prominent position. One has to wonder, If Sununu had not made that quick decision without thinking, would I have gone to Washington with him? We'll never know.

An important by-product of my assignment to the Job Training program was Sununu's choice of Fred Gagnon, the outspoken CEO of the Kollsman Instrument Company, as the program's business leader. Mutual friends were convinced that because of our fiery personalities, Fred and I would be a disaster together. We developed a mutual respect and became a very productive management team. We also became extremely good friends. Fred was always there for me when I needed an ally. I still appreciate our strong bond.

John Sununu asked me to come in one night (so the press would not see us meeting) to get my input on the major decision of his life. Should he run for another term as governor or position himself to accept George H. W. Bush's offer to go to Washington with the new president? He was truly in a quandary. He loved being governor, but he was being offered an opportunity to be a major player on the national scene. In typical engineering fashion, Sununu had developed a pro-and-con list for both options. We spent more than an hour discussing his choices. He had not arrived at a decision. I could tell by his emphasis on the various options that he would end up going to Washington. He was forty-four years old. He realized that this should be his peak earning period.

He had eight children, all with plans to attend college. The governor of New Hampshire earned $45,000 at that time. His pay in Washington would start out around $70,000. He would have to have two residences, one in Washington and one in New Hampshire. He would have to do a lot of traveling between the two homes. There was not any real economic difference between the two options, as he found out.

I have always believed that the reason he made the fateful decision to accept the free airplane rides was economically driven. Happily, he is now in a position to put those kinds of problems behind him.

John Sununu is an extremely loyal friend. When my job was under fire in the Gregg administration, John went out of his way to seek me out at a political event. He said, "How's it going, Marshall?"

I said, "Fine."

Sununu said, "Marshall, how is it really going? I know what's going on. What can I do to help you?"

I will always remember that! Here was the president's chief of staff going well out of his way to ask what he could do to help me.

One of Sununu's major weaknesses was that he didn't suffer fools easily. They tell the story that when a senior congressman approached him at the White House, asking for support of a new bridge in his district, Sununu peppered the congressman with questions. What is the population of the two communities involved? What is the traffic count on the current highways? What is the peak traffic count? The congressman couldn't answer the questions, but pleaded for White House support for this bridge. Sununu told him to come back when he knew what he was talking about.

Mike Dukakis had the same problem. Massachusetts politicians would tell you that "the Duke," as they called Dukakis, had no sense of humor. I found that Mike had a good sense of humor, but he also did not suffer fools gladly.

Ironically, Sununu and Dukakis, who were very much alike, did not get along well at all. They were probably too much alike. Dukakis was miles apart from Mel Thomson philosophically, but they were good friends personally. In retrospect, the biggest mistake I made when I managed Mel's memorial service was forgetting to invite his friend Mike Dukakis to speak.

I have always regretted that oversight.

John Sununu is probably the smartest man ever to be our governor. He has almost total recall. His SAT scores, which he would never let me use in any of his campaigns, were 800 (perfect) in math and 772 on the verbal. He has a great sense of humor and is an extremely loyal friend. As I mentioned, he did not tolerate fools. As a result, he was not always popular with members of Congress. I got a lot of kidding from friends in Congress when they found out I was a major player in first getting him elected.

CHAPTER 62

Governor Judd Gregg

The first time Fred Gagnon and I met with the newly elected governor Judd Gregg, Fred had me prepare a decision briefing paper. We outlined what the JTPA program was doing. We also outlined our plans for it. We listed the decisions we wanted from the governor. With each problem, we listed the various options we were considering.

Fred and Sununu had always operated that way. Fred stressed to me that we must be organized and not waste the governor's time. Judd discussed our option paper with us, but he made no decisions. He kept telling us that he would get back to us. He never did.

Don Reed was the businessperson in charge of the Private Industry Council. He was a telephone company executive whose main job seemed to be to get on all kinds of public service committees and spread goodwill for the telephone company. John Sununu, Fred Gagnon, and I had been determined to run the JTPA on a businesslike basis and not load it up with political hacks, which is the way CETA had operated. It got CETA into all kinds of trouble. Several members of the Governor's Executive Council, with a new governor, started pushing me to hire a bunch of unqualified political hacks. I refused. The councilors complained to Reed, whose job was to curry favor. I'm sure that they also complained to Governor Gregg.

Gregg was busy trying to build his own staff. As usual, there were a lot more applicants than positions. Someone convinced him that my job was a political plum that they could fill with one of their own. My job was one of the higher-paid jobs in state government.

Thus, Gregg made the prompted decision to fire me. This caused a battle royal. I called in all the chips I could muster. I had all of the living governors call Judd on my behalf. I researched all of his political contributors lists. I asked all Gregg's big contributors whom I knew to call the governor and plead my case. I left no stone unturned. Eventually, there was a compromise. The JTPA program was split in half. I headed one division and Judd's guy headed the other division. My pay remained the same. I proved to the governor that he couldn't fire me, but he took away my programmatic powers: a typical political solution.

There was a sidelight to that skirmish. Eli Isaacson, the president of Isaacson Steel, was the new head of the Private Industry Council. He became the governor's hatchet man in the effort to get rid of me.

A few years later, Eli used his political clout to supply steel for the huge Ronald Reagan Building in Washington. Eli was way over his head in that arena. The big Washington builders set a trap for Eli's under-capital-ized business. The Washington bureaucracy withheld Eli's hard-earned payments. They nearly forced him into bankruptcy. Eli brought his prob-lems to Congressman Bill Zeliff. Bill told Eli, "Marshall will know how to straighten out your problems. I'll put him on it Tuesday when I get back to Washington."

Eli blanched. He said, "Marshall will never help me. I worked hard for Judd Gregg trying to take away Marshall's job. He'll never help me. Isn't there anyone else who can help?"

Bill told Eli, "You don't know Marshall. If there are north country jobs at stake, Marshall will save the New Hampshire jobs. Then he will tell you that he is by far a bigger man than you."

I saved the jobs, saved Eli's company. I had a few words for the obse-quious Eli afterward.

Judd and I had major differences when I worked in his administra-tion, despite the fact that I had been heavily involved in his father's cam-paigns. Yet when I had my quadruple heart bypass and valve job, one of the nicest letters I received was a handwritten note from Judd. It meant a lot to me.

CHAPTER 63

The Z Team

When Bill Zeliff made his run for Congress, he immediately started romancing me to work on his campaign. I held off for months because I didn't think he had a chance. I had no desire to be unemployed again after the election.

Bill was persistent. The make-work job I had with Judd was fraught with tension. I had completed my term as chair of the National JTPA Liaisons Group. Thus, I was more vulnerable to increased efforts to fire me. I decided to take my chances with Bill Zeliff. I negotiated a promise that he would take me to Washington with him if he won.

I jumped into his campaign. He was way behind. A poll showed him at 5 percent, with Larry Brady, the *Union Leader*'s candidate, at 29 percent and former House Speaker Doug Scamman Jr. at 31 percent. There were only thirty days left until the primary. At my urging, we went into attack mode. I knew that Scamman had voted for broad-based taxes. I sent some of our interns up to Concord to research Scamman's voting record. We compiled a list of every tax increase and fee increase he had ever voted for in his lengthy legislative career. Pat Griffin's advertising team put together a coordinated newspaper, radio, and television blitz, utilizing this information and featuring a ringing cash register. The long list of tax and fee increases that Scamman had voted for was laid out for the taxpayers to see.

We received a list of Larry Brady's Washington lobbying clients and the required forms that he had filed as a lobbyist. I noticed that some of the forms were titled "Registration as a Foreign Agent." We held a press conference in front of a shoe company that had closed due to foreign competition. We proclaimed that Larry Brady was a registered foreign agent. We followed the press conference with a paid-advertising campaign with the same lead slogan.

As a result of my attack campaign, skillfully packaged by our advertising team, we were now in a horse race. All of this was accomplished in the final month of the campaign. To this day, Larry Brady and Doug Scamman Jr. are bitter about my tactics.

Election night was the most hectic that I have ever been involved in. I told Bill he won by 314 votes. Later that night, after consulting and comparing our numbers with the *Union Leader*, I told Bill that we had won by a margin of 276 votes. Bill took the podium and claimed victory at

1:05 A.M. An hour later the press pool announced that it had made a mistake and that Brady was the real winner. I was on the phone most of the rest of the night trying to reconcile our voting figures with those of the press pool and the *Union Leader*, which also had usually reliable voting figures, and Secretary of State Bill Gardner, who was in charge of official voting records. Brady was insisting that the press pool numbers showed him winning. By three o'clock in the morning we had again contacted every town in the district. I was convinced that our figures checked out and that Bill had won by about 250 votes.

That night was an emotional roller coaster of unbelievable proportions for Bill Zeliff, his family, key supporters, and me. Every nugget of new or clarifying information raised or dashed our hopes and our emotions. I will never forget the bonding that took place that night. It is probably one of the main reasons that Bill Zeliff still declares, "If I go to war, I want Marshall Cobleigh in the foxhole with me."

By about seven A.M., we were convinced that Zeliff had won. Using the figures that we and the *Union Leader* had jointly developed and verified, they proclaimed us the winner by 376 votes. At 11:30 A.M. the Associated Press declared Larry Brady the winner, using its own figures. Gardner, the secretary of state, called us shortly after noon and verified that our figures, not Brady's, were correct. It seems that in the town of Sandown, the AP had accidentally shown Larry Brady with 711 votes when his actual total was 71. At 1:30 P.M. it was officially declared that Bill Zeliff had won by 314 votes, out of 48,460 votes actually cast. Of course, there was a recount. I managed Zeliff's recount team because I had had experience in that area. The recount established that Bill Zeliff was going to Washington as New Hampshire's First District Congressman.

Brady was the ultimate sore loser. After the recount, Brady protested to the State Ballot Law Commission, the Federal Election Commission, and probably all the ships at sea.

Ironically, the last recount in the First District congressional race was in 1980, when I beat Bob Smith by 1,261 votes. That recount lasted seventeen days (almost all paper ballots then) before Smith conceded. I thought Smith was a sore loser who cost me a real chance to win by impeding my fund-raising for more than three weeks. Compared to Larry Brady, Bob Smith was a paragon of virtue, despite his sore losing tactics in my case and then again the only other time he lost, to young John E. Sununu.

It was eventually established that I was going to Washington with

Bill after a number of fits and starts that held me on tenterhooks for several weeks. I was not going to be chief of staff. Bill decided to go with Brian Flood, who had Washington experience. We had a difficult relationship from the start. Brian was jealous that Bill listened to me on New Hampshire political matters.

You didn't have a secretary in Washington. At age sixty, I had to learn the computer, typing, and how to be my own secretary. My manual dexterity was extremely limited. I was a klutz at best.

Brian used my limited clerical skills to bad-mouth me to Bill constantly. It was a frustrating experience. Appearance was important to Bill. Coming from a hotel background, he was afraid that the guests wouldn't check in if we were all not neat as a pin. I kept telling him I was not a goldarned bellboy.

My lifetime experience in political fields was an irritant as well. People of all types would come in and tell Bill that he was "lucky to have Marshall." They meant it as a compliment. Bill took it as an insult to his capabilities. From my past endeavors with state legislative leaders groups, the U.S. Jaycees, national Republican politics, the Republican Congressional School, and the insurance industry, and because of my age, I knew many congressmen personally. Bill also resented this, particularly in the beginning, when they knew me and not him.

Bill told me not to hang around Bullfeathers, the congressional watering hole, as his predecessor had. "With your reputation and mine we will get in trouble," he told me. Every time something good happened to him, such as his appointment to the ad hoc committee to deal with the banking crisis, he would say, "How did that happen?" I would tell him, "It's the Bullfeathers connection." In time, he let me drink where I wanted to drink.

Eventually Brian got himself in trouble and Bill named me his chief of staff. I was extremely happy in that role, and we accomplished a lot.

My biggest accomplishment was the creation of the A-to-Z spending cut plan. This moved Zeliff from unheralded back-bencher to nationally known leader in Congress.

I was frustrated at the congressional leadership's tendency to package every issue into a huge take-it-or-leave-it vote. There was no opportunity to strike bad items unless you were on the Appropriations Committee, which was off-limits to new members. I did not buy the argument that it could not be done in a 424-member House of Representatives because I had repeatedly done it in a four-hundred-member New Hampshire House when I served as Speaker. I piggybacked on an idea that Senator Bob Kerry of Nebraska had tried.

The A-to-Z plan simply let every member propose one cut to the budget. It is debated for ten minutes by each side. Then there is an up or down roll-call vote.

I talked Bill into going with me to see Senator Bob Kerry, and he gave us permission to expand and try his plan in the House.

We looked at all members whose names started with the letter *A*. We chose Rob Andrews, a Democrat from New Jersey, to be our cosponsor. (This caused me a lot of grief from my best friend among the Congressmen, Jim Saxton, also from New Jersey. Jim didn't like Andrews.)

Bill set up an appointment with Andrews. I explained the concept. He eagerly joined our cause. The A-to-Z spending-cut plan was born. We had a meeting of the fiscally conservative groups and sold them on A-to-Z.

Interest groups supporting the A-to-Z spending-cut plan included:
American Conservative Union
American Legislative Exchange Council
Americans for a Balanced Budget
American Small Business Association
Americans for Tax Reform
Association of Concerned Taxpayers
Christian Coalition
Citizens Against Government Waste
Citizens for a Sound Economy
Free the Eagle
National American Wholesale Grocers Association
National Federation of Independent Business
National Taxpayers Union
Pennsylvania Leadership Council
Small Business Survival Committee
United Seniors Association
U.S. Chamber of Commerce

The *Congressional Quarterly* wrote: "The appeal of the 'A-to-Z' Spending Cut Plan put the House Leadership in a precarious position— our plan for a historic spending cut session taps into members' frustration and their desire to make a statement on the deficit." The article added, "Few predicted last August that a brash plan to shut down all other business in the House and devote at least seven eight-hour days to nothing but debate and votes on spending cuts would ever get anywhere." The *Congressional Quarterly* went on: "But House Democratic leaders have been rudely surprised before by the power of the deficit—or perhaps more precisely, by the frustration and powerlessness felt by many legislators when they push for deeper cuts. Such feelings, together with a mix of political gamesmanship and raw opportunism, have galvanized a bipartisan majority of the House rank and file. And despite increasingly anxious efforts in recent weeks to find a way out, leaders now find themselves teetering on the brink of what would be a historic embarrassment.

"Over the strenuous opposition of senior Democrats, the controversial A-to-Z plan to set aside at least 56 hours of debate for dozens of as yet unspecified spending cut amendments has come within just 15 signatures of the 218 needed to discharge it to the House floor.

"If chief A-to-Z sponsors Robert E. Andrews, D-N.J., and Bill Zeliff, R-N.H., find enough members willing to sign the discharge petition, they would strip leaders of control of the floor for a week or more and hand over management of spending cut votes to four Junior House members.

"Democratic leaders have managed to stall A-to-Z signatures at 203 with an alternative spending cut plan of their own, but they are bracing to stave off another push for signers before the Fourth of July recess."

The article went on: "Some members, particularly relative newcomers like Zeliff and Andrews, say they are frustrated that when they try to push deficit-reduction proposals, they are often blocked by Democratic leaders' ironhanded control over the committees and the floor debate process.

"House Appropriations Chairman David R. Obey, D-Wis., has fought back by introducing his own competitive version of A-to-Z, which would allow only amendments that cut a project in the district of the member offering the cut. Obey calls his measure the 'Anti-Hypocrisy Deficit Reduction Act of 1994.'

"Few thought we had much chance of success then, but less than a year later, the momentum behind their movement has forced the House leadership to concoct an alternative plan. Zeliff and Andrews have gone from obscurity to fairly high profiles for a couple of second-term House members.

"The plan's largely Republican backers (167 of the 203 members on the discharge petition are Republicans) style themselves as underdogs fighting an autocratic, out-of-touch House leadership, and they have deftly played on that argument in building support outside Congress."

I convinced Bill to go the national talk radio hosts annual convention.

This meeting and the talk show invitations we all subsequently received gave the A-to-Z plan great new momentum.

The *Congressional Quarterly* went on to say, "Rush Limbaugh and other conservative talk radio show hosts have devoted air time to the cause, but perhaps the most effective support has come from the editorial page of the *Wall Street Journal*, never a big fan of the House Democratic leadership. The *Journal* has kept up a steady fire of editorial support for A-to-Z, capitalizing on the change in House rules that makes the heretofore secret names on discharge petitions publicly available. Under the headline 'Look Who's Hiding,' the newspaper recently named nearly three dozen House members who earlier backed A-to-Z but so far have refused to sign the discharge petition.

"Singling out members like that is designed to put enormous pressure on them back home, and the weight has been particularly heavy on Republican appropriators, some of whom originally backed A-to-Z but then hesitated to sign the discharge petition after colleagues on the committee warned them that they were in effect cutting their own throats.

"Rep. Robert L. Livingston, R-La., originally held off but then signed the petition and now refuses to discuss the matter at all. Fellow GOP appropriator Jerry Lewis, Calif., said he caught flak after the *Wall Street Journal* editorial named him, but that constituents sympathized with his argument that A-to-Z could cut projects vital to his district.

"A-to-Z sponsors said they plan eventually to convert enough members like Lewis to get the 218 signatures this year, but even if they do not make it, they are even more bullish about their prospects next year, after midterm elections that are expected to make the House more Republican and more conservative than it is now.

"'We've got a grass-roots issue here that people understand," said Zeliff. "If we don't get it this year, it'll be a no-brainer next year."

Pat Buchanan pointed out in "Why Special Interests Fear A-to-Z": "A-to-Z is the *Nightmare on Elm Street* of the special interests. And they are horrified that a discharge petition to get A-to-Z out of the rules committee ... A-to-Z is the gravest threat in modern times to the legislative process ... It would give a line-item veto to the full House. All those backroom deals where votes are swapped for pork could be undone on the floor."

Buchanan went on to say, "Comes now, however, an idea that may just work, an idea that at least will sort out the serious budget cutters from the phonies.

"A-to-Z is the prescription for a revolution that could lead to the real majority seizing power over the purse from the speaker and the committee chairmen.

"The beauty of A-to-Z is that it would expose the fakery of so many Congressmen who talk fiscal conservatism back home but vote to keep the money rolling in D.C. It would define both parties with clarity and give us a new accountability to our politics. It would force congressmen to make hard decisions, right on C-Span, to show whether and where they were willing to cut the federal budget. By forcing the House to vote up or down 56 straight budget items, every voter would be given a detailed report card on each member, a report card that separated the spenders from the budget cutters.

"With A-to-Z, the newer, younger members closer to the electorate (Zeliff and Andrews have been on the Hill only three years) would be empowered at the expense of legislators who have sat there decades, and accommodated themselves to the ways of the House. If it catches on, A-to-Z special sessions could be conducted several times a year.

"With so much at risk House leaders are threatening the rebels with retaliation-terminated projects in home districts—if they vote for the discharge petition. But the bullying is not working. As of June 18, 203 members had signed the discharge petition, and supporters were working on the 26 Democrats and nine Republicans who claim they support A-to-Z but have yet to sign.

"But time is running out for a special session this summer and the leadership may yet prevail. If it does, voters should retaliate against those who killed A-to-Z and, when the new Congress arrives in January, with dozens of new members, it should be brought up again. As it shall. For it fits perfectly the rebellious spirit of our times," Buchanan concluded.

The *Wall Street Journal* continued to support our cause, saying, "The Beltway establishment is striving mightily to kill the A-to-Z Spending Cuts Plan, but somehow we suspect the movement to drive down federal spending is not going away.

"So far a majority of 229 members have co-sponsored A-to-Z. The idea is simple: Call a special session of Congress to focus just on spending cuts. A minimum of 56 hours of debate would be held and any member could propose his or her favorite idea to trim wasteful or harmful government programs. For once, the Rules Committee wouldn't be able to block floor amendments it didn't like. For a few brief days, the House would be a working democracy where junior Members (who represent nearly half the country) could have a say.

"Reps. Rob Andrews and Bill Zeliff came up with the A-to-Z concept after learning that Congress never really debates the direction or size of about half the federal budget—mostly entitlements on automatic pilot. 'The only way to have enough money for worthy programs today is to set priorities,' says Rep. Andrews, a New Jersey Democrat who says voters want members to stop saying yes to every special interest. 'The only way for my party to be politically insulated from the building tax revolt is to show we're willing to kill off some dinosaurs.' *Wall Street Journal*

"The problem is that kind of long-range thinking is an anathema to the House's own dinosaurs. Speaker Tom Foley has called A-to-Z 'the most poorly thought out proposal' he's seen in many years. He and Appropriations Chairman David Obey have passed the word that members who sign a discharge petition to blast A-to-Z out of the Rules Committee and on to the floor will regret it. That's largely why 58 out of the 229 co-sponsors (46 Democrats and 12 Republicans) haven't yet put their signatures where their principles are and signed Discharge Petition No. 16.

"'Some good members are leaving because they can't legislate and are frustrated,' says Rep. Tim Penny, a Democrat who is retiring this year.

"Win or lose, the A-to-Z battle will separate the budget's hawks from the chickens.

"Empires rise and fall, whole species die off, but through it all there is one constant: Government bureaucracies never die. And therein lies another reason why the A-to-Z Spending Cuts Plan, now under full-scale assault by the House's Democratic leadership, deserves to be given a chance.

"Since Congress routinely condones such waste, it'll take radical measures to drive a stake through the hearts of some of these 'undead' programs. The A-to-Z spending bill would be a start, forcing Congress to re-examine—and vote—on its fiscal priorities. Better still, voters can ward off future predations of bureaucratic vampires by electing fiscally responsible lawmakers this November," the *Wall Street Journal* concluded.

In another editorial, the *Wall Street Journal* said "[Reps.] Rob Andrews and Bill Zeliff will begin circulating a discharge petition to bring their A-to-Z Spending Cuts Plan to the House floor. So far, 229 members have co-sponsored A-to-Z. If a House majority of 218 members also signs the discharge petition, A-to-Z will bypass the Rules Committee's graveyard, and a special session will quickly be held. In addition to the 229 co-sponsors, another 21 members have signed a pro-A-to-Z letter but haven't taken the more meaningful step of signing onto the legislation. Their names appear nearby.

"Now, about two-thirds of the budget is almost immune from budget cuts. Entitlements are on autopilot; they aren't even part of the appropriations process. This is preposterous. Under A-to-Z, every program would be subject to a budget-cutting amendment.

"Naturally, House leaders are aghast. They've told the bill's co-sponsors that projects in their districts may be wiped out. Speaker Foley has warned Democrats there may be other negative 'consequences' if they sign the discharge petition.

"But while the leadership twists arms in private, it has little stomach for debating A-to-Z in public. Yesterday, C-Span couldn't find a single House Democrat to appear with Rep. Zeliff. Instead, Brookings Institution scholar Thomas Mann went on. Mr. Mann was last heard from defending secret discharge petitions. This time, he argued that a special session would disrupt the normal legislative process and its focus on spending cuts would sidetrack Congress from other issues. That sounded just great to most C-Span callers," the *Wall Street Journal* declared.

The *Portland Maine Press Herald* said, "Getting all federal spending on the floor for discussion is a worthy idea. Let's do it."

The *Washington Times* wrote, "This is a politically attractive reform issue. It could lead to real cuts in spending and fundamentally change the system. The anti-reform leadership of the House—Speaker Tom Foley, Majority Leader Dick Gephardt and Majority Whip David Bonier—had all strongly lined up against this very real opportunity to cut some spending from the federal budget.

"The A-to-Z Spending Cuts is the first reality check Congress has experienced in the post-sunshine era. A-to-Z Spending Cuts has majority support in the House and threatens to make Congress accountable to the people. Tom Foley, Dick Gephardt, Danny Rostenkowski and the rest at the trough have cause for concern.

"Reps. Robert Andrews and Bill Zeliff are on a hypocrisy hunt. If 218 members sign the A-to-Z discharge petition, their bill will come up for a vote, against the wishes—and frantic arm-twisting—of the Democratic leadership. Not all lawmakers who were happy to put their names on the bill last August are willing to do so now. The reason? Because posturing for the folks back home is one thing, but crossing the powerful House leadership is another thing altogether.

"Lawmakers trying to weasel out of signing the petition will no doubt quote House Speaker Tom Foley that the A-to-Z bill will be a 'three-ring-circus.' Just imagine: each member of the House being allowed to bring one spending cut proposal to the floor for debate and a vote—Anarchy! For obvious reasons, the idea of open votes on specific spending questions is terrifying to a House leadership that is used to wielding power by controlling the federal purse strings. For equally obvious reasons the prospect frightens the voting public not in the least.

"In fact the prospect is appealing and exciting for an electorate savvy enough to know that most of the Capitol's real decisions are made off-camera. There is no chance under the A-to-Z bill for the kind of conference committee shenanigans that allow members to take empty, phoney votes in favor of popular measures with the full knowledge that the provisions will be stripped once behind the closed doors of conference. Instead, lawmakers will be accountable for their votes, which will be clear, specific and open to voter scrutiny.

"But clear, specific and open votes are somehow a threat to the legislative process, according to the opponents of A-to-Z. All those lawmakers taking all of those votes—where will be the time for the thorough deliberation necessary for careful lawmaking?

"What a lot of hooey. Anyone who has sat in the House or Senate gallery at the end of legislative sessions and watched billions of dollars spent on weary voice votes knows just how much careful deliberation goes into the legislative process. Take the Intra Modal Surface Transportation Act of 1991, overwhelmingly approved by the House in late November of that year. The bill wasn't even finished being written when debate began at about 4 in the morning. Two hours later, the vote was taken without a single member having looked at, let alone read, the text of the bill, so goes $151 billion.

"That vote was not an aberration. By contrast, the A-to-Z procedure, which calls for debate and votes on simple, straightforward spending cut proposals, is a paradigm of democratic virtue," the *Washington Times* concluded.

I enlisted Ross Perot to come to Washington and speak out for the A-to-Z cause.

The diminutive Texas billionaire supported our bipartisan plan to cut government spending by letting House members demand debate and a floor vote on specific budget cuts.

"We still think we're the last superpower in the world and we don't want to look at the instrument panel and see that we're running out of fuel," Perot said in endorsing A-to-Z.

"Though the bill's advocates say it would lead to real spending cuts by circumventing procedures that House leaders use to safeguard pork," House Speaker Tom Foley said, "it would create a 'free-for-all' on the house floor and eliminate the hearing process that ensures bills are thoroughly scrutinized."

The *Arizona Republic* said, "The rabble rousers are dead serious about forcing members of Congress to put their money where their mouths are on the subject of cutting federal spending, and it's about time. At issue is a nifty little proposal called the 'A-to-Z Spending Cuts Plan.'

"Despite the opposition of House Speaker Tom Foley and every committee chairman, the A-to-Z plan has gained 221 co-sponsors. This is sufficient to force the matter, over the leadership's objections, to a floor vote. And once authorized, the session is expected to be held next month.

"Zeliff's office predicts that most members will offer proposals to cut only one or two specific projects—a million here, a million there. But as the late Sen. Everett Dirksen once put it, in time you're talking about real money.

"Indeed, Congress' deficit-spending binge began with a million here and a million there, and the deficit probably will have to be reduced in much the same way. There's no better way to begin than by an A-to-Z accounting of Congress' commitment to real fiscal reform," the *Arizona Republic* declared.

Noted columnist George F. Will said: "Hence the charm of this tax season of the A to Z Spending Cuts Plan proposed by Reps. Rob Andrews (D-N.J.) and Bill Zeliff (R N.H.).

"House leaders will throw up every possible procedural impediment to prevent this happening, because the spending system depends on obscurity, secrecy and hypocrisy. Back home, members preach parsimony. In Washington they practice mutual logrolling.

"We shall see who has the courage to cut, or the courage to defend, say, peanut subsidies.

"A-to-Z would be a step toward establishing the responsibility of individual legislators for what the legislature does. That would serve the cause of resistance to taxation," Will pointed out.

The *Birmingham News* said: "That's what a group of representatives led by Rob Andrews, D-N.J., and Bill Zeliff, R-N.H. (A-to-Z, get it?), wants to do next month. If they succeed, Congress will take a big step in the direction of winnowing out the huge federal budget deficit. And now is the time to do it. The economy is strong, and deficit-cutting sentiment is high on Capitol Hill.

"It would make all those cuts that are now off limits fair game. And it would mean individual members of Congress would no longer have any easy excuses for not trying to reduce the deficit. Their votes would be out in the open for everyone to see.

"A shocking idea, isn't it? No wonder the czars of the Capitol don't like it. And all the more reason for the rest of us to be for it, of course."

The *Philadelphia Inquirer* said: "The A-to-Z Plan would make Congress put up or shut up on the deficit.

"A whopping total of 234 representatives—a clear majority of the House—signed a letter supporting it. Alas, the legislation that would trigger this process is going nowhere fast.

"What happened? It's simple. The fellow who got this letter, Speaker Tom Foley, made it clear that he doesn't support such an exercise in democracy. Neither does President Clinton. So right now, fewer than half of the plan's original supporters have signed on as co-sponsors of this bill, which is bottled up in a House committee.

"To get it to the floor, Reps. Andrews and Zeliff will have to get a majority of the House—that's 218 members—to sign a 'discharge petition' to get the bill out of the committee to a vote in the House.

"They ought to succeed—that is, unless the public and the news media let dozens of Democrats and Republicans get away with talking out of both sides of their mouths.

"Citizens Against Government Waste (CAGW) was one of the very first organizations to support this proposal and will seek to have a bill introduced and passed during this session of Congress. CAGW believes that in such an environment, members of Congress who normally are stifled both by the procedural roadblocks and the Rules Committee, will be able to overcome the institutional bias of deficit spending and take the first few steps toward fiscal sanity and accountability."

The *Los Angeles Daily News* quoted me: " 'The key to the whole thing is accountability,' Marshall Cobleigh, Zeliff's administrative assistant, said Monday. 'The American people want us to cut spending, and they are frustrated with the Clinton [five-year budget] plan, which put tax increases in the beginning and spending cuts in the [later] years.'

"And Cobleigh notes that lawmakers who don't vote for an open rule 'would leave themselves vulnerable to the people back home. If Andrews and Zeliff can get a majority of lawmakers to force an open rule, Congress may have to approve the spending cuts that come to a vote out of fear of alienating the voters. That moment of truth could be at hand soon.'"

Even the *Concord Monitor* said, "Our gut reaction is more power to him—go ahead with it. Why not try something new—nothing else has worked. Congress has racked up $3 trillion in new debt during the last decade.

"House Speaker Thomas Foley has been unsupportive, no doubt because he doesn't want Republicans to get credit for spending cuts while Democrats get blamed for taxes."

The *Christian Science Monitor* wrote, under the headline "Push to Cut Budget, A-to-Z, Gains":

"Tired of higher taxes, red-ink spending, trillion-dollar budgets, and bloated bureaucracies? Two members of Congress think they have an answer. It's called 'A-to-Z.'

"A-to-Z would also put members on the spot. They would go on record—aye or nay—on dozens of specific proposals to trim the size of government. It would point the finger directly at big spenders. The two original sponsors, Rep. Robert Andrews (D) of New Jersey and Rep. Bill Zeliff (R) of New Hampshire, say their A-to-Z plan would attack runaway federal spending by returning significant budget powers to individual members."

Foster's Daily Democrat said, "Bill Zeliff is pushing some of his free-spending colleagues into a corner. It's called the A-to-Z Spending Cuts Plan. And it can result in some real spending reductions and some red faces. Isn't it satisfying to know that the people of the 1st District in New Hampshire have someone working for them? And his name is Bill Zeliff."

I knew that A-to-Z could work. I had presided over the four-hundred-member New Hampshire House, where we routinely let members propose amendments to spending bills. It's called democracy.

Bill Zeliff and I went through so much together that there will always be a strong bond between us. I have always believed that my job was not to mince words with my bosses. There are thousands of sycophants who will tell them what the sycophants think they want to hear. I deeply believed that my role as their administrative assistant was to tell my bosses what they needed to know and did not want to hear. This often rubbed Bill the wrong way. We came to a breaking point when I fought fiercely with him at a staff retreat over comp time for our staff, who averaged about eighty hours a week. Bill had a bad experience with a local police chief who wanted to get paid for his accumulated comp time, and was afraid he might face the same issue with his Washington staff. Bill replaced me as chief of staff and moved me to a spot on his committee staff because I fought him too fiercely on the comp time issue.

As a team, Bill and I had a significant impact on ending forty-six years of Democrat control of Congress.

The A-to-Z spending-cut plan that I created could not have succeeded without the editorial support of John Fund of the *Wall Street Journal*, who picked up our idea and promoted it extensively. A key role was also played by our intern Charles "Chip" Griffin, whose computer knowledge, creativity, and staff contacts were crucial to our success. He was rewarded with a well-deserved paid position on Zeliff's staff. Barbara Riley, Zeliff's press secretary, also played a significant part in our promotion efforts.

Another memorable moment occurred during my tenure with Bill Zeliff. John Mongan, the former mayor of Manchester, who finished third behind me and Bob Smith in my infamous hamburg-carrying campaign victory for the First District congressional seat, came to see Zeliff. Bill palmed him off on me, and John had the nerve to ask me, "Marshall, did you ever think that if Bob Smith didn't demand a recount after he lost by twenty-five hundred votes, and if I didn't threaten to run as an independent, you would be a U.S. senator today?" I emphatically told him, "John, I think about it every night when I go to bed!"

CHAPTER 64

Today's Problems

I believe the disease of public polling to determine not only public policy positions but also how to frame your advocacy of those positions to the unwashed public is one of the greatest threats to both New Hampshire and America as a whole. Harry Truman, who made more tough decisions than most of our other leaders, had a popularity rating of 28 percent when he left office. Today most historians rate Truman as one of the greatest presidents of our lifetime. A poll can never look into the future. He knew that a poll is only a snapshot in time. Mel Thomson was the same way.

In a time of slick thirty-second TV commercials—sound bites—when the White House spends more than four million dollars a year conducting weekly public opinion polling, political candidates of both parties, all across America, at every level, would not think of taking a position on any issue without checking with their pollsters. We must seek out and elect leaders who have the guts to take a stand without consulting an issue pollster.

Mel Thomson didn't need a pollster to tell him what was popular, because he didn't care what was popular. Mel simply asked, Is it right or wrong?

What a renaissance it would be for New Hampshire and America if we had leaders who ignored pollsters and temporal issues, future leaders who would stand on principle and simply do what they believe is right.

What can you do? First of all, on both a state level and in presidential elections, seek out candidates who will look you in the eye and tell you that they disagree with you on some issues. Support decision making at the lowest possible level. Look for courage and fortitude in our leaders both in New Hampshire and in Washington. We don't need leaders who tell us what they think we want to hear. Get involved in your government. At the very least, become informed about your candidates and find out what they really believe!

CHAPTER 65

Farewell

I *told my retirement party in 1997:* As Confucius said, "It is far better to
have your friends gather like this when you are on the right side of the
grass."

I appreciate each and every one of you taking the time to be here
tonight.

I always thought that the Barbara Streisand song "He Touched Me"
was a great description of a politician. I am proud to be called a politician.
If I touched your lives in a positive way, then I have answered my calling.

Churchill once said, "If you are not involved in politics, be prepared
to be governed by someone less able than yourself."

I've been involved in a lot of important fights on behalf of the people. With Pete and Stewart, Jack Bradshaw, we changed New Hampshire's
obsolete tax structure so that instead of taxing unsold inventory, we taxed
business profits. This led to New Hampshire's unparalleled economic
growth.

Mel Thomson started the movement to downsize government that
is sweeping America today. He taught me that government will always
spend more than you give it. That is why I no longer support broad-based
taxes.

Mel also taught me not to split infinitives, and I loved him.

John Sununu gave me the opportunity to be a pioneer in the fight to
let the states, not the federal government, run programs like job training.

I found out the real significance of the A-to-Z spending cut plan
when I attended, with Bill Zeliff, Tom Delay's cocktail party for the incom-
ing 1994 Republican congressional members. I was wearing a name badge
stating my name and the magic words CONGRESSMAN BILL ZELIFF'S
STAFF. Newly elected member of Congress after new member came up to
me and Bill, saying, "Thank you for helping to get me elected to Congress. I
could not have won without A-to-Z. I wrapped it around my incumbent
opponent's neck. I told the voters that I would sign the A-to-Z Spending
Cut Plan. I demanded that my opponent sign A-to-Z or be replaced by me.
I pointed out that my opponent was in bed with the Democrat leadership,
not the taxpayers of our district. A-to-Z was the key reason why I won."

Bill got the same type of message in spades. It was the first time that
the Republicans controlled the U.S. House of Representative in forty-six

long years. The national press corps from Washington gave all the credit to Newt Gingrich's Contract with America. The individual new members gave the credit to our A-to-Z plan. Yes, young men can change the world!

Little did Bill Zeliff and I realize when we first talked about the A-to-Z spending cut plan that it would directly impact congressional elections all across America. It led to the election of seventy-three new GOP members of Congress. A-to-Z allowed Newt Gingrich to become the first GOP Speaker since Castro has controlled Cuba. It was a proud moment. At that first freshman orientation, when the seventy-three newly elected members of Congress came up to Bill and said, "A-to-Z was a major factor in my election," I was extremely proud to have been a key part of causing that transition.

One of the great frustrations of my career came at the start of the first congressional session run by the GOP. Newt Gingrich convinced Bill Zeliff not to pursue the A-to-Z plan because it would hurt the GOP's efforts to stay in power. This was the first indication that we were going to be as bad as the Democrats were. We were putting staying power in place of principle.

There are tangible monuments to my career that will last a lot longer than we in this room will last, such as the Nashua Technical College; the turnpike extension to the Massachusetts line that spawned Nashua's economic boom; the New Hampshire Health Career College, from which my oldest daughter graduated twenty-two years after I sponsored the legislation to build it at Pete's request. Yes, the turnpike liquor stores are a very tangible part of my legacy as well.

I'm proudest of my children, Laura and Kim, and their children. More important than the buildings are the people whom we helped on a daily basis, and the friends like all of you we get to know and love.

There were many proud moments, like the election victories of Pete, Mel, John Sununu, Ray Wieczorek, Bill Zeliff, and countless others. There are my own victories as vice president of the U.S. Jaycees, Speaker of the House, and my congressional nomination with my pound of hamburg.

There were also many downtimes such as my divorce; the time Aristotle Onassis took more than a year and a half to pay his bills that were charged to my credit card; and, of course, the periods of unemployment when my friends and neighbors voted for candidates other than my choices.

But, as I told you before, what is a man? What has he got? I won't recite the whole thing, so I showed you. But you know I took the blows and did it my way.

I close by thanking you all for being here and repeating one more time my credo:

I am only one, but I am one; I cannot do everything, but I can do something; and what I can do by the grace of God I will do.

There's a great vignette about the Illinois orator and senator Everett Dirksen and New Hampshire's Norris Cotton. Dirksen said to Cotton one day when he was a freshman member in the Senate, "Norris, I'm going to do an experiment with you. You see that big marble column over there? Go over and smell the marble for me, would you please?" Cotton went over and said, "Marble doesn't have any odor, I can't smell anything."

Dirksen says, "When you can smell the marble, it means you've been in Washington too long."

APPENDIX 1

*WE HONOR House Speaker Marshall Cobleigh by
remembering what has been said about him.*

Former Senate president Stewart Lamprey: "Cobleigh has been a tower of strength in rule revision and legislative innovation."

Former governor John W. King: "He can make important decisions."

House Majority Leader Harlan Logan: "For organizational experience, energy, determination, unlimited willingness to work for what he believes in, and consistent mental alertness, Marshall Cobleigh gets my vote."

Portsmouth Herald: "It's a hard path Cobleigh has chosen to follow, and we can but express our admiration for his willingness to try."

Nashua Telegraph: "Marshall Cobleigh has risen high in state politics—to a point where his moves and pronouncements are closely considered."

New Hampshire Profiles Magazine: "Energy, determination and a multitude of eighteen hour days have made Marshall Cobleigh one of New Hampshire's outstanding businessmen and community leaders."

APPENDIX 2

What Kind of Guy Is Marshall Cobleigh?

"A man of high principle who has the grit to do what is right."
—*Concord Monitor*

"Marshall Cobleigh 'calls it as it is . . .'" — *Peterborough Transcript*

"Cobleigh is a refreshing figure on the political scene. He's one of those too-rare politicians who usually says what he thinks and believes, without evasion and double-talk." — *Keene Evening Sentinel*

"Cobleigh more than any other leader in the Republican Party, tells it like it is." — *Portsmouth Herald*

"Marshall Cobleigh chooses to meet problems head on." —*Lebanon Valley News*

". . . Marshall is doing what he deep down inside believes in. Rather than change his position on the tax picture he took it like a man, criticism, cartoons, the whole works. His interest lies not only for the people of Nashua, but for the entire state of New Hampshire. For this he gets an A!" — *1590 Broadcaster*

"He studies problems and issues, reaches a conclusion and then says what he thinks without equivocation or fanfare." —*Concord Monitor*

"Cobleigh is unpopular, but don't under-rate him. He's forgotten more about slick parliamentary maneuvering than most members of the House or Senate will ever know." —*Manchester Union Leader*.

"He made enemies, but he also won the admiration and respect of the solons for his ability to get things done. He stepped on a lot of toes, but he is considered an able legislator who knows every political angle." — *Nashua Telegraph*

From the *Concord Monitor*: "Candidate Cobleigh is a tough, sometimes abrasive legislative veteran of the new school of politics. He often has invited defeat at the polls by saying bluntly what he thinks. His quick smile and bubbly sense of humor mask a steel intellect and a talent for boring to the core of a problem.

"Cobleigh is a student of the American legislative process. He has done more than any person on the public scene to modernize New Hampshire's cumbersome, archaic legislature. He is both responsive and responsible with a strong streak of independence that sometimes is dismaying to Republican regulars.

"He is not a lovable candidate. But he certainly could be relied upon to provide forceful representation and even, if he were reelected, to shake up some of the stodgy nineteenth-century traditions that bind the Congress to selfishly-oriented inactivity.

"We often have disagreed with Cobleigh. No person is his master, and we're confident we'd squabble with him if he won.

"But we respect his ability, his tenaciousness and his devotion to the same ends that we espouse even if the means often differ. We admire his knowledge of the American governmental system, which means that, if he were elected, he wouldn't have to go through on-the-job training."

"He says what he believes without evasion or double talk, regardless of the political consequences. He says the same things before election as he says after election." — *1590 Broadcaster*

"Marshall Cobleigh was a tower of strength in our administration and is a wonderful friend." — Governor Meldrim Thomson

"Marshall Cobleigh has exhibited the highest qualities of leadership and integrity." — Governor Walter Peterson

---

APPENDIX 3

Career Achievements

National vice president, U.S. Junior Chamber of Commerce; and past president, vice president, and national director, New Hampshire Jaycees

Listed in *Who's Who in the Eastern U.S.; Who's Who in Business and Commerce; Who's Who in Insurance; Outstanding Young Men in America, J.C.I. Senators; Dictionary of International Biography*

Member, National Alumni Council of Boston University

Former trustee, Oberlin College, School for Mutual Insurance Agents

Constitutional Convention delegate, 1964, 1974, and 1984

President, New Hampshire Association of Mutual Insurance Agents, 1955–1956

Senator, Junior Chamber International

Former member, Uniform Code for Motor Vehicle Laws Revision Committee

Director, Nashua Chamber of Commerce

Director, New England Society of Association Executives

New Hampshire Chairman, Junior Olympic Program

Chairman, Sub-committee on Administration-Vocational Rehabilitation Planning Commission of New Hampshire

Twenty-year member, J.E. Coffey Post American Legion, former chairman of its Legislative Committee

Member, Boston University Varsity Club

Past vice chairman, Nashua Citizens Traffic Committee

City chairman, Muscular Dystrophy Drive, October 1962

Has served on fund drives, such as YM-YW Building Fund, March of Dimes, Salvation Army Christmas Drive, Community Chest, and many more

Nashua chairman, Teenage Safe Driving Roade-O

Past vice chairman of the Hillsborough County Republican Delegation

Past vice chairman of the Nashua City Republican Committee

Former member International Association of Approved Basketball Officials

Past president of Greater Nashua Young Republicans Club

Past president, Nashua Junior Chamber of Commerce

New England Rehabilitative Association Man of the Year

A Lifetime Record of Moving to Top of Every Field of Involvement

Senior administrative assistant and alter ego to Governor Meldrim Thomson of New Hampshire. Key liaison man and decision maker for 112 department heads who employed 10,000 people with a million-dollar budget

Moved from research assistant to Governor Thomson's administrative assistant in fourteen months

Elected Speaker, New Hampshire House of Representatives, chairman, National Republican Legislative Leaders Conference, Executive Committee Council of State Governments

Chosen Key Man by American Society of Association Executives

Board of Directors, U.S. Chamber of Commerce Association Division

Named Mr. Mutual Agent of 20,000-member National Association of

Mutual Insurance Agents

First enlisted man ever named athletic director of Patuxent River, Maryland, NAS. Chosen for duty on President Truman's yacht, the U.S.S. *Williamsburg*.

Elected National Chair of Job Training State Liaisons Group

Bachelor of science in business administration, Boston University, College of Business of Administration

Associate of arts, College of General Education, Boston University

Valedictorian, Travelers Insurance Company Home Office Insurance School

Valedictorian, School for Mutual Insurance Agents at the University of North Carolina

Honor graduate of the Institute for Organized Management at Syracuse University, 1967

First New Hampshire man to receive Chartered Association Executive Designation, 1970

Outstanding Alumnus of Boston University in field of public service, 1971

House Speaker Marshall W. Cobleigh succeeded Walter Peterson and served 10 years in the House. In 1969, at the age of 38, he was elected Speaker and served for two terms. The State motto, "LIVE FREE OR DIE," was adopted during his tenure as Speaker. In 1971 on the occasion of the 50th anniversary of women being able to serve as house members, Speaker Cobleigh was paid tribute by the then legislative historian, Leon Anderson. This is what Andy said. "The youthful House Speaker Marshall Cobleigh set an all-time record for feminine appointments to committee leaderships for the 1971 Golden Anniversary session of women in the legislature. He named five to chairmanships and another five to committee vice-chairmanships—a display of confidence in feminine lawmakers unequalled by any previous Speaker." Marshall was elected a member of three Constitutional Conventions. He later served in the executive branch of state government with Governor Mel Thomson and in the legislative branch of the federal government as legislative assistant to Congressman Bill Zeliff.

APPENDIX 4

A Sampling of Proposals Sponsored by Marshall Cobleigh That Are Now State Law

The technical-vocational school in Nashua

Health Careers College in Concord

The turnpike liquor stores in Nashua, Portsmouth, and Hooksett, which have raised over a quarter of a billion dollars for the state to help finance unmet needs

Support of the turnpike extension in Nashua, which has spawned a sixty-store shopping center and an eight-million-dollar industrial plant

Originated the integrated toll road concept, which will develop over the next ten-year period

Permitting cities, towns, and counties to put welfare recipients to work as a condition for receiving welfare funds

The surcharge on delinquent fathers who did not maintain their child support payments, which resulted in decreasing our welfare costs

Requiring Social Security numbers of divorced people to be furnished by the Probation Department to help us cut down on our aid for the Families with Dependent Children program

Legislation providing welfare abuse penalties

Increases in unemployment benefits

Fought to retain New Hampshire holding the first-in-the-nation presidential primary, which does so much for this state's public relations and promotion program. The primary in itself is worth an estimated ten million dollars to our economy.

Requiring ramps on all public buildings for the physically handicapped

An interstate compact for the cleanup of the Nashua River

Providing for a property tax survey committee

Providing for a study on the feasibility of an east–west toll road

Making the right-to-know law apply to all actions of this legislature and its committees

Improving our parole procedures

Memorializing Congress to pass federal-state tax-sharing measure

Reduced residence requirements to thirty days for presidential elections

Limiting administrative costs of charitable fund drives to 15 percent

Twenty-five-year retirement program for police officers

Constitutional amendment providing for freedom of speech in the New Hampshire Bill of Rights.

Included in the budget additional funding for psychologists and psychiatrists at the State Industrial School

Construction of an infirmary at the State Industrial School to provide for both medical and rehabilitation care in drug abuse

Banning habitual traffic offenders from driving

Setting up a concentrated attack on drug abuse and including funding for our best-in-New England undercover narcotics squad as well as funding for drug education and rehabilitation. Regulating the sale of hypodermic needles

Eliminating the waiting list at the Laconia State School

A new facility at the Soldiers Home in Tilton

Allowing the New Hampshire College and University Council to buy through the director of Purchase and Property

Establishing the rights of policemen and prohibiting police strikes

Providing free tuition for children of prisoners of the war in Asia

Increasing the salaries of state employees and establishing a personnel study commission

Increasing the limit of earnings of retired teachers and state employees

Controlling the sale of unsafe flammable fabrics with special emphasis on children's nightwear

"A-to-Z: A Case Study in Policymaking"

Marty Schram, in his nationally syndicated column, used the A-to-Z plan as a "Case Study in Policymaking."

A-to-Z Spending Cut Plan was a key factor in electing the first Republican House of Representatives in 46 years.

The making of ideas into policy is a Washington cottage industry in which success happens sometimes because of merit. But mainly, it happens because of unabashed marketing and uninhibited massaging of the media.

The popularity and power of the "A-to-Z Spending Cut Plan" has emerged as a classic triumph of marketing and massaging, Washington style.

It is a conservative and rather roguish notion, born in the office of a lowly New Hampshire congressman, that (just as its carefully constructed name implies) suggests any House member should be able to force an up-or-down vote on any item of spending that may have been camouflaged in a large, popular bill and slipped into law.

A-to-Z has never won a vote on the House floor. But it was championed by conservative editorial pages, propelled by talk radio motor mouths and chronicled (belatedly) by the mainstream news media. And, after it seemed to strike a populist chord, it was co-sponsored by a majority of representatives.

So A-to-Z, though unapproved, has become a force unto itself. It forced a hidebound House majority leadership that sought to bury it in committees to bend more than just a bit. The House Democratic leadership, pressured by defecting moderates, forestalled a move to bring A-to-Z to the floor for a vote by agreeing to permit at least some up-or-down votes on items of spending.

Now, anyone who wants to know how Washington really works had better study the inventive maneuvering of A-to-Z. It is perhaps typical of today's Washington that the story starts with Z.

Two-term Rep. William Zeliff, New Hampshire Republican, a marketing kind of guy who used to sell antifreeze for Du Pont, was sitting in his office one day last year with his chief of staff, Marshall Cobleigh, a wily and rascally veteran pol who was once New Hampshire's Speaker of the House.

They were watching the television news of President Clinton's budget fight and began talking about how any member of the House ought to be able to demand an up-or-down vote on any appropriation item, no matter how large or small. Time could be set aside for this at the end of each congressional session.

Mr. Zeliff, the artful salesman, and Mr. Cobleigh, the artful pol, saw a potential marketing master stroke: Forgo ego-gratifying tradition; don't call it the "Zeliff Spending Cut Bill." Call it the "A-to-Z Spending Cut Bill" and it'll sell coast-to-coast.

But they needed an A-name as a co-sponsor. Better yet, an A-name Democrat, to create an image of bipartisanship. So they perused the House roster and, lo, there he was: Rep. Rob Andrews, New Jersey Democrat, a young conservative two-termer. Rep. Zeliff telephoned Rep. Andrews, pitched his plan, they met, and "A-to-Z" was born.

Rep. Zeliff worked out front as the lead salesman; Mr. Cobleigh worked the media behind the scenes. The *Wall Street Journal* editorial page began singing rhapsodies of praise. One day Rep. Zeliff did back-to-back radio talk shows of two mild-mannered masters of understatement— motor mouths Pat Buchanan and G. Gordon Liddy; Rep. Zeliff's phones were jammed the rest of the day as listeners called long distance to pledge support. Rep. Zeliff worked the talk-show hosts' convention in California and came away with a grass-roots bonanza of invitations to appear.

Even Ross Perot came calling. He endorsed A-to-Z at a Capitol Hill news conference.

House Speaker Thomas Foley warned that a day of voting on any spending item, A-to-Z, would be like "A Day at the Circus." Indeed it would. Members would be confused about what they were voting on (as many are now). Vital social programs might get the inadvertent ax along with the cuttable comic stuff like the helium reserve fund (created back when we thought a U.S. zeppelin fleet would assure national security) and the $5 million for zebra mussel research.

But understand the appeal: For years, deficit-trimming notions like "Gramm-Rudman" evoked mainly yawns outside the Beltway; now everyone everywhere can grasp the simplicity of the meaning and message of A-to-Z. It may well be voted into law in the new, more conservative House expected next year.

That's the case that the earnest 37-year-old Rep. Andrews is making these days. The A-man of A-to-Z is selling with the zeal not of a conscript but an architect. But he laughs upon being reminded how he achieved his instant fame. For as the irrepressible old pol and packager, Marshall Cobleigh, recently reminded Rep. Andrews in a moment of mock seriousness:

"Don't forget, if your name was Pantagoulas, you never would have even gotten the call."

APPENDIX 6

My Credo

I am only one
but I am one
I cannot do everything
but I can do something
and what I can do
by the grace of God
I will do.

INDEX

Green, Sam, 27, 28
Green, William S., 114, 142
Greer, Ben, 95
Gregg, Hugh, 1, 3
Gregg, Judd, 231-232
Griffin, Bob, 4
Griffin, Charles, 246
Griffin, Pat, 233
Guild, Larry, 78

H

Hall, Charles Francis, 4,14, 86-87
Hall, Gus, 88
Hall, Raymond, 142
Hampton, N.H., 97
Hampton Beach, N.H., 22, 39, 66
Hancock, Betty, 218
Hancock, Mary Louise, 63-64
Hancock, Parker, 63
Hancock, Stuart, 52, 53, 59, 63
Hanna, George, 89
Hanover, N.H., 22, 96, 114
Hanover Police Department, 113, 114
Hart, Irene, 68
Hart, Robert, 45-46, 68
Hartigan, Winnifred, 116
Harvard Business School, 161
Hawaii, 215
Hayes, Donald, 141
Health and Welfare Department, 58-62
Health Careers Technical College, 119, 184, 249, 256
Hebron, N.H., 9
Hell's Angels, 12, 21-22
Henry, Patrick, 195
Hersey, Irving, 27
Highway Beautification Act, 182
Highway Department, 24

Highway Hotel, 6, 10, 26, 114, 115, 154, 165, 167-168, 172, 197
Hill, Leonard, 47,81
Hillsborough County, 78, 100, 170
Hillsborough County Republican Delegation, 254
Hoff, Phil, 50
Hollis, Franklin, 26-28
Hooksett, N.H., 184, 186, 198, 256
Horton, Mildred McAfee, 89
House Appropriations Committee, 37
House Bill 47, 12-21
House Bill 111, 181
House Bill 405, 150-151, 152-153
House Bill 602, 65
House Journal, 123, 124, 197
House Judiciary Committee, 21
House Majority Leader, 117-134
Howard, Kenneth, 76
Howard, Nelson, 16-17, 48, 124
Howard, Russ, 174
Hundred Mile National Championship Road Race, 22
Hunt, Charlie, 46
Hunter, N. Doug, 78

I

Intellectual Freedom Committee, 87
Interim Committee, 119
International Association of Approved Basketball Officials, 254
Intra Modal Surface Transportation Act, 242
Isaacson, Eli, 231-232

J

Jackson, Andrew, 187
Jackson, James, 85
Jefferson, Thomas, 137, 187